VILLAGE DIARY OF A HERETIC BANKER

notionpress
.com

VILLAGE DIARY OF A HERETIC BANKER

Moin Qazi

notionpress
.com

Notion Press

5 Muthu Kalathy Street, Triplicane,

Chennai - 600 005

First Published by Notion Press 2014

ISBN: 978-93-84049-53-9

For

A Ramesh Kumar

My mentor, boss and guide

Moin Qazi has doctorates in Economics and English literature and has spent more than three decades in the development sector working in India's, largest commercial bank. He was a Visiting Fellow at the University of Manchester. He has also served on deputation to the Grameen Bank of Bangladesh, International Fund for Agricultural Development, Rome and Ministry of Rural Development, Government of Malaysia. At college he was awarded the UNESCO World Politics Essay Gold Medal and the Gandhi Centenary Essay Gold Medal. He has contributed articles to Indian and foreign publications.

If a free society cannot help the many who are poor, it cannot save the few who are rich.

John F. Kennedy, Kennedy's Inaugural address of 1961.

I will give you a talisman. Whenever you are in doubt, or when the self becomes too much with you, apply the following test. Recall the face of the poorest and the weakest man [woman] whom you may have seen, and ask yourself, if the step you contemplate is going to be of any use to him [her]. Will he [she] gain anything by it? Will it restore him [her] to a control over his [her] own life and destiny? In other words, will it lead to swaraj [freedom] for the hungry and spiritually starving millions? Then you will find your doubts and your self melt away.

Mahatma Gandhi (One of the last notes left behind by Gandhi in 1948, expressing his deepest social thought)

I firmly believe that we can create a poverty-free world if we collectively believe in it. In a poverty-free world, the only place you would be able to see poverty is in the poverty museums. When school children take a tour of the poverty museums, they would be horrified to see the misery and indignity that some human beings had to go through. They would blame their forefathers for tolerating this inhuman condition, which existed for so long, for so many people.

Muhammad Yunus, Nobel Laureate

I expect to pass through this world but once. Any good therefore that I can do, or any kindness or abilities that I can show to any fellow creature, let me do it now. Let me not defer it or neglect it, for I shall not pass this way again.

William Penn

CONTENTS

ACKNOWLEDGEMENTS

There is no greater agony than bearing an untold story inside you.

Maya Angelou

I owe much to a lifetime of collegiality of steadfast colleagues, enthusiastic bosses, supportive peers and juniors who have helped me learn and practice development finance. I owe deep gratitude to so many people for their help that if I were to put down their names it would make a formidable list. They all shared the physical and emotional adventure both in the workplace and the field. They also assisted me in my task of building a cogent narrative out of the impassable maze of my notes built up over three decades of work in development finance.

Before all, I must record my debt to the thousands of women in the villages and low-income urban clusters of developing countries who so lovingly shared their time and taught me about their enterprises, their finances, and their lives. Most were poor in economic terms but rich in wisdom. My knowledge of the rural society is largely derived from them.

Let me thank the following individuals for the usual as well as several unusual reasons:

First and foremost, I acknowledge the extraordinary support of A. Ramesh Kumar to whom this book is dedicated. Kumar was my boss during my assignment at my bank's state headquarters in Mumbai. The vibrancy of the Self Help Group movement in Maharashtra has much to do with Kumar's revolutionary approach. He has also pioneered a unique model of housing microfinance in India. He and his wonderful wife Usha have been my ardent well-wishers and have played a critical role in my career. I am indebted to them for their constant encouragement and support. Creativity or talent is a wild river till it is tapped and harnessed into energy or power. The responsibility for nurturing and suckling these talents lies with us.

My thanks to Eknath Kalbande and Ramesh Ringe, my bosses at Nagpur when I was an independent manager handling development finance. They taught me both the science and the art of development finance with their highly practical, hands-on approach. Thanks to Jaya Kotian for his selfless support during my posting at Wardha.

I thank my senior colleagues who have been my bosses at various stages of my career and have so whole heartedly lend support and encouragement to my endeavours: Arundhati Bhattacharya, S.R. Iyer, Ashok Kini, Arun Shandilya, Diwakar Gupta, S.S.Ranjan, Sangeet Shukla, Sharad Sharma, Abhay Chaudhari, Sunil Pant, B.A.Tiwari, S.B.Bejalwar, A.P.Pathak and A.S.Rao.

Thanks to my colleagues S.Jayaraman, S.S.Roy, Prakash Khandekar, Raj Kumar Singh, Sasi Dash, Raj Chaterjee, Rajendra Benodekar, P.V.Subbaraman, Ravindra Nath, Ajit Bhide, Vinod Karnik, S.Hari Prasad, V.S.Kumar, P.D.Deshmukh, Surendra Jain, Zafar Qureishi and Narhari Sethi for support in my career as also at a more personal level. I would prefer to call them friends and well wishers rather than colleagues.

I had the happy company of B.A.Karpate, Ramesh Bagde, Vinod Yeramwar, Tukaram Kohad, Sanjay Gogte, Shriram Joshi, Satish Parate and Shishir Ninawe in my rural development work in Chandrapur district. They journeyed outside the mapped territories of their roles. Let me thank them for their selfless assistance, unfailing support and ever cheerful demeanour during the five years I spent in that district. I also thank my childhood friend Azhar Khwaja for his warmth and understanding and consistent and unfaltering support. It was great to have him on my side.

If this book is to have a hero, it is G. Srinivas Rao, an exemplary employee whose work forms the bulwark of my career. He was the kind of guy who would never flinch. He'd work harder than everyone else and stand his ground when he believed he was right. His integrity was unassailable. I was truly fortunate to have him in my team. My profuse thanks to him.

I am grateful to my nephew, Sameer Siddiqui, who supported me in the writing of this book by playing both collaborator and critic. Sunayna Roy provided excellent copywriting support. I doff my hats to both of them.

It is to R.H.Bhave, Narayanan Raja, Abhay Singh and Ajay Swaroop that I am most beholden for constantly encouraging me and providing extraordinary support in my work.

I thank the entire team at Notion Press for their commitment and their rare insights and support that helped shape this book.

Above all, I want to thank my wife Nahid, and sons Salman and Wasim, who supported my career with patience and endurance, in spite of all the time it took me away from them. They ungrudgingly tolerated my persistent absence from their lives and put up with the absence of a 'migrant worker' from their household. Without their support, the book would not exist.

My sisters, nieces and nephews have been my most dependable fans and supporters and I thank them for all their good wishes and prayers.

I have been extremely fortunate over the years to have had so many friends who taught me so much and who have supported me through thick and thin. I cannot name them all, and I would hate to forget someone, but they know who they are. All these people have given me just about everything else that is important in life and I cannot quite think how to thank them for it all. To all of them I owe my warmest thanks and deepest gratitude. I hope I'm able to give back in ideas some part of what I have received from them in wisdom.

I owe a special note of thanks to many colleagues who, for various reasons, were (and may still be) sceptical of my approach. Without that scepticism and close scrutiny, there would be far more weaknesses and errors in this book and related works. Their guidance was extremely worthwhile in my career as a development banker. Those who know me are aware that I love a good argument and enjoy defending my theories. For that reason, this acknowledgement is especially heartfelt. We are a very special community in that, without the dialectic, we would be so much less than we are. I hope we never lose that quality. In the same spirit, I hope this book provokes some strong reactions— positive or negative.

I feel blessed to have lived to tell you that even when my hours were at their darkest, I drew strength from the belief that some day, I could share my experiences with others. This book is a reflection of my struggles; the battles have kept my spirit alive. To struggle is to strengthen my faith, my hope and my belief in humanity.

My final thanks are reserved for the institution which has been at the centre of all my learning and practice: State Bank of India. I deem it my great fortune that I was part of it in several turbulent yet defining periods of India's development history. I owe an immense amount of gratitude to it for allowing me full freedom to deploy my talents and ideas while keeping within patterns and standards. I consider it a highly benign institution with much to teach those who are willing to learn. The bank's family is a huge fraternity and I found an abode in the homes of legions of strangers. I would like to thank all of them in Tagore's words:

Thou hast made me known to friends whom I knew not. Thou hast given me seats in homes not my own. Thou hast brought the distant near and made a brother of the stranger. I am uneasy at heart when I have to leave my accustomed shelter; I forgot that there abides the old in the new, and that there also thou abidest.

Finally, I seek forgiveness of all those who have been with me over the course of the years and whose names I have failed to mention. The gifts were theirs, the gratitude mine.

Introduction

I shall now therefore humbly propose my own thoughts, which I hope will not be liable to the least objection.

Jonathan Swift

This book is more a diary rather than an instructive guide. It has my own thoughts, but let me frankly admit they are liable to as many objections as possible. Fallibility has been the mark of all adventurers and I must honestly admit I had a fair share of disasters. My diary provides the flavour of my personal experiences as a rural banker, my professional safari through the jungles of my bank's vast and deep network and its engagement with the poor in the remote crannies of India. It may serve as an antidote to much of the euphoria generated these days about the development programmes and the benefits of economic liberalization. But let me assure that it is a very faithful account.

I am a committed believer in the economic philosophy that guarantees equitable and just development. I have tried to faithfully portray the Indian rural development scene and document my personal experiences in a wide range of roles - grassroots worker, field officer, program manager, policy maker and academic. I have presented the facts plainly without any colour or gloss of ideology. I run the risk of rebuke from many quarters for my chilling candour. But I had grown so weary of the inane sophistry that marked the stance of my bosses, peers and fellow academics that I had become desperate for furrowing a new path.

My journey through rural India and through my three decade career in development finance was both rough and stormy as I kept rebelling against traditional approaches. The goal of my heretical act of questioning certain conventional assumptions was to shed light on the actual practices of the development sector that were not delivering the desired results and to prompt changes that could skew the odds in favour of the poor. My diary drifts and tacks like a sailboat but has a clear leitmotif. The seed around which the book crystallises is the intrinsic tenacity and grit of poor rural women that can be harnessed into energetic powerhouses to drive our rural society onto the road to prosperity. The book carries in its pages my poignant nostalgia for villages but it is also tinged at places with rage and despair.

Rural banking in India has been a great hurdle race ever since the government nationalised major commercial banks and mandated them to focus their thrust on villages. The official commandment to public banks was not just about barefoot banking, but was a directive to run into unfamiliar terrains to establish their flag posts. The expectations were that this would bring about both an economic and social revolution. The players were untrained and unwilling participants in the marathon. Their captains were equally unprepared. But the umpire was stubborn and unrelenting. He brought more players into the race and changed the rules of the game many times. At some stages, it appeared as if he himself had lost interest in the race. But the race continues, proceeding in different directions. The roadmap of financial sector reforms bypassed rural banking time and again despite repeated exordiums from developments pundits. Meanwhile the reconciled barefoot bankers continued to walk amidst the debris of the populist programmes. The official emphasis on financial inclusion keeps re-emerging in policy documents but little earnestness is shown by bankers in pursuing it on account of a plethora of constraints.

The eighties of the last century saw an unplanned and indiscriminate expansion of bank branches most of which later became an economic deadweight. Between 1977 and 1990, the Reserve Bank of India mandated that a commercial bank could open a new branch in a location that already had bank branches only if it opened four in locations with no branches. This regulation was part of a social banking program that tried to expand access to financial services in rural areas. The additional burden arising out of the mass opening of rural bank branches adversely affected the resilience and viability of banks. The extension of commercial bank branches was inspired by the need to fill credit gaps in the rural economy which the uneven and inadequate development of the cooperative movement had left. The politicians believe banks can bring economic revolution through rural credit, which is just like expecting a midwife to deliver a baby. In a developing country, it is not enough just to provide credit for production. Production itself must be increased with the adopting of improved technology.

The branches mushroomed and there was an exponential increase of rural branches of banks. Villages began to be courted by bankers. This phenomena gave rise to a popular adage: "A village could be known as uninhabitable only if it did not have a branch of a bank." Such was the explosion of rural banking. The depth and outreach of the banking network in the late seventies grew at a sizzling pace on account of tough government mandates. This was at a time when the transport and communication infrastructure in the country was abysmally weak, unlike today when mobile phones, email, SMS and Skype enable you to communicate anywhere any time.

Financial market imperfections that limit access to finance are key in most development programmes. Lack of access to finance is often the critical mechanism behind both persistent income inequality and slow economic growth. Hence financial sector reforms that promote broader access to financial services should be at the core of the development agenda.

Providing better financial access to the non poor micro and small entrepreneurs can have a strongly favourable indirect effect on the poor. Spillover effects of financial developments are likely to be significant. Hence, to promote pro-poor growth, it is important to broaden the focus of attention of finance for improving access for all who are excluded.

While the positive social and economic impacts of nationalization were quite evident, the experiment was also an eye opening lesson in the disaster that mindless bureaucratic programmes can become. Most development programmes are a grim reminder of how mechanically trying to meet targets can completely undermine the integrity of a veritable economic and social revolution to such an extent that a counter-revolution can be set into motion. But we refuse to learn lessons particularly because populist politicians consider it a sure way to burnish their electoral fortunes.

The poor have skills, are politically conscious, and are aware of the need for schooling for the children and taking care of their health and also planning a future for their families. However, their lack of income makes it impossible for them to monetise their skills and thereby improve the quality of their life. Providing investment capital for additional income generation can unlock their potential to solve many, if not all, of the manifestations of poverty. This has to be supplemented by skill development, proper marketing support and appropriate monetary compensation for their skills and produce.

During my efforts in development finance and rural development work for over three decades, I have seen projects and strategies succeed as well as fail. I have seen misguided project designs, poor implementation and squandering of large sums of money. But I have also witnessed incredible achievements. When development works well, it can transform lives by providing the underprivileged the capital and knowledge that can open up opportunities for them and reduce their poverty.

The development community seems constantly and restlessly in search of a singular approach that will solve poverty, unveiling new buzzwords every few years only to toss them aside. The fundamental flaw with this system is that each new approach fails to break out of the underlying technocratic and specialized paradigm.

We must understand that there is no precooked blueprint for replication. Individuals can make a difference in fighting poverty when ways are found to institutionalize creative ideas. Replication of successful models continues to be a guiding mantra of development programmes. But an associated caveat when examining specific experiences with replication in mind is the personal charisma of inspirational leaders and organisational synergies, both of which are not readily transferable. We must respect the fundamental truth that charisma and passion cannot be transfused. We need to have charismatic and highly motivated leaders to lead programmes. It is equally important that we must appropriately reward and recognise good performance so as to further enhance the quality of leadership. Leadership finally remains the most crucial element of the success of any new initiative. There is vast difference in being a rural banker by choice and in being one by chance. So is the case with any other development institution or agency. Imposing of unwilling leaders has been the bane of most development programmes.

There is a glut of information on rural development. There is now a mountain of scholarship and a huge circuit in operation: dissecting statistics, furrowing through the libraries, wracking the brains and pontificating. Most development finance academics are researchers with little real world experience. Leadership in rural development programmes is a clinical art and people need experience. The fact is that what works in Haryana does not seem to work well in Bihar. What works in India is not automatically transferable to Peru and vice versa. It is not certain as to the exact reasons for the different disparities, but can be mainly attributed to cultural, social, economic and structural differences.

Consultants have for long been the key people in policy mechanics and there have been many incidences of glaring overdependence on them. It is extremely necessary to moderate the reports and prescriptions of consultants with ground realities that can be ascertained from grassroots leaders. There are those who have been making points that if the consultants are so confident of their advice, and plans, why they themselves don't execute it. The old adage about teachers gets changed slightly: "Those who can, do; those who cannot, consult." I feel consultants must seek a more active engagement with the poor so that they have a truly authentic feel of the reality. We must remove our academic blinkers to get an accurate picture of the society we want to serve.

I have been inspired mostly by people who have followed their printed blasts with long tiring journeys in inhospitable terrain to demonstrate their solidarity with these people. Consultants have never lived down the description of them in Robert Tomasend's *Up the Organization* as people who borrow your watch in order to tell you the time. There are too many consultants willing to give advice most of which is descriptive and very rarely contains prescriptions. This is the hubris of the consultant who believes he can wear down the problems with sheer studiousness. Consultants are like burnished glass: they live their whole lives off the reflected glory of the organisations whom they were privileged to provide consultancy. They keep on using the word "holistic" very liberally like the way the environmentalists use the word "sustainable". It's the world's most pretentious word I have ever come across. Consultants have abused its original connotation and stripped it of its dignified place in development lexicon.

Nevertheless, consultants do have a role to play. There is always something of continuing value about bringing an outsider in. If the consultant is experienced, he or she can sniff out problems. A wide knowledge of the way many other organizations have coped with similar problems can help provide solutions that the organizations by themselves could never have stumbled across. In addition, consultants can act as disseminators to the real world of the latest thinking in the academic and practitioners' worlds and of their own often considerable inner research.

Poverty reduction is not a discipline. You can't get somebody from a university who has done a Ph.D. in poverty reduction. Nor is there a talisman for eradicating poverty. It may not be possible to locate a common denominator for a successful rural manager. It may also not be possible to lay down a standard blueprint for a rural development programme. From their own experience, rural banking veterans can spell out the ingredients that one may need to be successful. But the new managers shall have to work out their own recipes for blending these ingredients in the right proportions. There is so much cultural diversity even in neighbouring villages that a blueprint for one village may need a drastic change for a village next to it.

The policy makers who dominate most discussions on the problems of the poor keep waxing rhapsodic about the great possibilities of their plans and strategies serving each sentence like an expertly bowled cricket ball. They release their epigrams like pet doves. The palatial décor of the conference rooms is what is talked about in ostentatious tea breaks. Conferences are substituted for work. Perquisites are substituted for truly earned rewards — and there are no penalties for corruption, laziness and divisive rabble-rousing. Adept at diplomacy and wordplay, these leaders obscure the real concerns behind a fog of jargon and euphemism.

No wonder the villages distrust all these urbanised gentry who jeep themselves into the village, complete with their pageantry, exhorting the local population to produce fewer babies and more food for the benefit of their urban brethren. There is no mention of the exploitative prices for their produce, that has been the key cause of their impoverishment. They deliver these messages to the villages, and hastily jeep their way back to their urban environment. The policy wonks and mandarins keep barricading themselves against the political or journalistic assaults with their trained staff ringfencing them. They would make a valiant and often brilliant pitch to sway the young lot but mostly the pitch would be badly off key. Much disservice has been done to the cause of rural development on account of this schizoid approach: alternating engagement and withdrawal. It is easy to dish out lectures on development finance; but it is an arduous experience to practice it.

Though much rural development is welcomed by the whole population and does not involve outsiders in personal risk, much also involves conflicts of interest where the weak are dominated, exploited and cheated by the powerful. Where that happens, many of the rural poor and those who work with and for them face abuse, discrimination and danger; the bravest and most direct are often threatened; some are assaulted; and some are even killed. There is much innovation and even heroism and sacrifice by staff of banks and development agencies known only to villagers and other staff, which is not only left anonymous but undocumented. Even when programme results are reported, the names and actions of the individuals who made the process successful on the ground are seldom known.

We should really applaud and honour ordinary men and women, who have nobody to back them, yet are working doggedly to keep projects rolling. Nobody can fathom the mental and physical suffering they and their families are undergoing. I doubt whether outsiders like me, protected by passport, police and the state, can be justified in urging others to risk their livelihoods, their families' well-being, or their lives. To take risks for oneself is one thing. To encourage others to do so is quite another. As Adlai Stevenson has so pithily commented: "It is easier to fight for principles than to live up to them".

The failure in practice of so many normal professional solutions points to re-examination of the perceptions and priorities of professionals — those normal, non-poor, urban-based elites who define poverty and what should be done about it. The other is to examine the perceptions and priorities of the poor themselves. Neither has received much attention in anti-poverty discussions. Most professionals — politicians, bureaucrats, scientists, academics and others, and including ourselves — have plunged into debate and action in the middle, without questioning what has brought us there, what we are conditioned to see and to believe, or what others see and believe. We have had neither time nor incentive to examine ourselves and our predispositions, nor that of the poor.

There are development panjandrums and authors and writers on rural development and planning who arrogate to themselves the right to hand out certificates on best practices. These people shut themselves from the world and give lengthy opinions on the basis of reports and statistics appearing in journals. I have found even senior executives turning into glib talkers on poverty. Even while publicly proclaiming their commitment to a public cause, they don't hesitate to speak in a different voice at internal forums.

The best advice I can proffer to young managers is not to drain themselves in sterile debates, but to keep focussed on action at the grassroots:

Much to cast down, much to build, much to restore;
Let the work not delay, time and the arm not waste;
Let the clay be dug from the pit, let the saw cut the stone,
Let the fire not be quenched in the forge.
(*Choruses from the Rock* – T.S. Eliot)

I firmly believe it is possible to eliminate poverty in our country—provided we re-examine the received wisdom of our assumptions. The poor are poor not because they are unskilled or illiterate but because they cannot retain the returns of their labour. They neither own capital, nor does anyone give them access to credit, except on the most unreasonable terms. They live on the edge, in constant fear of a catastrophe or tragedy. But they have no insurance because insurance companies consider them a losing proposition. The State's social safety nets are not only grossly inadequate but mired in corruption and bureaucratic red tape.

We need to bring in the poor to the conversation. Interventions that take the end user into account almost always have better success rates than top down decision-making ones. Many social enterprises are still not talking enough to their poor customers to find out what they really want, and too often policy makers have no idea what their end beneficiaries really need. Let us hope that the expanding use of technology across all segments of society will help to create platforms for exchange of ideas, so that people can better express their needs and there is a more meaningful exchange of information,.

The message in this book is that there is no grand, universal formula for poverty reduction. The battle has to be fought on several fronts and what works in one place does not necessarily work everywhere. The way forward lies in grassroots field experiments for understanding the causal relationships in poor people's behaviour and in learning by doing. My faith in poor people's ability to climb out of the poverty rut is unshakeable and my core belief is gradualism. I believe that lasting social change most often—and perhaps always—comes slowly rather than in a burst of revolutionary fervour. It is this belief that has shaped my work. I also believe that lasting change can be effected only when women are given equal opportunities for financial empowerment. If you're poor, you're disadvantaged; but if you're poor and also a woman, you are doubly disadvantaged. A poor rural women's status is best portrayed in Maya Angelou's poignant words:

I've got the children to tend
The clothes to mend
The floor to mop
The food to shop
Then the chicken to feed
The garden to weed
I've got shirts to press
The tots to dress
The cane to be cut
I got a clean up this hut
Then see about the sick
And the cotton to pick
Shine on me, sunshine
Rain on me, rain
Fall softly, dewdrops
And cool my brow again

In this book, I have said things which may sound critical, wounding, and even angry. In expiation, I can say that I have been as bitter about many societies, including my own. I do not mean to be hurtful to a warm and generous people who have never been other than kind to me; wherein I have seen things cruel and hostile it is because they are cruel and hostile to India itself.

Speaking out, I felt, would relieve me of a load of agitated thoughts and emotions.

Speak, your lips are free.
Speak, it is your own tongue.
Speak, it is your own body.
Speak, your life is still yours.

See how in the blacksmith's shop
The flame burns wild, the iron glows red;
The locks open their jaws, And every chain begins to break.
(Faiz Ahmed Faiz)

This is not to say that I have been estranged from my bosses or peers. I set out to write this diary because I wanted to tell the story rather than let it ferment into discontent. I firmly believe that my younger colleagues would be able to put the lessons herein to good worth. The more important part, however, lies in the opportunity this diary affords to publicly acknowledge the debt I owe to so many people: villagers, volunteers and the staff of banks, government and development agencies who put up with some of my wild adventures in the rural planet and made serious attempts to give them both workable and doable shape.

This book is built entirely on anecdotal evidence. I never wanted to submerge the central idea in a deluge of statistics nor did I want to swamp the readers with mind-boggling figures. These figures are available in tomes and tomes of government reports already. I was keener to profile the trajectory of individual lives of grit, tenacity, determination, and above all, the honesty which is what has given the women in this book the status of star borrowers in the eyes of bankers. There is a minefield of data, but it has not been able to generate the sort of wisdom that can guide us meaningfully. To quote T.S. Eliot:

Where is the life we have lost in living?

Where is the wisdom we have lost in knowledge?

Where is the knowledge we have lost in information?

There is now an explosion of information. Facts have supplanted understanding, and knowledge is no longer able to generate wisdom. Every school of thought has contrived its own language of clichés and jargons understandable only by its own exclusive devotees who jealously guard the entry of any new initiate. Human knowledge has become too great for the human mind; every science has begotten a dozen more, each subtler than the rest. But even after the knowledge explosion, all that remains is the scientific specialist who knows more and more about less and less and the philosophical speculator who knows less and less about more and more.

I am always reminded of *The Little Prince* by Antoine de Saint-Exupery, in which he makes the telling point that adults think that only those things that can be described by numbers are true, whereas it is much more interesting to describe things the way they really are:

Grown-ups love figures. When you tell them that you have made a new friend, they never ask you any questions about essential matters. They never say to you, 'What does his voice sound like? What games does he love best? Does he collect butterflies'? Instead, they demand: 'How old is he? How many *brothers has he? How much does he weigh? How much money does his father make?'Only from these figures do they think they have learned anything about him. If you were to say to the grown-ups: 'I saw a beautiful house made of rosy brick, with geraniums in the windows and doves on the roof,' they would not be able to get an idea of that house at all. You have to say to them: 'I saw a house that cost $20,000.' Then they would exclaim: 'Oh, what a pretty house that is!'*

Development literature is packed with figures and tables. All our policy formulations are based on analysis of data which may several times not be authentic, thus severely distorting the picture that emerges. We have found several times that enumerators have reported highly contrasting data for the same sample of population. How does one tell the story of a statistic? One man is a person, a thousand are a community and a million are a statistic. Or as Joseph Stalin exclaimed "A single death is a tragedy, a million deaths is a statistic." I decided to write something that wouldn't reinforce the statistics that make India's millions but would look instead for the faces behind the figures. As each face becomes a person, numbers cease being an abstraction.

The problem is that anecdotal evidence often seems much more compelling than dry statistics. However, the social scientists are wary about the use of stories as evidence for a claim. Therefore, anecdotes that are not backed up with systematic and rigorous comparative data are not trusted. True, anecdotes are the weakest form of evidence, but they are also often the most persuasive. Even scientists can be moved by a telling anecdote that contradicts a mass of statistical evidence. But anecdotes must always have to be used with care, precisely because we are psychologically susceptible to them. Anecdote is not analysis, nor should it be. Yet as a way of taking a society's temperature, I can think of no better.

Can we get a better picture of the plight of the Indian farmer than the one portrayed by Rudyard Kipling:

His speech if of mortgaged bedding,
On his kine he borrows yet.
At his heart is his daughter's wedding.
In his eye foreknowledge of debt
He eats and hath indigestion
He toils and he may not stop,

His life Is a long-drawn question

Between a crop and a crop

(The Masque of Plenty)

Equally poignant is Jawaharlal Nehru's description:

I listened to their innumerable tales of sorrow, their crushing and ever-growing burden of rent, illegal extraction, ejectments from land and mud hut, beatings; surrounded on all sides by vultures who preyed on them – zamindar's agents, moneylenders, police; toiling all day to find that what they produced was not theirs and their reward was kicks and curses and a hungry stomach

My diary provides neither a macro-narrative nor any catch-all explanations. My intent and direction lie elsewhere. My overarching goal is to provide a flavour of the evolving rural India, through its people, through their hopes and their passions, their opinions and their perceptions. Such an approach is unapologetically subjective.

All our development programmes give primacy to mathematical analysis and computer remodelling. There is an overemphasis on technology. The top management feels that the investments in technology can address all development issues. Tech savvy and business school boys seem to be the answer to the problems of managing and scaling development programmes. All this makes difficult for a normal professional development worker to understand and serve the local, complex, diverse, dynamic and unpredictable realities of rural life. All the issues flagged by field workers are sorted into fixed templates and solutions.

I had little fascination for figures and at least in the initial years banking appeared more a number cruncher's delight. I found hard to cope with the tedious job of wading through an endless maze of figures. I was delighted more by peering beyond the dry lifeless figures that statistics appear to me and observing the millions of human actions that these figures represented. Analysis is not my strong forte; still, one would expect a creative writer to seek out individual experiences to tell stories of the changes in peoples' lives and emotions wrought by wider historical processes. It is all too rarely that a sense of style and an eye for beauty are found to co-exist with a head for facts and figures. I was fortunate in being reasonably endowed with both. Numbers may have never amused me but I had developed a fair degree of flair for them.

Successful rural bankers do believe in writing intricate business plans. But they also focus their energy, intelligence, and skills on creating businesses that can thrive in a challenging environment where social skills are as important as financial skills. Rural development, even if it means deployment of financial resources, has social levelling as one its overarching goals. Since you are part of a financial planet you have to work through equations honed by financial experts, and then create your own. But you cannot find all the convincing answers in spreadsheets and databases particularly when you are dealing with people in villages where formal documents and hard data are difficult to come by. Human behaviour is far too complex to be captured by mathematical models.

Forecasting does not require tremendous prescience; all it needs is to connect the dots using theoretical frameworks thrown up by credit analysts. Business plans, which contain stereotypical optimism, all appear maddening. The old rule of forecasting was to make as many forecasts as possible and publicize the ones you got right. The new rule is to forecast so far into the future that no one will know you got it wrong. Experts including the celebrated author of *The Black Swan*, Nassim Nicholas Taleb and Stanford finance professor Anat Admati have written that banks can twist data to make predictions ungrounded in the real world yet sufficient to pass government-mandated stress tests.

What is needed not just for rural banking, but for banking as a whole, is proper judgment of human attitudes and an ability to grasp a wide phalanx of human traits and attributes. It requires an open mind that is willing to learn and mastermind the dynamics of all types of societies. The biggest misconception about banking is that the people think one should have a degree in business or finance to do well in this industry. Banking is a generalist profession dealing with diverse industries. An educational background in economics or finance may help one understand banking concepts in the beginning. But in the long run it is the person with the right mix of personal qualities and managerial skills who will rise above the rest. These include the ability to learn quickly and continuously, openness to new challenges, a disciplined professionalism, an outgoing and inquisitive nature, an analytical and systematic mind, and negotiating savvy and personal integrity.

In my early days, working in a bank seemed like intellectual vegetation. Figures held no fascination for me and the initial flush of enthusiasm soon faded in the thick of mainstream banking with its then-prevalent focus on retail business and housing finance. The day-to-day pressures of the job and the weight of administrative responsibilities put on hold my dream of full-time engagement with villages.

However, the building blocks for my future work were slowly being assembled when I first experimented with my own wildly adventurous plans in development finance at Chandrapur almost two decades ago. My part-time experiments soon blossomed into full-time immersion in the world of India's villages.

There are many authors, papers, institutions and country case studies that have been seminal to our own understanding of the theory and practice of development finance. There is in fact a vast pile of scholarship. It will be vain to claim my book to be in the same league. To be honest, this not a scholarly work and if any reader is anticipating some rare and astounding revelations, he will be disillusioned. The book only reinforces the wisdom gleaned from the experiences of great bankers, sociologist and development experts and thousands of anonymous names across the country.

I hope that, in different ways for different readers, the book will challenge received wisdom and provoke richer understandings of political, social, academic, economic and financial institutions combining lessons from the classroom and the field.

1

A Banker To The Poor

There is no limit to what a man can do or how far he can go if he doesn't mind who gets the credit.

Robert Woodruff—Coca Cola CEO 1926 -1954

A small body of determined spirits fired by an unquenchable faith in their mission can alter the course of history.

Mahatma Gandhi

There is no passion to be found playing small in settling for a life that is less than the one you are capable of living.

Nelson Mandela

The difference between what we do and what we are capable of doing would suffice to solve most of the world's problems

Mahatma Gandhi

I joined the rural banking bandwagon at a critical period in the history of development banking, during a time of unresolved conflict between two tendencies in developing countries: the emergence of a huge range of creative solutions to the problem of lending to poor people, all of which interfered with the market mechanism, and the universal pressure from global financial institutions for removing these interferences. I was fiery with passion and enthralled by the heady slogans of the period, exhorting youth to lend their hand to eradicating poverty.

In his famous speech, broadcast on the radio at the midnight hour of India's birth as an independent nation on August 15, 1947, Jawaharlal Nehru, the country's first Prime Minister, articulated the new nation's promise to its people in words whose soul-stirring resonance still echoes today.

The future beckons to us. Whither do we go and what shall be our endeavour? To bring freedom and opportunity to the common man, to the peasants and workers of India; to fight and end poverty and ignorance and disease; to build up a prosperous, democratic, and progressive nation; and to create social, economic and political institutions which will ensure justice and fullness of life to every man and woman.

My father remembers how fired he and his friends were by Nehru's sincerity and determination; indeed, how some of the venerable elderly elite who listened to that historical speech commented that they felt like the old and decrepit war horses who spring back into action propelled by the bugle call. They felt like they were hearing the Delphic oracle.

Nehru's vision remains as inspiring today as when he first spoke the words but the goals remain equally elusive. India's poor still wait for opportunity and justice; too many of their lives are still fraught with poverty, ignorance, and disease. No doubt, some of the worst exploitation of human beings occurs in India—indentured servitude, sexual trafficking of women and children, child labour, female feticide and infanticide—and the less dramatic but just as debilitating daily violence of poverty, disease, and hopelessness.

To again take the help of the inimitable Faiz:

...this is not the morning we'd fought for,

In whose eager quest, all comrades

Had set out, hoping that somewhere

In the wilderness of the sky

Would emerge the ultimate destination of stars...

Indeed Gandhi had proclaimed that freedom could not be complete unless we relieve the masses of their poverty. After we gained formal independence, that is freedom from British dominion, the other freedom struggle was in the vanguard of all development policies and programmes. This was the journey towards the second independence, the true but elusive freedom, the freedom from poverty.

Nehru reiterated Gandhi's vision of independence:

Mahatma Gandhi taught us to view our national struggle always in terms of the under-privileged and those to whom opportunity had been denied. Therefore, there was always an economic facet to our political struggle for freedom. We realised that there was no real freedom for those who suffered continually from want, and because there were millions who lacked the barest necessities of existence in India, we thought of freedom in terms of raising and bettering the lot of these people. Having achieved political freedom, it is our passionate desire to serve our people in this way and to remove the many burdens they have carried for generations past. Gandhi said on one occasion that it was his supreme ambition to wipe every tear from every eye.

It was this emphasis on those excluded from the formal financial stream that led to a slew of measures in the field of finance and drove so many bankers into the arena of the battle against poverty. When I started my banking career, many of the developing-country practitioners with whom we worked at the time put their finger on the key questions arising out of the conflict between those advocating market led solutions for fighting poverty and those who believed that sustained grants and aids from the State were absolutely essential for combating poverty. The latter school believed in perennial extension of social safety nets. There was a plethora of baffling questions that confronted planners, a section of which felt that subsidies were distorting the economic climate and retarding the efforts of the poor for fighting poverty. Some of the pertinent questions were directed mostly at the relevance of the State's continued aid to poverty alleviation programmes. When and where is intervention at the bottom end of the financial market justified? Of what kind: direct intervention, subsidy, regulation or something else? The literature of that time, which consisted more of polemic and counter-polemic than of empirical investigation, did not answer all these questions. All we could do was to get a flavour of the aggressive debate in the hope that it might stimulate us to forge solutions that might at least have validity within our own local working environment.

As in other areas of development, the use of public funds is easy to justify in the interest of improving access and thereby promoting pro-poor growth. Such subsidies of course need to be evaluated against the many alternative uses of the donor or scarce public funds involved, not least of which are alternative subsidies to meet education, health, and other priority needs for the poor themselves. In practice, such a cost-benefit calculation is rarely made. Indeed, the scale of subsidy is often unmeasured.

But an even more serious problem is the possible chilling effect of subsidies on the commercial provision of competing and potentially better services to the poor. Subsidizing finance is likely to undermine the motivation and incentive for market-driven financial firms to innovate and deliver. It is this danger—that subsidies will inhibit the viability of sustainable financial innovation—that can be the decisive argument against some forms of subsidy.

It is not subsidization of the poor that should be questioned: the poor need help and subsidies in many dimensions. Subsidies to cover fixed costs (for example, in payments systems, especially when these generate network externalities) may be less subject to this chilling effect than those that operate to subsidize marginal costs. But every case must be assessed on its own merits.

While still at university, studying economics, politics, anthropology, journalism and sociology, I dreamt of a full-time career in research and academics, writing critical notes on development programmes. It was only when I came in close contact with rural realities that I decided to start as a ditch-digger and learn the ropes of rural development by myself. I always remember Walt Disney's classic quote, "The way to get started is to quit talking and start doing." Che Guevara, whose handsome face I had seen on posters and tee shirts, also came to mind. I did not know who he was till I read this passage attributed to him, "The merit of Marx is that he suddenly produces a qualitative change in the history of social thought. He interprets history, understanding its dynamics, predicts the future, but in addition to predicting it, he expresses a revolutionary concept: the world must not only be interpreted, it must be transformed."

That was the moment of epiphany for me, an experience nearly universal for social entrepreneurs, reinforcing that their work is less about money and profits and more about innovating unique and revolutionary solutions to the tough human problems that elude answers. The satisfaction derived was immense and was always deeply personal. From that time on, an active association with development programmes focused on the empowerment of the poor, especially women, has been my sole preoccupation. Like every social entrepreneur, I kept constantly testing and retesting ideas, processes, and procedures.

I was born into a family where hard work and education were of paramount importance. I admire both my parents for the way they inculcated in their children the values of hard work, justice and commitment. My father was a highly successful jurist and public figure who taught me the values of professionalism while my mother passed on to me her artistic sensibilities. These formed the twin strands of my genetic code, though other threads bind us together as well. They taught me that life was a struggle to achieve excellence in every area that one touched.

For a million reasons, my dad was my hero. He was a master of humorous anecdotes that turned into morality tales. He was my greatest coach, and he still shows up in my head, forcing me to work harder, to be better, whenever I feel like quitting. He gave me a feedback loop for life. My parents taught me the importance of getting the argument right. I do not always measure up to the exacting standards of precision they set for themselves but I came to understand what the right standard is. They instilled in me a sense of social justice and impatience with the injustice one saw in the world around oneself and the conviction that it is a supreme moral obligation to strive relentlessly to undo it.

In particular, I was aware of what was fair and what was not. The notion that you can always question authority—that just because someone is in a more powerful position than you doesn't necessarily mean that he's right—was very important to my parents; they had worked their way up the hard way. That you can always question the way things are, and then try to do something about it. I grew up surrounded by talk of revolution and justice, and I have consistently jousted with titans on behalf of the poor who have been my key constituency in my entire professional career. A part of me, which comes from my parents, always wanted to do something useful for the world. It is the only way, when you work in the development sector, to get an intuitive sense of how people really live their lives. It also hoes your mindset and worldview.

My entry into banking was more by providence than by intent. I wrote the examination, faced the interview, got through and decided to give it a try. I was fascinated by development finance and decided to stick to it. I owe my romance with rural banking to a posting as credit manager at State Bank of India, India's largest bank. I first learned directly about the power of the formal finance sector for the social and economic development of low-income people from the famous 1954 All India Rural Credit Survey. The great novelist Aubrey Menon, while being interviewed by the press, was asked to name what he considered the most important book written in India since Independence. He replied: "The 1954 All India Rural Credit Survey." I was fortunate to have read it in college and it had left a dramatic effect on me. The best part of the survey was not that it was highly comprehensible, but it was inexhaustible; it rewarded rereading. It taught me and changed me as I grew older with it.

This survey's recommendations foreshadowed initiatives by governments and international organizations across the developing world to expand access to formal credit in rural, unbanked locations. The report's rationale for such initiatives was founded on two key premises. First, supply-led inexpensive formal credit was necessary to displace evil moneylenders who exploited their monopoly to charge high rates of interest and were therefore net contributors to rural poverty. Second, state-led expansions of cheap credit were necessary to allow poor, rural households to adopt new technologies and production processes, and thus to escape the cycle of poverty and indebtedness.

My foray into rural banking was a radical move. If someone wants to do work in a village, the formal education system discourages him. The mindset that this system inculcates in students is that going back to the villages is a losing proposition. Remaining in the city is considered a success.

When I decided to take up a rural assignment in the bank, most of my friends thought I was crazy. My parents were appalled and aghast. "You can't possibly go and stay in a village for months and years. The very idea is preposterous. It's good as a tourist but not as one who will be working with them. You'll take to drink, the toddy that is the staple hospitality drink served by the villager. When broken in mind and body, you will creep back to the city, looking and behaving like a tropical tramp off a banana boat, good intentions ridiculed and rejected. You'll be met with hostility and suspicion by co-workers, politicians, and even the intended recipients of aid." When they saw my determination, my mother was reluctantly supportive, and my father came around slowly. My bosses were also very hesitant to let me go to a village but conceded when they found me passionately determined. They prodded, quizzed, needled and unsettled me for days until finally they stopped, satisfied that I knew what I was choosing.

I had always been on the side that criticized and evaluated the government and other public institutions, first as a journalist and then as a civil society activist. Now I was entering the very structure that I had questioned all these years. Most people who knew me were surprised at my decision—"You and the establishment?." After all, a public sector institution was also a State controlled body. To some extent, so was I. But beneath the trepidation, there was excitement. As a journalist, I was often frustrated at not being able to bring about a change. I could see and show, hear and be heard, but that was it. I remember, after one particularly passionate outburst in which I felt like joining a protest rally against corruption which I was actually covering for my newspaper, my mentor warned me, "You are a journalist, not an activist."

Something about rural India was just calling me. I wished to connect with my roots and to explore my own spiritual relationship with the villages on a much deeper level. I have always had a passion for development and social service, so it was only natural for me to go to villages to work in this arena. At college, I had visited villages in connection with my reporting assignments as also part of my internship with the National Service Scheme. But my exposure to the intricacies of rural problems and local social and economic tyrannies that had bedevilled the poor and marginalised populations was sparse because I had been too wrapped up in my own agenda.

I was a city-bred youth educated in Cambridge-affiliated schools in Nagpur and Bombay and brought up in the archaic curriculum of Shakespeare's sonnets with an elementary literacy in Marathi, the regional language. My school was a Presbyterian institution which taught me the first basic lesson of life—not to show off. If you do not acquire the fine art of suppressing your ego when you are young, that ego will surely overtake you when you are older after which it becomes an incurable disease. The tendency to show off is quite natural, but that tendency has to be tamed or subdued or else it usurps one's sensibilities and starts corroding those finer qualities of the heart that define an individual's aesthetic and humanist responses. As Groucho Marx said, "Humility is a strange thing; the moment you know you have got it, you have lost it."

I had the most snobbish, exclusive education imaginable and could have qualified for any lucrative job. But I was always assailed by a terrible guilt. "How is it possible that some people live in such penury—and we who go through the best of education don't give anything back?" I wondered. It was this combination of a prickling conscience with compunction and anger that drove me to seek a career in rural finance. It really didn't involve too much of a sacrifice. The bank for which I was working didn't have a very steep difference in salary between a posting in a metro centre and one in a village. The only difference was that the employees didn't think it sufficient compensation for the discomfort and hardship which a posting in a rural centre entailed. The city postings carried attractive allowances and incentives such as having the status of financial philosopher kings in the making. You also got an opportunity to acquire a robust set of financial skills that could help you leapfrog ahead in your career; one also acquired an appendage of an exalted nature: forex expert, wealth manager, corporate banker, and credit head.

To me it seemed that the physical, intellectual and emotional adventures the job provided were adequate compensation for those truly passionate about serving villages, despite the monetary loss and mental and physical hardship one suffered. This optimism was not shared by most of my peers, who felt that the management ought to compensate those working in villages by way of additional career rewards. I must admit that the city bankers were certainly looked upon with a mixture of disdain and envy in both social and financial circles. Those days we didn't have the new generation private banks we have today and the so called elite bankers in our organisation monopolised most financial events. They soon became perfumed young men with shiny attaché cases, and welcomed as banking yuppies. Their assignments were a sure passport to the charmed circles of the bank.

The rural and corporate branches of a bank were worlds apart. Visiting a rural bank office, you could expect to see the staff in casual street clothes instead of the flamboyant corporate bankers' impeccable three-piece pinstripe suits and Hermes neckties with matching pocket squares. You were more likely to find a rusty motor scooter leaning against a tree outside an archaic-looking, weather-beaten and sparsely furnished office than the polished marble counters, carpets and luxury cars parked in reserved spaces of metro offices.

While we rural managers survived on snacks infested with marauding flies followed by poisonous-looking syrupy tea, our glamorous colleagues cruised in fast cars and their modes of entertainment were Jazz Yatra concerts. Men wore suits and fat-knotted ties, yellow and pink; women frilly dresses. Their assistants would be dressed preppily in polo shirts and khaki pants, hair tied into taut ponytails and speaking with a coolly British accent or the upper crust Indian version of it. In contrast, rural bankers had to put up an attire acceptable to the rural culture. Hazardous roads made sophisticated two wheelers out of the way. Instead, the hardy but clumsy looking Yamaha, used by dairy owners for carrying milk to nearby towns, were the staple transport for not just bank officers but for all government staff working in villages.

I knew there were no rewards for working in villages. Even today when unemployment rates have zoomed and amenities in rural areas have improved considerably, it is still considered a stigma to be posted in a village. In our time, you lost out on promotions and languished in obscurity on the matrimonial map. At worst, you suffered the image of having been punished for barking at the management by being posted to God-forsaken places. I had known a multitude who would make nothing out of rural careers except returning with a baggage of headaches and blisters.

But there were brighter sides also particularly if you were imbued with an adventurous spirit of transforming the society around you. I believed there were so many wonderful development programmes that were not reaching the poor. If one could risk an adventure, there could be sure rewards for a determined individual. I had taken a rural assignment out of my own desire for an engagement with development programmes in villages. I had spent my days in school and college in a metropolis and was not professionally suited for rural work, but I was convinced that I had the temperament that could make up for other deficiencies. It is true that I was a professional banker taught and trained in the hard and coarse grammar of banking, but at the same time I knew I was a developmental worker at heart, always keen to empathize with the poor and their cause. I wanted to stretch my brains on something that genuinely excited me.

A college education is not always essential for being groomed as a banker but if, in addition to the liberal culture gained at a university, a man acquires a special knowledge of finance, economics, sociology, psychology, history and the science of governance, he is better fitted to handle the varied problems of both traditional and modern banking. A background in social anthropology and agriculture can be of immense help for bankers handling rural financial operations.

Any achieving banker will soon find himself thrust out of a comfortably known field into an unfamiliar one. He must be open to challenges. He must learn the ropes by himself before he can guide others. A banker must master and micromanage details. A banker knows the surface of many disciplines but depths of none; he should be ready to unlearn certain theoretical assumptions if his life experience warrants him to do so.

Although I began my career in the exciting and turbulent world of industrial finance, development finance (which in lay terms means here financial services for the poor) became for me, in the years that came, an abiding passion and a lifelong obsession. Even when I was posted in assignments unconnected with development finance, I kept myself involved in the field and always kept abreast with newer developments through academic journals and workshops and seminars. I would also use my annual Social Service Leave for joining village rehabilitation camps. The roots I had put down were not so shallow that I could pull them up when my assignment ended. I have cart-wheeled across the country but have remained always anchored to thoughts of village life. When my bosses reminded me, "Well, then don't sit in air-conditioned rooms and make policies without knowing the people for whom these policies are being made," I knew I had found true kindred spirits.

My first banking assignment had disillusioned me after the failure of a big cotton mill financed by our bank. I knew it was the type which would never allow me to sleep peacefully. If I were unlucky it would also mean endless enquiries, charge sheets and lawsuits. It was then that I realized that I'd find working for the poor more satisfying as there were so many development programmes that provided both a learning opportunity and a chance to assist the poor, particularly in rural areas. Moreover, working so hard for the poor gets you an avalanche of goodwill from your bosses and colleagues. As it is there are fewer people wiling to take up rural assignments, and it is a very welcome development for the management if there is a person voluntarily offering himself for the task. There is a full possibility of you enjoying relative autonomy even at junior level, something that cannot be visualised at the senior levels also in urban banking. Rural banking provides an endless scope for experimentation with one's creativity and the managements are normally glad enough to let your imagination soar.

But my job was not without its bagful of hazards. You can understand the hardships my family must have suffered, aside from the mental acrobatics needed to adapt to an alien culture, where one had to spend several nights without electricity, potable water, proper food grains and cooking oil. In those days, villagers were not so health conscious nor did their income levels permit the quality products they now afford. Wheat and rice, now consumed even by the poorest, were then a luxury for even the wealthiest in the villages.

It was my love and passion for books and literature that sustained me and helped keep my communication skills alive, enabling me to compete with officers who waxed eloquent on rural development at seminars and conferences even when none of them stayed overnight in a village. When the bank made rural postings mandatory, the darlings of the management and unions were posted at industrial branches situated barely outside the municipal limits of urban centres, though by virtue of their location beyond the city limits they qualified as rural centres. They did not serve the poor but rather the big industrialists. The buddies of the management were posted to these branches and were shown in official records to have completed their mandatory rural assignments. In this way, the bank made a sham of so-called rural assignments. The management and unions, normally at loggerheads, would always strike a truce on postings for their buddies at convenient centres.

I knew full well that I was an outsider in a strange civilisation. I would never be able to understand the area quite as well as a local person. But I also had a special set of experiences and a critique of development processes born out of varied experiences. My academic studies in anthropology gave me an insight into rural and tribal societies. A stint as a journalist had equipped me with useful insights into the realpolitik of the country's development programmes and familiarized me with the rural ecosystem. I was going without any mental baggage of biases and prejudices which could colour my worldview.

It was in a mood of adventure that I took the bus for my first rural job, in the village of Bina in the district of Nagpur. Since it was the day of a cricket match, the atmosphere in the bus was charged. Men, women and children—some standing in the aisle and others on the seats—huddled around the transistor set straining to catch every word of the commentary. I watched the driver push harder on the accelerator as he took his hand off the wheel to raise the volume of the transistor on his dashboard. The commentary over, he switched off the radio and drove in silence. At some stage he turned it on again, flitted between channels, located some crackling pop music and then, with a grunt of displeasure, turned it off. Everyone had fallen into a scared and frozen silence while the driver was concentrating on his high speed.

A man hanging on the back of the bus constantly yelled our route. Near a village, he screamed, "Refreshment and freshening halt; strictly five minutes." The driver coasted to the kerb, yanked the hand brake and parked the bus to let passengers off at a little thatch-roofed tea shack where a smell of cooking oil and tobacco hung in the crisp air. On the highway, a "dhaba" is a catchall term that can include truck stops, car parks and sometimes nothing at all, with string cots lined up so that you can lie down and relax after a happy meal. We discovered that our "dhaba" was a cafe. The cafe owner brought us sweet tea, puris, pakora and dollops of chutney and pickles and watery tomato sauce which he leaked out frequently from the plastic bottle.

At a raffish highway town, we stopped to switch buses. In each village, a man carrying a large mailbag would be waiting by the bus stop in the village square, who would look at first confused and then furious as the bus roared by him without slowing. I could also see an area at the back of the bus, separated by a wire mesh partition, that was piled high with mailbags just like those held by the angry, fist-shaking men in the village squares. "Yes, stop, stop," the passengers begged (anything to make him slow down), but the driver only accelerated. "Too late," one of the passengers yodelled gaily. The driver shouted back, "Already it is far behind. Requests must be more promptly made if I am to comply."

Finally the bus stopped and the driver shouted, "Bina". "Bina"! " Get down here." I realized it was my turn to disembark. The bus roared away, leaving me on the roadside in the dark. There was no sign of any village, let alone one called "Bina". I had planned to arrive during daylight, but the bus left late and then spent two hours in a greasy mechanic's yard on the plains, as the exhaust pipe had detached from the engine.

All the villagers who had disembarked with me had shuffled off to their homes. Night was falling, the cicada buzz was rising, and I began to get that panicky feeling that the city-coddled may experience while alone on the roadside in a remote village. An old auto rickshaw roared up and slid to a halt near me. The driver was swathed in an outsized jacket and a monkey cap, his eyes barely visible. I told him the name of my host and he nodded towards his rickshaw. I hopped in the backward-facing seat at the rear of the auto, joining other passengers already there. I held on for dear life as we travelled at breakneck speeds over pockmarked paved roads, then unpaved roads, then off-road rocky terrain. Wind whistled through our tuk-tuk's open sides, so we wore all our clothes, thus also saving on luggage space

I was amazed that a seventy-year-old patient from the health centre was able to clamber in the back with me and endure the bone-jarring journey. We drove on dark dirt roads that seemed to lead nowhere. I didn't speak fluent Hindi, only pidgin Marathi corrugated with English and Hindi. I had no idea where we were going and why there was no town and I was terrified. Over and over I repeated to myself, "Please, God, don't let me be murdered tonight."

We arrived in a small village about 30 minutes later, clearly not my destination. Though my Marathi was a little rusty, I asked the driver where he had taken me. He told me he had brought me the wrong way and tried to extort money to take me to my real destination, but finally drove me to the right signpost. I gave the auto-rickshaw driver a huge tip for not murdering me. It was pitch dark. Not a soul in sight. Even the stars had forgotten to light up the sky. To my relief, I could see somebody flashing a torch. My caretaker.

My first shock did not appear in my office, but rather during the first night of my homestay. It was so quiet I could hear the goats' hooves clattering on the cobblestones, the murmuring of the distant monkeys. A long bulb glowed dimly, threatening to go out at any moment, casting surreal shadows on the walls. I writhed on the mattress, succumbing to all the aggressors: the heat, the mosquitoes, the stabbing bedsprings. I woke up scratching the blisters on my shoulders. The night had been a frenzied experience, and all morning the nostalgia lingered: making the house seem dreamlike, dreary, looming, like a set of a great mystery film.

The first morning contact with a village is normally pleasing. I vividly remember my first day at the village where I spent two years as manager of a village bank. It looked like a painting of an old pastoral village, with tiled roofs jigsawed together and mud-brick houses faded to pastel where successive coats of lime-wash had been diluted by foul weather. It was a dusty warren of thatched huts, tiled roofs and brightly painted temples. I followed a footpath down the hill, deserted but for a herd of goats, and crossed the stream where women washed laundry, whacking clothes on boulders and drying them on shrubs. Elderly men cogitated while supervising small herds of cows.

A gentle thunder grumbled around the hills; the monsoon was not far off. The scent of the cypress hedges was everywhere. Half a mile away, a herdsman was sitting on a hillside singing quietly to his cows—a long and seemingly formal song, inexpressibly soothing.

With a pure heart a peasant sweats
The drops fall on earth
The rain clouds burst
The land turns green
The flower blooms
The grain ripens
I knead my bread
That gives me life

I found the change - the slow pace of life, the stillness and silence, the smoky fire, the stones in the rice and the domestic chores - just really hard to adapt. The zeal of a volunteer in the village can erode quickly. That incredible stoicism is everywhere. It appeared to be a bitter medicine, but I guess I needed it. I quickly grew impatient with poignant snapshots of Indian squalor: the ribby children with flies in their eyes and other emblems of abjectness that one can't help but see within minutes of walking into a village.

I had arrived in Bina with an overblown sense of my own nobility and preparedness and, more naïvely, under-equipped for the responsibilities. I also deeply underestimated the cultural baggage I unwittingly carried everywhere with me. I started my work in the village driven by the notion that I was going to help the poor, but discovered that noble missions do not necessarily add up to great achievement. There were the usual linguistic faux pas and cultural gaffes that contribute today to my repertoire of comical stories to tell at gatherings, but there were more serious mistakes.

I soon saw what happened when the 'educated' tried to 'help' the poor—how bureaucrats gave subsidized loans for high-yielding Jersey cows which died in tough drought conditions, leaving the poor worse off. How the veterinarians fleeced villagers, charging what top physicians and surgeons in cities didn't dare to charge affluent patients. How education failed to prepare poor children for getting a job, yet alienated them from their traditional economies. The whole experience purged me of pretensions and made me realize my own inadequacies. I found my mind had been filled with flabby conclusions drawn from sloppy reading. I substituted journals, books and films on rural projects for the fiction I intended to read in the coming months.

Going into my internship, I was unclear what rural development entailed. Unprepared, with no road map, no tools, insufficient gear, and no protective layering I decided to spend time with the people, listening to the communities. Early into my journey, I realized that my pre-conceived notions were hindering my understanding of the issues and concerns. Rather I needed to look at the problems of the poor through their eyes. My pre-departure vision was one of heroically entering remote villages, and after briefly surveying the problems, rapidly coming up with solutions to better the lives of the villagers. I did not realize how crucial it was, for the sustainability of any project, that the villagers plan their own schemes, and not the "development experts".

I had always imagined that the poor were ignorant and uneducated. Most people whom I consulted before embarking on my rural mission admired my aspiration but moderated my enthusiasm with caveats. "They know a lot more than we do. You can at best learn from them." "Don't try to supplant their culture; that will be the greatest disservice." I initially wrote off these responses as an attempt to unnerve me. Later I realized that these advices were not pure banter.

My fertile, overheated conscience was further stung by my academic reading of the sufferings of people in Latin American countries. Driven by guilt, buried under the weight of my attractive job and haunted by the sight of excruciating poverty every day, I volunteered to spend the weekends off from my office with villagers, trying to make up for the fact that I had so much while they had so little.

I put away my books and immersed myself in the rhythms of villages learning from the poor and understanding their problems, trying to see their culture and society through their own eyes. I had to invert everything I'd learned in economics classes. My status as a qualified sociologist was worth zilch. The heaviness of being successful was replaced by the lightness of being a beginner again, less sure about everything. That status did make me a little ashamed at my inadequacies, yet it freed me to enter one of the most creative periods of my life. I was able to turn my ideas into workable goals. The humble beginnings taught me life as only a villager can know. It brought me to terms with the inadequacy of my learning. I realised I had to become part of the villagers' heartbeat to be in a position to help them.

I have never been hooked by the bookish definitions of poverty: this much income or that much calorie intake. I define poverty as the absence of adequate nutrition, clean water, basic sanitation and health care, education andenforced constitutional rights. Poverty may be defined as the inability to secure the minimum consumption, requirements for life, health and efficiency. Poverty is insufficient supply of those things which are requisite for an individual to maintain himself and those dependent upon him in health and vigour. The problem of poverty is considered as the biggest challenge to development planning in India. High poverty levels are synonymous with poor quality of life, deprivation, malnutrition, illiteracy and low human resource development. Poverty can be defined as a social phenomenon in which a section of the society is unable to fulfill even its basic necessities of life. When the poor are living on the edge of subsistence, a minuscule misfortune can push them down into a tailspin. With nearly four out of five Indians living in poverty, millions are caught in a lethal web. Illnesses become a financial sinkhole for village women; they are often forced to drop out of the labour force as they provide most of the care. TB has now at least gone from being a death sentence to a manageable illness. The government has been building awareness of malaria by popularising blood tests wherever any one has fever. Similarly, polio has now been virtually eliminated. Mosquito nets and repellents are being liberally used even in remote villages.

The real tragedy of the poor is that their voice is unheard in forums, even at those which are exclusively devoted to their problems. As the Madagasy proverb goes, "poverty won't allow him to lift his head, dignity won't allow him to bow it down". They are shouted down by those who consider them illiterate and uninformed and who abrogate to themselves the wisdom and the right to speak for the poor. The oppression of impatience came home to me only when I was on the other side, years later. It is not pleasant for anyone to be pushed away with an "All right, now sit down," when that person is halfway through expressing an issue of life and death. And of course, the public places where such meetings are held are designed to keep the poor away from any scope for voicing their problems.

No amount of reading or instructions could have taught me what I learnt in these years I spent in the hinterland. Henry Miller once said, "One's destination is never a place, but a new way of seeing things." I had been handed a rare opportunity to connect with my country and its people, to see and understand the everyday realities of the life of the rural poor. I learnt to be less judgmental. I saw first-hand the consequences of all that ails our system. Yet, for the first time, I realized how easy it was to blame the government for everything; stepping inside and instituting change was much more difficult. I recognized how isolated we all are despite being connected through the news and media. The peasants, I believe, might have a keener understanding of development and its implications than the economists sitting in the rarefied atmosphere of Yojana Bhavan.

It is this distance that has grown between the planners and the people in the rural matrix that has plagued the rural financial system. Too much dependence on data and much less direct engagement with the poor has been the major cause of failure for most state mandated development programmes

I sometimes feel that the younger managers are now loath to accept rural assignments not just because of the hazards they entail but because they have not been properly mentored. Something has gone askew somewhere in the alchemy and we have been unable to build a new generation of committed rural bankers.

So, are development practitioners born or made? For me, the answer has been both. It is through a combination of following my instincts and being in an environment that cultivated and directed my talents in the service of the poor. I also got an opportunity to use my creativity for bringing about both economic and social transformation. My successes spurred me on, and in the process I grew passionate with my mission.

Banking claimed me but could not hold me a hostage to its rules, as I craved for innovative ways to break out of the age old and hardened paradigms. I rarely worked within the realm of conventional assumptions and was never impressed by the rarefied starched-shirt world of banking officialdom. I was not a rebel but I felt it was important to lead life the way one knows best.

We used to spend evenings with the village headmen, trying to understand the local culture, and how best we could tailor schemes to meet the local needs. The *Village Adoption Scheme*, introduced by the government country-wide, was an innovation that helped banks build up professional credit culture in villages and empower the rural population with information about new agricultural technologies and development finance. Fortunately, politics had still not seeped the rural fabric and there were few factions in the villages. The village society had a monochromatic character. The village headman (*sarpanch*) would be selected by a consensus of village elders. The headman was usually a sober, just and committed individual. Unlike today, the village headman would ensure that our programmes were enthusiastically embraced by the villagers.

One feature I discovered was that villagers may be uneducated, but they are extremely clever and good at telling an outsider what they think the outsider wants to hear. The truth of a village may come out only slowly, with time—time for trust to build between the villagers and outsiders, and time for the outsider to peel away all the layers to get at the truth. I was there in the villages during the blistering heat of May, the chilling cold of December, the spring harvest festival and the September election for the *sarpanch* (headman). When the electricity failed, as it so often did, I would scribble notes by candlelight. I would drive through the sodden winter fogs to be in time for the meeting with the villagers. Most of them would leave home quite early for their fields. A delay on my part would mean a meeting lost. The entire trip would amount to a waste.

It could be a drive in the milky whiteness of the dawn or the blazing darkness of the night along rutted paths as the warm air swirled over my face, my thoughts whirling me into a trance. I might have to plod through rain and slush. My hair would get as dishevelled as the thorn bushes we passed on the road, and the villagers wondered whether I'd combed it properly in the first place.

During my engagement with the poor as a bank manager handling rural finance, I found in them a reservoir of grit, wisdom, tenacity and courage that enabled them to cope with severe adversities. I had not known how brutal poverty could be until I encountered it almost daily, but the memories haunted me over the years. How the sick went without medicines, children dropped out of school because parents could not afford education, how young children went cotton picking to add to the family's kitty. Amartya Sen argues in his book *Development as Freedom* that poverty is 'capability deprivation'. These adolescents, facing a volatile situation at an early stage of life due to economic insecurity, are not simply poor but rather 'incapable' individuals who lack the basic means to enjoy the rights and freedoms enshrined in the Indian Constitution. In highly patriarchal societies, sudden access to skills and money can alter the dynamics of a woman's relationship with the people around her in unpredictable ways.

I had always wondered why rural poverty had defied all solutions. My exploration led me to a unique conclusion: first the poor lacked capital and second insurance against tragedies wrought by nature, to which the poor were particularly vulnerable. The poor had a disproportionately larger share of tragedies and had ver little or no insurance coveragThis was my learning during the extension work I did for the National Service Scheme as a university student.

I have learnt and understood many things in working with poor people, but nothing more clearly than that poor people do not have to remain poor forever. The poor remain poor because they are powerless. Once empowered, the poor are able to overcome seemingly impossible odds. But people cannot transform their lives all on their own. The first step is to change the overall perception of development academics and policy designers about poor people—from needy beneficiaries to active architects of their own development.

I had set myself a clear vision: create new space and terms for poor village women. I knew my limitations and I had decided not to extend my agenda beyond this limited horizon. I always made it clear that I was not there to drive the existing agencies out of business. Nor was I going to supplant the government welfare departments. I always warmly embraced the various functionaries in the development apparatus. I felt this limited agenda should help me to endear myself even to my worst opponents. Prejudices exist in the most open of cultures which is why society requires tempered radicals who can act as catalytic agents, bringing in change without tearing down established and respected structures and picking out rotten apples without upsetting the apple cart. I always felt that the best way to finish an enemy was to make him a friend. As events unfolded, I was happy to find that I had taken the correct route. In fact, my good equation with the village leaders helped me in getting the help of the government. With time, even the rage of political leaders had all but gone, or mellowed.

I learnt the hard lesson that helping improve lives and fostering economic development is difficult, often because of locals' scepticism about the work of 'development experts'. "We don't hate you," they would tell me, "What we hate is what you represent." As I tried to grapple with rural realities, I began to view the village and its environs more like a native than an outsider. Not only did I get used to the smells, dirt, dust, winds, noise, insects and vermin and the lack of privacy, I learned to distinguish good land from bad, the various properties of the plants and trees found in the area and picked up insights into good veterinary practices. The canvas of the story was ready to stretch wider, move further and include new friends: villagers from the neighbouring villages, local rural leaders and a huge planet of development practitioners.

I saw how some of the world's poorest and most oppressed people are changing our world. But nowhere was my journey through development more influenced than in an unassuming village where I stayed whenever I had the chance over the last fifteen years. This village, Wanoja, became a microcosm of all I saw elsewhere, stuck as it was in centuries of tradition. Only the names changed. It provided me with friends and joyful moments and sometimes gave me hope in human progress. But, just as often, it crushed that hope in the nasty friction between irresolvable social divisions. Even in the violence that submerged my village I saw the hope of people breaking the status quo and gaining a voice. I saw women grappling with intense poverty. I heard the struggles of the women at the grassroots. Initially I often broke down in confusion, not knowing what contribution I could make, but over time I decided that my future lay with these poor but tenacious women who were fighting daily misfortunes to build a decent future for their families.

More than any other professional unit, a rural bank branch requires a special set of skills particularly when there are few people willing to work in villages and when your priorities are not the affluent famers but poor, helpless and disadvantaged women. There is no point making anyone in your team feel needlessly inadequate. I was never a slave of my own opinion. Instead, I listened to others. We must focus on each person's strengths and manage around his or her weaknesses. We shouldn't try to perfect each person, but help each one to cultivate his or her talents, become more of who he or she already is. There may be a moody person in your team, but careful handling may enable him to deliver the most wonderful results. There are a lot of people who don't enjoy the work they do. They tolerate it under duress and wait for the weekend. I have also met people who love what they do and can't imagine doing anything else. The expression we use is that they're in their element. It's their enthusiasm that has to be channelized.

A community will always make a better decision than an individual. An open system means more voices; more voices mean more discussion and criticism that leads to better decision. I always bounced my thoughts off my staff. That's why building consensus is important to the process. I wanted all these voices to come together in my projects. Getting all stakeholders to play a role in the exploration of a solution by giving them a voice in the process is an important way of accomplishing this. It helps also to be able to look at old problems in new ways putting a new twist on what has been tried before. Team-building, consensus-building and innovative solutions are the keys to success. I demonstrated both trust and faith in my team. As Ralph Waldo Emerson once said: "Trust men and they will be true to you; treat them greatly and they will show themselves great."

I always believe that people can do wonders, if their energy is channelized and focussed on a given task. Tomorrows are made by people. A lesson I learnt early in life is that great leaders don't teach. They touch and transform. They don't instruct; they inspire by their conduct and disposition. They help people discover within themselves the strength to find the pathway to the stars.

The talents of our people are greatly underestimated and their skills underutilized. Our biggest task is to redefine our relationship with our employees. The objective must be to build a place where people have the freedom to be creative, where they feel a real sense of accomplishment—a place that brings out the best in everybody. Just as an artist has many colours on his palette, a leader has a palette of employees with different skills. Like the effective mixing of colours helps the artist produce a work of art, the leader's effectiveness in channelling the skills of, and obtaining the best results from, each employee helps create an organisation that is always energised, enthusiastic and effervescent.

During the ten years I was manager of the rural branches of the bank, my staff never participated in strikes, because I was convinced that strikes would shutter our business. It wasn't because we were against the management or the unions. Most of our clients were villagers—the majority of them illiterate—who could not have advance notice of the strike in an era when even basic connectivity was light years away. We didn't want to cause inconvenience or discomfort to clients. An equally important reason was that neither the management nor the unions ever bothered about the problems of staff working in remote rural areas.

The outsiders believe that the cost of living in a village is cheaper when compared to cities. Contrary to what people believe, the cost of living in a village is higher than that in the nearby town. You have to depend entirely on the nearest town for your groceries. The local agents who ferry these items from nearby towns charge a heavy premium. In most cases, school and medical facilities and proper housing are not available and the family has to be based at the nearest town. This entails maintaining two establishments at a reduced salary because all the major allowances are reserved for larger centres. I know of staff assistants who spent their entire lives in remote areas because the unions were dominated by the urban elite who protected the interests of those living in cities. I was proud of the relentless work put in by my staff, despite the miserliness of the bosses in recognizing them. I always dinned just one instruction into the heads of my boys, "If the organization doesn't care for you, build goodwill with clients. That way the esteem and respect from the local population will neuter your frustrations."

It is on account of the high cost of maintaining two establishments that most managers prefer to commute from their homes in towns to their rural job centres. To fresh entrants in this field of development work, I can only suggest that one must live in a village, and not merely just drop by for the day, if one really wants to get full insight into the society in which one has to operate. I think many of our ambitious development programmes have gone awry because development workers, particularly the senior bosses, never had the patience to understand the problems and needs of villagers. During their official visits, they move through villages as if they were passing through revolving doors, rarely interested in dropping into a villager's house, afraid of catching infection in case they had to taste the villager's hospitality.

There are managers working in Naxalite areas who have shown personal courage and ingenuity in creating safe spaces in which they can pursue development work. Their reward is not early promotion or early transfer out of these disturbed areas; usually these boys would be the last to qualify for promotions because they have neither amenities nor instructors under whose tutelage they can prepare for departmental examinations. A large number of boys working in god forsaken places are highly qualified and have been rank holders in universities. Their families stay far away in towns where the facilities for education and health care are at least satisfactory. Their transfer is ruled out because there are no replacements to relieve them and management doesn't have the guts to post others, who have spent their entire career in cities, at least for short periods. These unfortunate ones are confined to a serfdom of an entire career in such abysmal conditions.

The management is helpless because they quail to take on the unions who want to create a safe haven for their chums. A person who has spent a career in villages will tell you of both the discomforts and hazards one has to put up with. Apart from the physical discomforts, one experiences a constant fear of physical insecurity. The government and corporates have not been able to induce their staff to agree to take up rural careers in villages in large numbers. All ambitious parents are driven by the desire to give the children the best amenities and education which cannot possibly be achieved if one opts for a rural career. Most individuals working in rural areas find it very difficult to lead a peaceful personal and family life. The family has to be located at the nearest township where a semblance of at least bare primary health and education facilities are available and the employee himself has to put up with the hard rigours of village life: no toilets, erratic power supply, lack of primary health care and above all, lack of intellectual company. The plight is similar to that of a voyager marooned on an island. Leave apart any guarantee of rewards, there is not even a token discomfort allowance. The lucrative allowances are reserved for those already enjoying the luxury of the company of their kith and kin in regally furnished official apartments in big cities.

Before I took up a full time career in development banking, I worked as a journalist focusing on development sector. I wrote extensively in both the national and international press and travelled extensively in the remote hinterland. This experience provided me a lot of insight into the problems of the rural folk and I decided to become a part of the development administration. As a journalist, I could never visualise the hazards of a career in villages. All along, I had been protected with an important identity card which provided me ease of access to even the most powerful bureaucrats. But most important, it gave me much needed security and protection from local leaders. A village is served in too many conflicting ideologies and your city breeding doesn't adequately equip you to deal with the crude and rustic manoeuvres of local leaders. It is just basic common sense that you can use to navigate the rough terrain of village politics. In the heady world of policy and investment conferences, it is easy for policy makers to forget the incredible tenacity and endurance demanded of grassroots development workers.

Our exposure to villages came from our homestays. This was known as a 'night halt'. This was not just a paper fad. The bank's regional offices monitored these night halts and we were expected to give a monthly report on them. Rural branches were opened in such remote hinterlands that the bank manager was the only literate denizen in some of these desolate islands. We lived the lives of the locals so that we would feel the pain the villagers felt. I remember once a poor woman telling me "Uncle, I will fetch rice from the village headman's house as what I cook is very dirty. It's so full of stones you'll crack your teeth if you eat it." When I checked the cavernous kitchen, I found her daughter trying to light the damp wood. She fingered the kindling gingerly for fear of the community of scorpions living, loving, and reproducing in the pile.

We had to tiptoe through a political minefield. It was a vibrant universe of fast hatching leaders of a rich diversity of stripes and hues. In fact, trying to patch up with these groups is like building relations between a wolf and a sheep. I had to play dumb on several occasions so that leaders didn't get irritated because earlier when I tried to send them packing out of my office they created a big ruckus in the village the following night. The burly mustachioed worthies who stalked me were a really ferocious and required diplomacy of a high order to pin them in their tracks. The temperature of the political rhetoric kept heating up. Bleeding the banks to aggrandize the rich farmers had become a favorite sport of the politicians. The politicians had been using banks as cash dispensers for populist programmes. Most rural branches were hobbled by a legacy of political interference. The greater part of the last decade of the twentieth century was spent by banks in cleaning their branches of the avalanche of bad loans in which they had been buried. The years of sloppy lending had left a vast hole in the balance sheets of rural banks.

I found rivalries between leaders were poisonous and based on the principle that if one could not succeed, others had to be seen to have played foul. Each man sought to demonize the other. A war of attrition started between us and the syndicate of village power brokers. It would keep on festering for weeks. People are only too ready to ascribe motives to you, or even run you down. They would jeer us at meetings. In fact, one had to develop a thick hide to stand up to the derisive campaign of some of the rowdy and garrulous elements in villages. I would always keep a joke ready to deflect any jeer.

Once I decided I would remain a permanent creature of the planet of the poor, I started religiously making myself part of the villagers' beats—interacting with people, speaking their earthy language, rallying the masses for meetings. Without a common language, we communicated through gestures and occasional local words which I had picked up from colleagues. Languages interest me very much—as the basis of communication, and in their own aesthetic right—but I have never been very good at learning them. My lingua franca was Hindustani which is itself a mongrel of two hybrid languages, Hindi and Urdu. In remote villages, I spoke pidgin Marathi. I made very serious efforts to respect linguistic sentiments and tried to avoid mangling any of the culturally rooted modes of communication.

It was only through long and close contact with the poor themselves and through our work with them that we were able to gain a deeper understanding and more balanced view of the local society. In this way, our experience was not that of typical non-governmental organizations (NGO), many of which work from within the confines of the project enclave or are based in urban centres from where excursions are made out into the villages by jeep. Sadly, many NGOs are far removed from the realities of poverty and often fail to reach those most in need. For me, the most surprising discovery was the simple human-to-human connection that let me overcome both linguistic and cultural barriers.

We have to get rid of the pernicious notion that the roots of poverty lie with the poor themselves and that cultural differences are responsible for the gap between less-developed countries and the industrialized West. I found the villagers had many of the same economic needs, beliefs and aspirations as the most capitalist of Westerners. Village craftsmen were keenly interested in profits, and entrepreneurship was in plentiful supply in rural India, having been part of the traditional culture for a millennium.

Underdevelopment in these communities resulted from a scarcity of capital, the allocation of which was a matter of politics, not culture. Anti-poverty programmes that ignored this reality had the potential, perversely, of exacerbating inequality because they would only reinforce the power of elites. Many government programmes inadvertently fostered stratification by channelling resources through village officials who used the money to fatten the existing rich classes. The fact that policies often fail for no good reason is annoying, but is certainly less depressing than the view that they are a conspiracy against the poor.

Now more than ever, it is important to reaffirm that significant advances are attainable for the rural poor, who are a potential source of great wealth and creativity, but who must first and foremost seek their own survival under present institutional, cultural and policy conditions. Their poverty deprives not only themselves but also the rest of us of the greater value they could produce under more conducive circumstances. I feel that the people who have pioneered the various programmes that have now become models, recognised this potential and sought to evoke it.

We should not forget that poor villagers are not just statistics but people like you and me, and apart from the poverty that they share in common, there is as much variety of humankind among them as anywhere else in the world: the hardworking, the lazy, the shy, the outspoken, the honest, the devious, the intelligent and the dull, the improvident and the enterprising. The people with whom we worked were all of these, though, in my experience, the positive characteristics almost always stood out.

An important advice I would proffer to the younger crop of rural managers is that they must always have the desire and urge to produce a superior thing. How you think and the way you handle relationships are what decide how well you communicate with your customers and relate to your team. Someone said that much of today's communications are like scrambled eggs—wholesome but messy. We must learn to be cogent and logical in our communications. I suffered from an irresistible urge to correct not only my own drafts and letters but also those of others, much to the distress of my long-suffering typists whom I must have driven up the wall many times and to whom I shall ever be grateful for their understanding and patience. With a low threshold of tolerance for inefficiency, I confess to being intolerant of slipshod work and irritatingly insisted on pursuing excellence in tasks which hardly demanded it.

While the world is indeed complex, we see that constraining 'circles', even if they are not always 'vicious', can be broken by initiatives that are well thought out but adaptable, conceived by leadership that persisted and shared credit widely, by melding so-called traditional and modern features into new attractive combinations.

Midway through my rural career, I realized I had collated a ragbag of half-cooked impressions, prejudices and preferences about the villages. I had no idea what my rambling outpourings of half-fangled ideas would amount to. I wrote to get things off my chest—a kind of catharsis. I was surprised that leading business newspapers gave prominent space to my despatches, presumably because I was the only writer reporting directly from the field. In quick time, I became a roving faculty member, lecturing at academies, and a one-eyed denizen in a kingdom of the blind. I scribbled in my notebooks. With the onset of computers I kept tapping away on my laptop, composing copious notes and sometimes angry missives, the words spawned from the depths of my rage and desperation. As an ex-journalist, I had learned the subtleties of the craft and the sensitive nuances of the profession.

I found that the word 'finance' conjured up images of cold-hearted bankers working with people they did not understand, an unwelcome stranger to the village. The rural banker seemed a remote figure: infinitely rational and too perfect to relate to mere human concerns. At worst, he would seem like a social naïf, if not an outright sociopath, a man who had intelligence and reason but was devoid of emotions. Yet bankers are not the horned, greedy villains the public tries to demonize them to be. They are decent, caring human beings. Because their business offers few anchors for their morality, their primary compass becomes how much money they make.

To me, the real story of development finance is neither the numbers nor rapid growth. In fact, it is about the slow movement—a value-based, de-risked, diverse, widely-spread, bottom-up social transformation. The exact opposite of the dizzying development in financial markets around the world. That's why it merits discourse. As a society, we have often looked for models that we hope will trickle down. Maybe it is just the right time for some lift. There are charlatans everywhere. There are also attempts to subvert the ethic, some by entrepreneurs pushing ultra-rapid growth and some by politicians who love to give away freebies at no cost to themselves. But there have been genuine attempts by innovative and committed managers that have brought new hope for the poor, particularly the women among them. It is now an accepted wisdom that villages present an ideal arena for improvisation of credit policies and procedures.I myself found innovative efforts at village level both easier and followed by rich dividends.

The poor are yet to find their voice, even as the media (for that matter, the entire establishment) have become the megaphone of the classes that are prospering. The preference for growth over social justice, indeed, the argument that economic growth is the road to social justice, is advocated over and above increased spending. But is it required for accelerated growth to translate into inclusive growth? The answer, I fervently believe, lies in inclusive governance. In the absence of inclusive governance, the people at the grassroots, that is, the intended beneficiaries of poverty alleviation programme are left abjectly dependent on a bureaucratic delivery mechanism over which they have no effective control. The alternative system would be participatory development, where the people themselves are enabled to build their own future through elected representatives responsible to the local community and, therefore, responsive to their needs.

Not only is responsive bureaucratic administration almost a contradiction in terms, the Indian experience of the last six decades would appear to confirm that bureaucratic delivery mechanisms absorb a disproportionately high share of the earmarked expenditure: up to 85 paise in the rupee, said Rajiv Gandhi; perhaps 85 paise, says the Planning Commission in a recent evaluation; not quite so high, says the Prime Minister. We can leave it to experts to argue how many angels can dance on the head of a pin; for our purposes, it is enough to note that 75% to 85% of expenditure on poverty alleviation schemes is absorbed by the delivery mechanism itself. No wonder outcomes are so derisory.

I am tempted to quote worse, precisely because (in India) over a hundred schemes are delivered to the same set of beneficiaries through mutually insulated administrative silos, set up by central government ministries intent on jealously guarding their respective fiefdoms. Convergence of schemes at the delivery point becomes virtually impossible, thus depriving beneficiaries of the multiplier effect that would operate if the beneficiaries themselves, through their locally elected leaders, were to have the authority to plan and implement the utilisation of these resources in keeping with their own respective priorities. So far, I am on well-trodden ground. But the argument for a systemic reordering of the delivery mechanism to shift from bureaucratic delivery to participatory development runs much deeper.

The priorities of senior managers keep rapidly changing. Very often, top managers take their eye off the ball once it seems to be within the goal and then the whole thing tends to fall apart. But it must be admitted that in most banks, successful micro-finance programmes are more individual-driven than institution-driven. The time has come when we must institutionalise the best practices through recognition of individuals who have innovated them. I have seen that most senior managers are thrifty in the matter of praising juniors. Recognition is a way of indicating an organisation's approval. Very often, these seminars resonate with buzzwords like *empowerment participation, sustainability* and *marginalisation* and end in copious policy statements. They would arrange discussions and seminars on microfinance over glitzy parties at swanky hotels.

I had a quick eye for vanity and I would perceive the frequent incongruities between the way people talked and the realities of the situation. Much disservice has been done to the cause of rural development on account of this schizoid approach: alternating engagement and withdrawal. It is easy to dish out lectures on micro-finance, but it is an arduous experience to practice it.

Any debate about the economic policy for the poor is usually tortuous, long-winded and insular. There is a tendency to stay away from the common ground for common goals, for the development of a desperately poor people. More than anything it obscures issues. To cut through the fog, we have to lend our ear to the voice of the people who are the stakeholders. "God gives us nuts but he doesn't crack them," says an Irish proverb. The world is not a finished product. We contribute to it by our sincere work to make it more perfect and ideal. We work to bring out a new earth, which will arrive when our works promote a better order in human society, uphold human dignity and promote love, equality, freedom, beauty and creativity. In the process we also perfect ourselves and thus our work becomes a means for our self-actualisation.

Fortunately, these common beliefs are misconceptions—only a small part of the explanation of why the poor are poor. In all corners of the world, the poor face structural challenges that keep them from getting even their first foothold on the ladder of development. Most societies with the right ingredients—good harbours, close contacts with the rich world, favourable climates, adequate energy sources and freedom from epidemic disease—have escaped extreme poverty. The world's remaining challenge is not to overcome laziness and corruption, but rather to take on the solvable problems of geographic isolation, disease and natural hazards, and to do so with new arrangements of political responsibility that can get the job done. We need plans, systems, mutual accountability and financing mechanisms. But even before we have all of that apparatus in place—what I call the economic plumbing—we must first understand more concretely what such a strategy means.

I must admit that I was considered a maverick, a heretic, a radical, an avant-garde and an anachronist in the realm of rural banking. I never toned down my ideas to ingratiate myself to the bosses, most of whom were parlour socialists and many of my suggestions would spark dismissive snorts from them, who found my uncompromising rebelliousness not in keeping with the ethos of the organisation. Honestly, I had grown jaded with the traditional approach but was blissfully unaware of the power dynamics at our headquarters. I was convinced that the staid arena of rural banking could be transformed into a stage for desperate improvisation and innovation. In the process, I treaded on some pretty powerful toes. There were regular missives of stinging criticism and sharp-edged admonitions from my superiors. I remember every time a programme got grounded, I had to seek their patronage to nudge the processes down below. Then there were the several hard-line strands within the management that were not willing to see beyond the mould of traditional banking. The most inspiring mantra that sustained me through such trying phases was ultimately the one given by Mahatma Gandhi—"First they ignore you, then they laugh at you, then they fight you, then you win."

The excruciating hardliners remained stuck in a time warp. Many of them had an innate dislike for rural banking. My peers and my senior colleagues would label me a "freak", "leftist", "deranged" and "populist". The critics in my organization would often scoff at my notion of getting much traction for an initiative but I persevered. But my close friends knew that deep within me I harboured a sensitive heart guided by the poignant words of Che Guevara: "Let me say, at the risk of seeming ridiculous, that the true revolutionary is guided by great feelings of love" I am a professional banker trained in the hard and coarse grammar of banking. But at heart, I'm a developmental worker, always keen to do my bit for the underprivileged.

I would get chafed at the restrictions my managers would impose on me. Banking certainly claimed me but could not hold me a hostage to its rules, as I craved relentlessly for innovative ways. I rarely worked within the realm of conventional possibilities and was never impressed by the rarefied starched-shirt world of banking officialdom. I was not a rebel but I felt it was important to lead life one knows best. It was a no holds barred, bottom up approach that refused to accept 'no', that defied stuffy Anglicized sticklers for rules that put human relationships above everything: commerce as it was played on the streets, not as a parlour game.

I kept on pushing the idea of including the poor in the dialogue, and not doing what we (privileged outsiders) think is best, but asking them what is best for them. Ask a non-swimmer what he needs before he gets in the pool. He might tell you that he wants to know how to keep his head above water. Maybe you decide to give him arm-floats, but what he really wants is for you to tell him how to keep himself afloat without props.

I have always been inspired by the rousing words of Theodore Roosevelt:

It is not the critic who counts; not the man who points out how the strong man stumbles, or where the doer of deeds could have done them better. The credit belongs to the man who is actually in the arena, whose face is marred by dust and sweat and blood; who strives valiantly; who errs, who comes short again and again, because there is no effort without error and shortcoming; but who does actually strive to do the deeds; who knows great enthusiasms, the great devotions; who spends himself in a worthy cause; who at the best knows in the end the triumph of high achievement, and who at the worst, if he fails, at least fails while daring greatly, so that his place shall never be with those cold and timid souls who neither know victory nor defeat.("The Man in the Arena" Speech delivered at the Sorbonne, in Paris, France on 23 April, 1910)
That inability to put oneself in the shoes of the poor and to keep on living the same way thinking "thank god I don't have to live THAT way" just doesn't work. Berating or patronizing rural folks is both culturally and professionally the most undesirable extension of any rural development executive's personal trait. Unfortunately most aid personnel have cultivated this mind-set and approach. Since they never had extended homestays in the villages they would always carry the stereotyped notion

of the poor as helpless people who need to be handheld through every stage.

Our clients lived miles apart down rutted dirt roads; travel between villages could take the better part of a day. This was before electronic contraptions made their appearance and accounts had to be laboriously copied and recopied by hand in ledger books stored in giant stacks, with all the mistakes and inefficiencies that the process entailed. We had to page through hand-written ledgers to produce periodic reports and data sheets for our Management Information System (MIS). After unwrapping and counting wads of cash collected from borrowers, I would begin entering the instalments into their respective ledgers by hand, a task that would take nearly two hours. Computers have brought a great relief to modern day managers whose time was once largely consumed in balancing account books.

During my assignments, I never maintained conventional dossiers on the geography or economy of villages served by my bank. Most of the statistics that had to be collated for beefing the dossiers once every year were culled from surrogate sources. For more practical purposes I organized essay and elocution contests for students in villages to get feedback on what the youth thought could be the ideal form of rural development for their village. Both girls and boys participated in essay or debate contests organised especially for the purpose on either Independence Day or Republic Day. The prize money, by village standards, was simply fabulous. My favourite subjects would be those that had something to do with the village where I was posted, such as 'My dream of an ideal village'; 'What is wrong with my village'; 'Ways of improving my village'; 'How girls were discriminated against by the family and why', 'How could the status of girls and women be improved' etc. The elocution and debate contest would have two sides, speaking for and against the motion. Local teachers prepared executive summaries of the essays and elocutions and footnoted them with their own independent observation. These essays became a permanent dossier for me and became the most reliable compass for my rural adventures.

My days in rural India were a colourful adventure. Puttering down dirt roads by motorbike to villages in the most remote of areas, with a cotton cloth wrapped around my head, tied below the chin, to protect me from the searing heat, interacting with people of cultures that seemed to exist on a different plane, long hours spent waiting at desolate, mice-infested bus stops in the middle of nowhere, greasy late suppers among the coloured neon lights and throbbing speakers of all-night "dhobis", the heat, the dust, the anxiety, the fatigue and the cold bucket-bath in a dismal flophouse at the end.

I was viscerally moved but this rich, rough life helped seed wonderful ideas. I met some of the poorest of my villagers, for whom life is a never-ending struggle and yet they have somehow survived. Some whom I knew as malnourished children have, against the odds, grown into adulthood, married and had children of their own. I marvel at their endurance and resilience. At the same time, I feel overwhelmed by the immense loss of all the latent talent, skill and accomplishment of so many millions of people, these inhabitants of another world who are denied the possibility of reaching their full potential. One glimpsed it in their innate skill, grace, artistry and physical stamina, but how much they might have been able to contribute to human knowledge and well-being will never be known.

I found spiritual solace in the symphonic cadences of Tagore:

Leave this chanting and singing and telling of beads!
Whom dost thou worship in this lonely dark corner
of a temple with doors all shut?
Open thine eyes and see thy God is not before thee!
He is there where the tiller is tilling the hard ground
and where the path maker is breaking stones.
He is with them in sun and in shower,
and his garment is covered with dust.
Put of thy holy mantle and even like him
come down on the dusty soil!

I had the privilege of watching the women acquire a sense of dignity once they were given tools for self-sufficiency. I discovered the power of creating a business with real accountability. And I learned, maybe most importantly, to listen with my heart. At every hospital, school or village where I would stop, people put their time on hold to provide me insights into how they lived. Even when recounting embarrassing truths (like not being able to pay a child's school tuition) or telling painful stories (like losing a baby in childbirth), it was done with grace and dignity. I think that was the moment when humility in its truest form—rather than an easy but false humbleness—began to creep in for me. For the first time in my life, being right had nothing to do with being successful or effective.

I think a manager's weight is measured by his sensitivity to the holes in his society. As far as a mentor or guide is concerned, a teacher helps in the initial stage only. Then you have to discover the teacher in yourself. A teacher can inspire in the beginning, instruct somewhat, but then you have to listen to your own inner response, your own voice. There may be bumps along the road, but they are part of every career road. You have to learn to negotiate the shoals of myriad challenges.

I spent time walking with farmers through their one-acre farms and enjoying a cup of tea with their families, sitting on a stool in front of their thatched-roof mud-and-wattle homes. It was no small hardship given India's chaotic and treacherous bovine trails that double as roads. A satchel slung over my shoulders filled with notebooks, camera and film rolls, a bottle of water and a canister of Baygon insect repellent were my constant companions.

I braced myself on my mobike as I wove my way out of the dirt lanes of the village and onto a narrow asphalt road. It was exhilarating to feel the air whipping around my face, the throb and bob of the machine gripped between my legs and an exuberant west wind sweeping the azure blue of the skies and the enchanting green of the verdant fields. Narrow sand roads twisted through the endless bush. It was easy to get stuck while driving, and I often lost my bearings on my way to some distant village, passing bullock carts piled high with fodder, tractors clanking toward the fields. I remember once clinging to a rope while standing on the tailboard of a roaring jeep jammed full of villagers going to the market. My accessories were a small suitcase cinched together with baling twine and a bulging burlap sack whose contents were as jumbled as the pieces of my own disorganized everyday life.

There were very few landlines in those days and most of those didn't work much of the time. If one phone conked out, it didn't work for months, only crackling with odd tones in spurts. During the rains they would make funny clicking noises, like tendons in terminal trouble. You had to walk miles to get to another phone. We had to spend nights without electricity even when electric wires drooped perilously overhead.

When the dawn arose, it would appear as if the villagers had bribed the night for this noble gesture.

No one in the government appeared to be bothered about the welfare of the poor, about doing something to resurrect their lives, to bring up their standard of living and to give them the basic amenities. Delivery systems of primary education, healthcare, rural roads and drinking water were rusty and decrepit. Hearing from Dalits, who had long sat at the bottom of the heap in nastily hierarchical villages, I observed that as more of them got a job, money or land, some of the old oppression began to visibly lift.

I worked hard to acquaint myself with poor, rural India by making numerous visits to remote, neglected villages, where I spent hours listening to villagers, sometimes sleeping in their huts or sitting cross-legged on their dirt floors, sharing their meals in their dark, sooty, windowless kitchens, awkwardly inhaling smoke from the clay oven over which the poor women rotated slowly inflating chapattis with a pair of rusty iron tongs. I would duck into ramshackle farmhouses, pat dirt-smudged children on the head and, with little prompting, nibble on a potato plucked from a twig-fuelled cooking fire. As night wore on, blinking open my eyes, I took notes, anaesthetized by exhaustion and despair. I would roll down on the bare *dari* for a wonderful soiree under the canopy of, not a three or five star hotel but a tremendous canopy studded with millions of stars.

My rumpled clothing and the stubble on my face would leave my origins unidentifiable to my people. I got stuck in traffic jams with goats and their herders coming in the opposite direction on narrow, sloping tracks. Technicolour butterflies lolloped by, as big as dolled-up bats. I remember I would often stop to inspect giant spiders, bodies the size of blackened plums.

As I travelled through rural and urban landscapes, too often devastated by the demands of development, I met people who have risked their homes, families and even their lives to effect real change in the world. The stories they shared so openly and warmly were not merely of economic or political success but stories of empowerment and hope that dramatically portray the potency of collective action.

Tiny villages huddled beside the road, and when an automobile approached, naked children would cower in fright, and then invariably, as panicky chickens do, dart into the car's path. Though kindness was quick, acceptance came slowly. One long-time native summed it up: "You're only a stranger for five minutes, but you're a newcomer for 50 years."

I was nevertheless heartened to discover that I was admitted with an instant affection that had as far as I could see no qualifications at all from the first day that we walked about the little compound together and shared our first food in the little house. I made it a point to address every village elder as 'uncle'; the all-purpose Indian honorific for men even marginally older than yourself.

A village assignment is however a unique experience despite the inconveniences that one has to put with. You can change lives and can turn a shriveled, stricken economy into a vibrant community where children go to school, health and nutrition improve, and poverty-driven horrors like starvation and prostitution are memories, not the future. Your vision and perspective of human development will be incomplete unless you have engaged with a village –it is the microcosm of the other and more exciting and creative India. It gives remarkable insight into the soul of real India –an India that cannot be ignored. If we want to ignore we can do so only at our peril. In his book *The Prince of Tides*, Pat Conroy writes: 'Once you have traveled, the voyage never ends, but is played out over and over again in the quietest chambers. The mind can never break off from the journey.*'* Like the lion in the jungle, my natural habitat was the field. Even as I kept climbing the ladder in my professional career making me bound to desk, I always kept returning to the field as if the fields kept beckoning me. I remember when I was posted to my administrative office I told my boss why I wouldn't fit in. 'I'm a field person. I can't sit inside all day and study programmes. I need to be up and about, to see, hear and learn.'

There is a lack of clear understanding of the social forces involved in rural India, of the real nature of caste systems, and of the actual potentials for institutional change. There are critics who believe that since the poor are so poor, we should not make them pay for things. My experience is that dignity is more important than anything else and that the poor already pay for things; so let's find a way to provide them things they can afford and want. That ethos underpins development finance. The mantra is, "Tell us what the poor want, don't tell us what you think is good for them."

Just as resistance movements need to reinvent themselves, to shed their fatigued, old slogans, development workers need to find new ways of doing what we've done in the past. And that includes me. Poverty is the biggest hurdle to empowerment. It is poverty that denies access to education; fails to create job opportunities; drives families to a demeaning life shorn of the barest dignity; forces a mother to give away her girl child in marriage. People live in such seething poverty and crippling penury that families are left with stark choices: should they sell an animal and send a child to school?

In one village where an untouchable was, a few years ago beaten, or worse, merely for letting his shadow pass over someone of a higher caste, I found castes could sit together for meals. That matters: social division may break down faster than economic inequality. During my school days I did not have enough money to buy all the prescribed gear—textbooks, dissecting sets, rulers, compasses, carpentry tools, special exercise books, pens and so on. I knew how deprivations could plague the educational trajectory of a creative mind

It sounds ridiculous to say so, but it can be expensive to be poor. People at the bottom of the pyramid tend to face more risks than wealthier people do because they cannot afford the same defences. In the absence of efficient, formal markets, they pay more for services than those living at the top of the pyramid—a phenomenon known as the "poverty penalty": they have to spend more of their income on basics than people who live in high-income areas with decent infrastructure. They must buy water from roving vendors rather than turn on a tap to their in-home connection to the water system. They miss work more often because of preventable illnesses caused by poor sanitation. They waste more hours commuting because of inadequate public transportation. Chances are that they don't have legal title to the land they live on. And since they have nothing to put up for collateral, it's almost impossible for them to obtain a loan. In an emergency, they resort to loan sharks that charge usurious interest rates.

I have always felt that poor people have very short time horizons to think about—daily bread, daily needs. They can't think more than twenty-four hours at a time. They think that by the following week, things may be better. Therefore microfinance institutions have two options. For ultra-poor families, the Grameen Bank gives soft loans coupled with food grains and grants provided by the government. For the marginally poor, the institutions provide financial counselling and try to tailor a daily or weekly loan collection schedule to the customers' daily cash flow. However, this sort of assistance is very rare with Indian microfinance institutions.

We could learn by bearing witness to the villagers' way of life. Their entire mental model is different—the multiplication of wants is replaced by the basic fulfilment of human needs. A farmer explained it to us thus, "You cannot make the clouds rain more, and you cannot make the sun shine less. They are just nature's gifts—take it or leave it."

A villager is at several levels a philosopher, too. When the things around you are seen as gifts, they are no longer a means to an end; they are the means and the end. And thus a cow-herder will tend to his animals with the compassion of a father, a village woman will wait three hours for a delayed bus without a trace of anger, a child will spend countless hours fascinated by stars in the galaxy, and finding his place in the vast cosmos. Life has changed inexorably in the two decades that have been powered by the internet, but remote tribal belts are still governed by the same hoary pattern.

All development programme managers must understand that the magic that goes with our immediate successes may disappear after we move to the next assignment. Our successor is already stung by the praises we have received and he examines every action of ours under a microscope. I found that during my career all my successors, without exception, painted me in negative colours. Much of it was justified, but there were also bright spots glossed over when they were determined to find fault.

I was always stubborn about what I thought was right—whether confronting powerful bureaucrats, fighting land sharks or helping flood-affected fishermen. I feel satisfied that my pugnacity and courage have given heart to many friends and colleagues. Being a maverick and an iconoclast in an ossified culture can help you. Yet being a loner can be a huge handicap when you are trying to tear down that culture, facing powerful, entrenched forces fighting you every step of the way. I feel that despite the loneliness, it was the unshakable self-confidence, unwillingness to compromise, unflinching hard work, a steadfast heart and a steely stomach that enabled me to push my plans. It helped me too that I had the ability to insulate myself from the controversies that raged around me and focus on the work instead.

My action would leave many eyebrows arched in the corporate office of my bank. There were many seniors who were keen to write my banking obituary.

I must thank Providence for having survived many attempts by my detractors to trap me. It was not baseless police complaints filed by local goons but the stinkers and admonitions I received from my immediate bosses that sank me into depression. There were swollen minds and bruised egos that had to be soothed while getting legitimate rural poor in the development plans. Sometimes when the government departments rejected subsidy claims because of my insolence, I would go on the defensive, trying to mend fences, having to swallow painful admonitions because I couldn't afford to have my poor clients lose government largesse. I had to keep colleagues to my point—the superior, the peers and the subordinates, in order to push my agenda. I remember every time a programme got grounded, I had to seek their patronage to nudge the processes down below. I honestly wouldn't trade this experience for anything else.

I firmly believe that a sensitive official alone cannot smoothly manage and drive a grassroots programme. Vision is one thing, creativity is another. But what can you do when you are up against a calcified bureaucracy, fickle-minded villagers who change their opinions faster than they change their clothes and local drunkard goons who can stab you without provocation?

Several development successes have occurred in less than optimal settings, often under appalling conditions: weak governance, widespread corruption, minimal infrastructure, deep-rooted social divisions and a poorly functioning judicial system. In each case, creative individuals saw possibilities where others saw only hopelessness, and imagined a way forward that took into account local realities and built on local strengths.

When we want to help the poor, we usually offer them charity, to avoid recognizing the problem and finding the solution for it. Charity becomes a way to shrug off our responsibility, but in fact charity only perpetuates poverty by taking the initiative away from the poor. It allows us to go ahead with our own lives without worrying about the lives of the poor.

My own background has taught me a lot about the power of investing in the poor, particularly the women, because you do end up feeding a family and not just an individual. For a solution to intractable poverty, we need a massive cultural shift. Foundations, universities, NGOs and financial institutions have to contribute educational, social and financial programmes that can deliver tangible, measurable progress as well as defining clear policy and position points.

I have known idealists whose revolutionary ideas were aborted by such hard conventionalists, and they would end their careers lamenting the verses in *Kathy's Song*:

And a song I was writing is left undone
I don't know why I spend my time
Writing songs I can't believe
With words that tear and strain to rhyme.

I did not belong to the tribe of development-mavens wanting to rock the boat of established development practices. Nor am I a development junkie. I am certainly not a proselytizer for the philosophy that breeds contempt for customs and traditions symbolic of the old order, but one shouldn't hesitate to make room for innovation. I always tried to resist the traps that could make traditions toxic: the temptation to use them as cover for prejudice and conformity, a refusal to change or stretch—we'll do it this way because we always have. In India, the general impression of the public sector is one of bureaucratic insensitivity and bland indifference with executives preferring to conform to byzantine traditions.

From the drawing board to delivery, you have to inhabit the product and the programme, living every detail, as if it were a living, breathing organism. You put so much of your life into this thing. There are such rough moments that I think most people give up. I don't blame them. You have to be burning with an idea, or a problem, or a wrong that you want to right. If you're not passionate enough from the start, you'll never stick it out.

First, the grand design of most development projects, typically hatched by outside development professionals, makes local ownership of this difficult. Second, the hierarchical structure of most public sector agencies in low-income countries, coupled with the implicit rules for allocating credit and blame, make committing to performance goals unappealing for middle managers and frontline staff. Third, in many low-income countries, the public views public sector workers as incompetent or corrupt, while public sector workers view themselves as victims of a dysfunctional system that encourages corruption and rewards inefficiency. Consequently, public sector workers assume an identity that does not promote accountability and professionalism.

It is against my natural inclination to present an idyllic picture of the villages I served or to view its inhabitants through rose-tinted glasses. I knew very well that some of the peasants I befriended were shrewd, calculating, cunning and often deceitful: they took satisfaction from turning the tables on a naïve urban banker. Yet, despite all the tribulations that I suffered—physical hardships, want of privacy and monotonous food—I came away from the villages with feelings of warmth towards their men, women and children which I retain even now.

Today, the most important need for a development worker posted in a rural area is the need to listen. Listen to what the people want instead of assuming one knows what the problems and solutions are. Listen to those who work in the field and live the day-to-day challenges. Respect opens many doors. Economic development and social change cannot be imposed from without. They must be sought and grasped by the individual pursuing opportunities for self-realization. Lasting change comes about so slowly that you may not even notice it until one day people and individuals don't want to be taken care of—they need to be given a chance to fulfil their own potential. If we can inspire people around the world to think differently about what it means to be poor, then we will have made a real impact.

When we design solutions that recognize the poor as clients or customers and not as passive recipients of charity, we have a real chance to end poverty. And I believe we can do that in our generation. This logic comes from the importance of empathy—not a form of empathy that comes from superiority, but one born from a profound humility. Unfortunately, there is a major lack of empathy in our world; too often our better-off citizens choose to ignore the woes of the rest of humanity. This trend has become pronounced recently because of the emergence of several unrepeatable fault lines in the development space.

In recent years, a development worker has to wrestle with political leaders, deal with lobbying by various groups, tolerate allegations of one's lack of personal integrity, and overcome opposition from government departments. The political arena in villages is no longer binary—the ruling party and the opposition party. Today we have a kaleidoscope of political parties of different hues and stripes. Yet it is true that if one is sincere about bringing about change or development, one will have to ride through these squalls. The nitty-gritty of the process of development is much messier than what people expect.

Poverty and vulnerability are not purely economic phenomena reflecting what people have; they are also social phenomena reflecting who they are. Rural society has been buffeted with the bane of various kinds of historically entrenched group-based inequalities. Caste ethnicity and religion exacerbate the economic dimensions of poverty and vulnerability through processes of cultural devaluation which assign certain groups of people a lower position in the social order.

In the introduction to their book, *Super Freakonomics*, Levitt and Dubner wrote, "If you had the option of being born anywhere in the world today, India might not be the wisest choice. Despite its vaunted progress as a major player in the global economy, the country as a whole remains excruciatingly poor. Life expectancy and literacy rates are low; pollution and corruption are high. In the rural areas, where more than two-thirds of Indians live, barely half of the households have electricity and only one in four homes has a toilet." I cannot contest this statement factually. However, being an Indian, I can say if I had a choice to be reborn, I would choose India as my place of birth. Not because I have had a wonderful existence in the country, but because of the challenges to which it exposed me that made my life richer.

With age comes wisdom, and now I increasingly realise that reason must prevail over emotions. I will have to make hard choices that go against the grain of my conscience shaped by the eternally-held values that I cherish. People may advise that positive thinking and big dreams can help us accomplish great tasks. I personally feel one has to bow before the altar of destiny and realise that we have to navigate our ambitions within the realms of divine will. Each one of us has a moral compass that shows us the limits of our talents and abilities. I think that is a more authentic guide than the well-meaning advice of well-wishers.

At certain turning points in my life, when I would have made the wrong decisions with my limited intelligence, I have felt as if my will was perceptibly bent by some higher power which saved me from myself.

There's a divinity that shapes our ends,
Rough-hew them how we will

(**Shakespeare**, Hamlet)

As Malcolm Muggeridge says in his autobiography, "In all the larger shaping of a life, there is a plan already, into which one has no choice but to fit." Ruskin's famous quotation has remained for me an enduring touchstone, "Quality is never the result of an accident. It is always the result of intelligent effort."

But now my voyage is over. And I return home. The reclining moon floats high in the sky, and has lost its dome, little by little tattering away from above. I don't feel as if I am returning from another world, but rather from an inner world, a world whose arcane existence is outside us. The world from which time departs and to which it returns, its waves caught in countless manifold simultaneity. Recollections keep filtering back to me, some sharp and stark, some a little hazy, others faint and blurred.

For the first couple of days after returning to a compulsory metropolitan assignment as a policy-maker and advisor, I felt a twinge of contrition every time I opened the fridge or flipped on the TV. But it's hard for a city-bred individual who has only ever attended great schools and lived comfortably to be truly thankful without a healthy dose of perspective. While I don't think I was overindulged, I lacked that perspective, and as a result took my education and possessions for granted.

I now firmly believe in the great truth enshrined by Gandhi:

We are inheritors of a rural civilization. The vastness of our country, the vastness of the population, the situation and the climate of the country have, in my opinion, destined it for a rural civilization. Its defects are well known but not one of them is irremediable. To uproot it and substitute for it an urban civilization seems to me an impossibility, unless we are prepared by some drastic means to reduce the population from three hundred million to three or say even thirty. I can therefore suggest remedies on the assumption that we must perpetuate the present rural civilization and endeavour to rid it of its acknowledged defects. This can only be done if the youth of the country will settle down to village life. And if they will do this they must reconstruct their life and pass every day of their vacation in the villages surrounding their colleges or high schools and those who have finished their education or are not receiving any should think of settling down in villages

(Young India, 7-11-1929)

Now that I've been back long enough to reflect a little, I see that there's a more constructive path to take. That path boils down to one word: "thanks". The words of the brave and courageous Steve Jobs keep resonating in my daily world—

I'm convinced that the only thing that kept me going was that I loved what I did. You've got to find what you love. And that is as true for your work as it is for your lovers. Your work is going to fill a large part of your life, and the only way to be truly satisfied is to do what you believe is great work. And the only way to do great work is to love what you do. If you haven't found it yet, keep looking. Don't settle. As with all matters of the heart, you'll know when you find it. And, like any great relationship, it just gets better and better as the years roll on. So keep looking until you find it.

2

ADVENTURES IN THE RURAL PLANET

There is in every village a torch - the teacher; and an extinguisher - the clergyman

Victor Hugo

I would say that if the village perishes India will perish too. India will be no more India. Her own mission in the world will get lost. The revival of the village is possible only when it is no more exploited

M. K. Gandhi

I would rather be first in a small village in Gaul than second in command in Rome

Julius Caesar

When I entered banking, I carried the impression that it was a high-profile job with an aura of greatness in which one could bask the whole day. The bank branches I had seen were in swanky contrast to government offices, which always presented a morose and mournful look through the dank corridors. My view of the career was belied when I found bankers so often hauled up for loans gone bad, for frauds perpetuated by clients whose culpability one could never know. I immediately forsook this bright career for an adventure in rural India.

The success of a rural banker lies in the way he relates to some of the resourceful people in the village. We must be able to jell with the existing rural ecosystem if we want to make a real impact on the rural society. We must have a strategy which ingratiates us to local partners. At the same time we should have the patience to learn and understand how rural people see themselves. Initially I found the change in villages is slow—the slow pace of life, and the slow response to our ideas and concepts. The village is actually chock-a-block with a variety of resourceful talent: postman, schoolteacher, anganwadi worker, the staff of the local Primary Health Centre. Through years of exposure to visitors, these people have developed an independent worldview and are neutral players on the village turf. They have been waiting in the wings to be empowered to play a role in the making of their village.

We as practitioners must learn to shun entrenched vested interests which stubbornly resist reformation in the existing social order which, in fact, perpetuates their feudal tyrannies. We must seek out people at the lowest rungs of society; these are the ones who really matter to the success of our development initiatives. At the same time, experienced veterans who have spent several years in villages and thereby learned a great deal about those villages too can serve as a prism into the worldview of a village. Gandhi's advice in this regard is worth recalling:

My ideal village still exists only in my imagination. After all every human being lives in the world of his own imagination. In this village of my dreams the villager will not be dull—he will be all awareness. He will not live like an animal in filth and darkness. Men and women will live in freedom, prepared to face the whole world. There will be no plague, no cholera and no smallpox. Nobody will be allowed to be idle or to wallow in luxury. Everyone will have to do body labour. Granting all this, I can still envisage a number of things that will have to be organized on a large scale. Perhaps there will even be railways and also post and telegraph offices. I do not know what things there will be or will not be. Nor am I bothered about it. If I can make sure of the essential thing, other things will follow in due course. But if I give up the essential thing, I give up everything."

(Letter to Jawaharlal Nehru, 5-10-1945.)

The village is the basic unit of the Gandhian ideal social order. Gandhi succinctly pointed out, "If the village perishes India will perish too.... We have to make a choice between India of the villages that is as ancient as herself and India of the cities which are a creation of foreign domination". Gandhi's ideal village belongs to the Pre-British period, when Indian villages were supposed to constitute the federation of self-governing autonomous republics.

According to Gandhi, this federation will be brought about not by coercion or compulsion but by the voluntary offer of every village republic to join such a federation. The work of the central authority will only be to coordinate the work of different village republics and to supervise and manage things of common interest, as education, basic industries, health, currency, banking etc.

The central authority will have no power to enforce its decisions on village republics except the moral pressure or power of persuasion. The economic system and transport system introduced by the British have destroyed the "republican' character of the villages.

Gandhi, however, admitted that in olden times tyranny and oppression were in fact practised by feudal chiefs. But, "odds were even". Today the odds are heavy. It is most demoralising." In this way in the Gandhian scheme of things the ancient 'republic', an Indian village without tyranny and exploitation serves as a model unit.

I have found in my career that most people have a psychological aversion to repaying bank loans. In the majority of the instances, the defaulters have sufficient assets and capital to redeem their debt but they will use every possible means to escape it. In many cases, defaulters of huge amounts have erected shrines to legitimize their new image as beneficent avatars. There was once a defaulter in a village close to my bank, whose debts caused the banker who had processed this debtor's case to lose his own job; the borrower had erected a very beautiful temple on the highway and earned huge popularity for his so-called God consciousness. Whenever I encountered the temple on my travels, I always felt compelled to nail a board on it indicating that the temple was unofficially hypothecated to the bank.

Personal experience taught me that when villagers need a loan, they will make endless trips to the bank, sitting meekly in office halls, beseeching the manager for help with obsequious supplications. "You're our God, you're our saviour. God will bless you with a hundred children." Once the loan is released, however, most of them start behaving like wily debtors who can be tamed only by the Cabuliwallah!

Villagers are often highly clever and cunning, contrary to popular urban notions of villagers being simpletons and dimwits. One reason for the villagers' recalcitrance could be that they have come to associate the signing of documents with cruelties and frauds. Stories are legion of fly-by-night operators duping villagers by posing as genuine financial agents and promising eye-popping returns. The villagers no longer wish to trust anybody, least of all politicians and other authority figures.

Bank officials must often waste precious time obtaining a particular document from a borrower to ensure that the bank doesn't lose its claim over the loan. The statute of limitation stipulates that, in case of default of debt, the claim must be invoked within a prescribed time limit, normally three years. Before the end of that third year, borrowers start performing vanishing tricks because they know that deferring the payment would permanently absolve them of their liability to the bank. Collecting these documents is one of the most humiliating experiences a bank manager can have. Villagers play clever hide-and-seek games with the manager, who may have to return empty-handed to his bank even after spending an entire day scouring the village. The process entails enormous costs for the banks, drains its precious manpower, and entails a mental struggle for the official. I am sorry to record that even well-established businesses make much fuss about signing these documents, using their signature as a negotiating tool to get part, if not full, amnesty on the defaulted amount.

The basic spirit behind the statute is that there should be a reasonable period during which the bank may take action against the borrower. Bankers do not want to file lawsuits against erring borrowers, especially in the case of smaller loans. Since lawsuits are both time-consuming and drain precious manpower resources and other expenditure, banks try to use the traditional methods for recovery of dues. Court proceedings will sometimes turn into such protracted odysseys that it is not unusual for the litigation to long survive the litigants themselves. The worst case is when farmers, particularly agricultural labourers, migrate to other villages. The manager has to do a lot of intelligence work to sniff out these borrowers. This is more complex at smaller bank branches, where there is a single officer handling hundreds of small loans. Since the farmers are in the fields during the entire day, the manager has to visit the village in the early morning or late evening if he wishes to meet them in person.

When the banker goes searching, there is no certainty that the borrower would be in the village. He may be labouring in the fields, shopping in the bazaar or groaning at the local hooch joint. Even if he is at home, the chances of meeting him there depends on where his dwelling is located. If it is in the deeper terrain, there is every possibility that word of the manager's visit has already travelled to him and he has slipped out of the house. Waiting for the banker at the doorstep of the house would instead be the wife or children, studiously parroted to recite the usual script. They would feign total ignorance, wearing a mournful look on their faces. "Sir, he is not at home. We will convey your message. He was telling us that he was planning to visit you to assure you of his commitment to relinquish the debt." Or it could be, "Sir, he has just gone to the city doctor as he is having fever for the last ten days. People say it *is chikungunia* (complex strain of malaria)." During those days, *chikungunia* was claiming villagers like a monster and every borrower would proffer it as a standard excuse for not paying loans.

During one such visit, I had a taste of the villagers' amazing ability to manipulate emotions. A particular borrower would give my staff the slip whenever they visited the village. Charurkhati, the key village served by our bank office, was connected with the main road by a two-kilometre stretch of rutted and treacherous path. I met a farmer on the trail, and he immediately recognized me as the local bank manager. I inquired about the whereabouts of the borrower whose signature was to be obtained on the documents. At first he pleaded ignorance and fumbled. Then his face became deceptive and he assertively asked, "What's the matter?" I told him that the borrower had not paid even a single rupee and the loan documents were to expire in three days. I had to get the documents renewed, and obtain a signature in token of the renewal. He fixed me with a stern stare and started haranguing me, "Today's managers deserve such ordeals. They made us make many trips to the bank before we could get a loan. Officials in the local government steal the funds sent from the government for our benefit, leaving us with a two-hour hike to the nearest dirt track. The closest well is an hour's walk away, and the nearest hospital is four hours away. We don't even have a proper path to the cremation site. Our elders are denied a decent funeral because the body keeps slithering on the slushy and broken path!"

It took me a while to recover from the sudden increase in his decibels. I felt hurt that he had lumped me with the stereotypical managers who had been posted here against their wishes and were therefore frustrated and ventilated their distress through harassment of clients. I assured him that I would be gentler and more accessible than my predecessors. My gesture of courtesy softened the intensity of his rage but I was already losing my patience, as the evening was wearing on. I asked him if he could help me in locating the borrower. He asked how serious the matter was, given that the manager himself had to come all the way to the village. I emphasised to him it was serious enough and that I might lose my job if I were unable to locate the borrower. The farmer, unruffled, insisted it would be futile to locate the borrower, as the villagers themselves were not sure of his whereabouts, and that I should waive off the loan.

I have been an avid believer and practitioner of Thomas Alva Edison's great dictum, "Many of life's failures are people who did not realize how close they were to success when they gave up." If I persisted with the manhunt, I would at least have the consolation of pursuing it to its logical conclusion. Like most astute villagers, who run their village administration more ably than B-school boys, this man tried to unnerve me, saying, "I think you better return, or else you'll get caught in the storm. It appears it will rain heavily." I told him I was not the one to be deterred and proceeded ahead despite the hovering clouds that portended heavy rains.

As I proceeded ahad, I found a weary farmer, with a pugilist's build, chain smoking under a tamarind tree. Without cracking a smile, he asked why I'd chatted so long with such a crooked farmer. It turned out that the man to whom I'd been speaking was the same farmer whom I had been relentlessly pursuing. I was stunned. He had tricked me, who enjoyed the reputation of being a great face reader, despite a half-hour conversation. I sprang back on my mobike to step up my pursuit of the deceitful man, who had, by now, slipped into the lanes crisscrossing the fields. I tried to put the ignition on. I tried to kick start my machine but nothing happened. It seemed my loyal and steadfast mobike too was in low spirits. I kicked again and the machine whined. I tried harder: the old engine groaned to life, kept sputtering and finally gained traction. Lightening crackled and speared down explosively and thunder shook the city like a bass drummer on LSD. The moon had already disappeared into the huge cloud of darkness. The battle appeared already lost. The experience was one of the most frustrating events in my life and has stuck firmly in my memory. It was a hair raising exercise and it definitely eroded not just my own self confidence but my confidence in the innate goodness of villagers.

Wait Mr. Postman
Please Mr. Postman, look and see
Oh yeah
If there's a letter in your bag for me....

These lyrics sung way back in the '70s by the Carpenters immortalized the humble postman and his role in a lovesick teenager's life. Closer to home, Rajesh Khanna did pretty much the same in *Palkon ki chhaon mein* ('In the Shade of the Eyelids'), as he sang *Dakiya dak laya* ('Come, the mailman has brought the mail'). These films and songs reflected a reality many middle-aged Indians were familiar with—the ineffectual man in khaki, his pants clipped firmly at the bottom to keep the well-starched fabric from getting smudged by the greased cycle chain, pedalling his bicycle and putting letters and postcards into eager hands.

In a village, the postman enjoyed a status unrivalled by his urban colleagues'. My experience of the city postman had not been very encouraging. The mailman would abandon the letters atop the boxes of residents and sometimes the letters fell, were trampled, and tracked back outdoors. For the villagers, the postman was a souvenir they treasured. The postman's social perimeter straggled around the constellation of villages he covered in his official errands. He had access to even the most intimate and private affairs of families; if the entire household was unlettered, he would read their letters aloud and would also write out replies on their behalf. When he brought good news, the recipient would reward him with whatever sweets there were in the house. During festivities, he would be an important guest and be treated to goodies that the family had prepared.

Gone are the days when he used to deliver picture postcards, letters to lovers, money orders from newly-employed sons, and goodies from doting grandparents. Gone too is the time he was the villagers' window to the world, a tenuous link with loved ones. In these high-tech times, lovers no longer write letters, instant banking has replaced money orders, grandparents rely on courier companies to send parcels of love. The ubiquitous telegrams have been consigned to history. The postman now visits the houses to drop off the official statements of the bank or the insurance company, or the telephone or electricity bills, or printed pamphlets for promotion of consumer products. He is now part of the communication transmission called snail mail, even though it may still be the most trustworthy mail.

The postman at the village where I was stationed was Vithal Batte, a demure man with a knack of striking up friendships with any stranger. With his grey hair and gentle demeanour, he cut a grandfatherly figure, but, as I quickly learned, he was a postal employee with a workaholic edge. Money was not a high priority for him. His wife was employed as a peon in a local school. The Battes didn't have children. For them the entire village was their family. Batte had a special calm ability for defusing tension; he was a natural mediator. He handled every visitor to the village with warmth and sobriety. On account of his affable nature and his charming manners, Vithal was a much adored man. He was everybody's family friend, the fond uncle for the kids.

After every short ride on his bicycle, he would waddle to a stop, lower his voluminous satchel, sending a few letters flying into the dust. Diligently he would brush off the dust and return them to his stockpile, don his satchel again and resume his daily rounds—a process which I watched with pleasure through the large window in my office. A dedicated postal carrier, he spent most of his day weighed down by letters as he navigated treacherous paths in order to ensure that the mail reached the remote villages in a timely fashion. He would sit using the seal to cancel blank postage stamps on letters, putting them into his old, worn out, discarded canvas bag that bulged with letters that had doomed addresses. It had also a seal, *'Returned Letters'*.

For me, the postman was more than just a benign messenger who delivered a trove of daily mail. He was an informal but highly resourceful member of the local bank family. He relieved us of a number of cumbersome and mundane tasks, made simple by his knowledge of the local geography and the social arcana. He didn't mind the long hours of work he had to put in despite his meagre salary. I think the greatest incentive for him was that he enjoyed the job and was able to realize his self-actualization needs. He always cared about the respect he could command. "Those who have known us, continue to respect us. In fact, people trust us more than the courier guys," he would chuckle. "There have been many a time when I have picked up letters dropped carelessly by the courierwallah and delivered them to the right address."

The postman was a key person in the village as he helped me with innovative solutions to intractable problems. One such problem was the difficulty experienced by the infirm and old customers in visiting the bank. A majority of the villages in our block were cut off by a river which had to be crossed to reach Bina, the larger village where the bank branch was located. The paths from other directions were treacherous, impassable for most of the year. People needed to be ferried across by canoes in order to transact their business with the bank. A large number of depositors were illiterate and could not sign their cheques. They had to be escorted by a family member who had to forego a day's wage for the purpose. I felt that a solution must be found to mitigate the hardship of these people. I was also losing precious time as I had to keep bobbing across to villages on a fishing boat just for the sake of getting simple formalities completed by marginal farmers and agricultural labour.

On the suggestion of the postman, I worked out an innovative method for addressing this issue. I decided to use the postman's services for delivering payment to those depositors. My staff compiled a list of such ailing or elderly customers and we decided to set apart a specified amount of cash to be delivered by the postman against cheques signed by the depositor. In case of illiterate customers, the postman would attest to the thumbprints. There was no provision of drawing cash from *suspense account*—an account which is normally debited in case of emergency expenses for the bank; so I decided to draw from my own account. Once the cheques were received and the accounts debited, my cash would get replenished. Since the postman was a contractual employee of the post department, I had absolutely no qualms about engaging him for this work. However, as a matter of caution and to circumvent the possible complications of labour laws, I decided to make the payment in his wife's name.

It was Vithal again who inspired me to become a strong adherent and later a staunch champion of the experiments which reinforced that even a small loan to a woman tends to have far more beneficial ripple effects for the family compared to one made similarly to a man. Sociologists may debate endlessly about the reasons why men tend to spend the money on themselves while women tend to spend on their families, especially their children, but an assignment in a village can reveal this truth in its starkest colours. Vithal's voice was not the only voice raised in the village in the favour of women but his was surely the loudest and most persistent, and—cumulatively—the most persuasive. He was such a zealous believer in the theory that he tramped through almost all the villages with me to demonstrate the creative potential of poor rural women in money management.

Another area where his advice proved to be worthwhile was in dealing with defaulters of loans. Our normal practice was to print tersely worded standard letters in which we would fill the particulars of the borrowers and mail these letters to them. The postman had been observing me generating huge volumes of correspondence with unimpressive results. The mounting postal expenses for dispatching these letters were blowing holes in the balance sheet without yielding commensurate benefit. I happened to discuss my dilemma and anguish with the postman. He suggested I send postcards for small borrowers and telegrams for bigger ones.

What was so new about this strategy? The post card is not a sealed cover; its contents are always open for public reading. In villages, the postman normally drops the mail at the doorstep of the villager. If the person happens to be away, his neighbour or any visitor is quite likely to go through the contents. Similarly the villagers get alarmed and curious when there is a telegram. A telegram in a village normally triggers an instant alarm. The informal communications network of any village is so efficient that even the bowel movements of every man are known to his fellowmen.

Losing face is a devastating thing in a village context, and the villager will normally do anything to avoid it. The news of the bank's notice catches immediate fire and the borrower becomes the butt of the village gossip mill. The villagers come up with wonderful theories about the likely fate of the poor borrower. This builds tremendous social pressure on the borrower's family, forcing him to take immediate steps to regularize his loan. This strategy served me well for almost a decade during my professional career and would have continued to do so, had the internet not decimated these channels.

It is strange that repayment ethics, so deeply ingrained in Indian culture, have been made foul words by politicians. The sanctity of repayment, no matter how deceitfully the debt was contrived and how cruel the costs, has been drilled into the Indian consciousness since the time of *Manusmruti*. Manu listed eighteen main categories of law for the king to decide on. Of those, wrote Manu, "The first is non-payment of debts." Manu held: "By whatever means a creditor may be able to obtain possession of his property, even by those means may he force the debtor and make him pay." Manu's code is divided into twelve chapters, and in the eighth chapter, there are stated rules on the eighteen subjects of law, which include both civil and criminal law.

Sir William Jones, who came to India in 1774 as one of the first judges of the Supreme Court of Judicature of Bengal, learnt Sanskrit and undertook an authoritative translation of the *Manusmriti*. He wrote in the preface of the translated work (published in 1794):

"The style of the Manusmriti *has a certain austere majesty that sounds like the language of legislation and exhorts a respectful awe; the sentiments of independence on all being but God, and the harsh admonitions even to kings are truly noble."*

What about disputes and debt recovery? Manu specified the punishments to be given in case of disputes arising about loan repayment and listed eighteen types of disputes. When a creditor sued the debtor for recovery of money, it was the duty of the king to ensure that the creditor got back his money. Manu permitted the king to employ all means, fair or foul, to recover the dues, which means might include killing the debtor's wife, children and cattle or obstructing his movements. Manu held the view that a defaulter could not absolve himself of his debt burden even by death.

Chanakya said that sons should pay with interest the debt of a deceased person or co-debtors or sureties. Was a spouse responsible for the debts incurred by a person to whom they were married? Yes and no. A wife was exempted from the debt burden of her husband if she had not given her assent to his borrowings. However, for the debt incurred by a wife, her husband was liable for repayment. Perhaps this was the background in which one of the committees on rural indebtedness concluded that "the Indian farmer is born in debt, lives in debt and dies in debt".

I do not want to make out a case for the moneylender. We cannot have outlandish justifications for stratospheric interest rates. However, the loans offered by banks for small loans in India are quite affordable. Added to this is the government subsidy. If it is not a capital subsidy, it will certainly be an interest subsidy. The legal system in India is inextricably linked with the English language: both were originally imported from abroad. Originally an English transplant with Anglo-Saxon roots, the legal system in India has grown over the years, nourished in Indian soil. What was intended to be an English oak has turned into an Indian banyan, whose dangling trellises are themselves as big as independent plants

We had to make frequent trips to the Block Development Office at Warora and the Collector's secretariat in Chandrapur for discussions on various rural development projects being undertaken by our bank branch. We believed that instead of individual clients going and sorting out issues, it would be wise for us to meet the Collector and discuss the issues collectively. My first visit was a unique experience. I had a young, agile youth volunteer, Moreshwar Chikankar, who would join me on my trips to these government offices.

In the1990s, India had some of the hardest-working bureaucrats in the world, but its administration had an abysmal record of serving the public. The sclerotic bureaucracy had plagued all development programmes.

Vijay Bhoge, a fifty-three-year-old civil servant, woke each morning to the screeching of peacocks outside his bedroom window. A scuffling attended him, as an armed guard, peons, gardeners and orderlies—tasked with catering to Mr Bhoge's various needs—hopped to attention. After a simple breakfast, he would leave his residence, a Victorian-style bungalow once used by a senior British police officer, and get into his car, a white Ambassador—the curvaceous clone of the 1948 Morris Oxford, complete with siren and flashing yellow light, which has symbolized officialdom in India for decades. Mr Bhoge would take the back seat; a policeman riding machinegun in the front, and in a few minutes they would arrive at Mr Bhoge's main office, the Collectorate.

There for the next four hours, beneath a portrait of a beaming Mahatma Gandhi, Mr Bhoge would receive a stream of poor people. A turbaned flunkey would regulate the flow, letting in a dozen at a time. Many were old and ragged, or blind. Most brought written pleas: for the resumption of a widow's pension that had mysteriously dried up; for money for an operation; for a tube-well or a sprinkler. Many bore complaints against corrupt officials. Mr Bhoge listened, asked questions and, in red ink, scrawled his response on the petitions. For desperate cases, he ordered an immediate payment of rehabilitation grants. More often, he wrote a note to the official to whom the petition should have been directed in the first place—or, wretchedly often, to whom it has already been directed: "Act upon this according to the law." If he was fully convinced about a particular case of injustice, his usual remark was "Kindly do the needful."

Supplicants had already begun besieging the Collector's office when I arrived that morning. Two greasy clerks presided over his antechamber, their desks overflowing with papers loosely bound in crumbling files held together with strings. Three phones rang intermittently, and were answered in a wide variety of tones, ranging from the uncooperative to the unctuous, depending on who was calling. Outside, a nervous line of saluting adjutants waited for signatures, permissions and orders.

All eyes were on the closed teak door in the corner, bearing the brass nameplate of the Collector, behind which their destinies were being determined. The huge hall appeared to be a neglected warehouse; admin papers piled high on the desk of every employee, paper-bound files held down by paperweights, metal filling cabinets rimmed with dust, an old, rusty fan wheezing away, a single huge padlock. We were directed to a small garret where we found the collector's personal assistant shooing away visitors like he was swatting mosquitoes. People crowded round the desks, seeking attention, thrusting slips of paper forward, folding hands in entreaty, shouting to be heard. Occasionally, a paper was dealt with and a khaki-uniformed peon sent for to carry it somewhere. Sometimes, people were sent away, though most seemed to be waved toward the walls where dozens were already waiting, weary resignation on their faces, for their problems to be dealt with. We saw a small board hung at the entrance of a dilapidated hall reading "Staff Recreation Hall". Two men sat on each end of a wobbly pew, both straddling the chessboard between their knobby knees, their noses directed at the muddle of pawns in the centre. We later realized that these were occupants of vacant chairs in different sections of the Collectorate. A man stood at the door to signal the likely entry of any official. Before we left, we witnessed one such signal. The players clattered pieces on the board and slipped out through a broken window.

"It's hopeless," I said to Moreshwar, who had accompanied me. "I told you we should have tried to get an appointment. We'll be here all day."

"How would we have got an appointment?" Moreshwar asked reasonably, since we did not yet have a phone in the village. "No, this is the only way. You go and give them your card."I did not share

Moreshwar's faith in the magical properties of this small rectangular advertisement of my status, but I battled my way to the front of one of the desks and thrust it at an indifferent clerk. "Please take this to the Collector Saab," I said, trying to look both important and imploring. "I must see him."

The clerk seemed unimpressed by my card. "You and everyone else," he said sceptically, putting the card aside. "Collector Saab very busy today. You come back tomorrow, we will see."

At this point, Moreshwar insinuated a currency note into the clerk's palm. The man's eyes lit up and sparkled. "Send the card in," said Moreshwar, "It's important."

"I am doing as you wish," the clerk said grudgingly, "but you will still have to wait. Collector Saab is so very busy today."

"You've told us that already," I replied. "We'll wait." He then called a clerk who was hidden in a cubbyhole desk in front of him. A peon wandered in, bearing tea for the clerks. Once the clerk at the desk had satisfied himself that his tea was sugared to his taste, he added my card to the pile of papers he gave the peon to take in to the Collector. "It will take some time," he repeated with a grin.

It didn't. Soon after the door had closed behind the peon, the black phone on the assistant's desk jangled peremptorily. "Yes, Sar. Yes, Sar," he said perspiring. "No, Sar. Not long. I have taken care of them. Yes, Sar. At once, Sar." He had stood up to attention during this exchange, and when he replaced the receiver there was a new look of respect in his eyes. "Collector Saab has called you in."

A long bank of windows ran along the side of the room. Mr Bhoge half rose to greet me, an effort which consisted of bracing his hands on the side of the chair and raising his sloping shoulders in a quick jerk upward to shake my hand. I offered mine, robotically expecting him to have a commanding presence, but his demeanour was modest and his tone warm. In a subdued stream of equally-accented, putt-putt syllables, he reeled out his priorities in development projects in villages. I couldn't resist the urge to broach the subject of corruption among lower babus, particularly those associated with development programmes. After a pause, he counteracted saying that the whole culture had to share the blame for the situation. I mentioned that, on account of the government's cranky programmes, we were sanctioning loans and writing them off ritually after three years. His eyes flashed with sardonic delight.

The leather top of his wooden desk was covered almost entirely by a dozen or more piles of documents, arranged in neat rows; in the space that remained there were two telephones. He leafed through the pages, signing some and pushing others to one side. A husky clerk came in, carrying a cache of documents and clutch of papers. Yellow and orange sticky labels indicated which pages required signing. Mr Bhoge fished out a pen from the tray, scribbled his signature in the requisite places and shunted the files down the table. The clerk hobbled out.

When he promised to issue suitable instructions on my pending issues, I was very happy to find a sensitive soul and a liberal analogue in the hard-fisted bureaucracy. The meeting turned out to be a forerunner for a lasting friendship. In the Collector I found a source of enormous support to us.

A village has a variety of quaint characters. In Bina, we had a venerable *maulvi*, known as *chacha*(uncle), who wrote out psalms from the Quran for the village folk to wear as charms or amulets and for the sick to swallow as medicine. He would use water tinted with saffron for the purpose. If this was not available, he would use ink of saffron colour. He had an amazing fund of anecdotes and proverbs which the peasants loved to hear, and would keep reciting doggerels in Arabic. He would twirl a one rupee note around the head of the person to bless him; the amount would be later given in charity. In the morning, we'd be woken by his beautiful, full-throated sound calling the faithful to prayer. He had the bushiest eyebrows I have ever seen: they seemed to join with his mutton-chop whiskers and full, Babylonian beard. The maulvi seemed to the young eyes of children very ancient and full of old-time lore. They used to snuggle up to him and listen, wide-eyed, by the hour to his innumerable stories.

His tone was emollient. He would mutter an incantation in Arabic and blow a draught of air onto the faces of supplicants. The visitors at his abode would sit down in the night to sing plaintive Sufi dirges and odes while listeners swayed in rapture, clicking their tongues at a particularly moving verse and sometimes throwing up their hands in uncontrollable passion. Sinners, supplicants and, yes, even scallywags, would hand over a few rupees for a crack at redemption.

We had a war veteran whose sons were running a massive brick unit with a labour strength of around 300. He used to transport the workers from Kamptee to Bina, the site of these units, in an unusually designed wagon. The buses of those hard times were not buses at all, but any self-propelled, privately owned contraptions that could move people or animals or both. Some were ancient trucks, some four-passenger cars whose bodies had been ingeniously transformed into trucks, while others were three-wheeled motorcycles made into trucks, with a penchant, under an unbalanced or restless load, for tipping over. All of them carried twice as many passengers as they should have. They had whimsical schedules, itineraries set by changing road conditions, and broke down more frequently than not, leaving passengers stranded in the middle of nowhere. From there, everybody was on his own: once you got on a 'bus', your tracks were lost to the world.

Automobile drivers curse the bullock carts for slowing down traffic, and highway engineers hate them because their narrow, iron-rimmed wheels destroy the surface of the roads, especially in the summer, when the asphalt melts under the baking sun. Yet they are as much a part of Indian life today as they were at the dawn of Indian history. And, judging from ancient temple sculpture, the bullock cart has remained unchanged throughout the rise and fall of countless kingdoms. The cart has two wobbly wheels about five feet in diameter and is drawn by two humped bullocks with the yoke resting on the bullocks' necks in front of the hump. The Indian peasant is poor in money and technology; the bullock cart still remains for most farmers the only vehicle they can afford or know how to use.

As I was to discover late into my rural adventure, the BIna village was endowed with a rich diversity of talents. We had rural artistes who had splayed the walls with a glorious profusion of colours and stripes of political parties. Since each alliance comprised several parties, and each party had its particular set of colours, rustic Van Goghs and anonymous Anjolie Menons were recruited in their hundreds to paint political graffiti wherever their creativity blossomed.

There was the ubiquitous but rapacious moneylender, the *sahukar*. Nearly all village inhabitants had been compelled at some time or the other to call on the *sahukar*, the jeweller-usurer, a pot-bellied man with a skull as smooth and shiny as a billiard ball and face blacker than the bottom of a cooking pot. No matter how much distaste he provoked, the *sahukar* was the key person in the village. He was its banker, its moneylender, its pawnbroker, and very often its vampire. One must ask, as I did while living in rural India, where the capital of the poor came from, since that is one thing that capitalism requires. I gained a significant insight into the answer to this question when I asked a street vendor how he financed his tiny business. He replied, "I get my money where everyone else does." I said, "Where is that?" He said, "Everyone knows. I get it from a five-six." I asked, "What is a five-six?" He answered, "It is the place where you borrow five rupees in the morning, and pay back six rupees in the evening." I suddenly realized why so many poor people stay poor despite their hard work. Their entrepreneurial efforts are severely undercapitalized and often financed by loan shark rates that can be as high as twenty percent per day. Try to get ahead paying those kinds of rates.

All dirt tracks converged at the house of the *sahukar*, like the threads in a spider's web, and along the tracks came desperate families. Some brought their wives' ornaments wrapped in bits of rags; others brought the produce from their fields. Sometimes the women would walk in and remove their glistening nose studs, their wedding chain, and bangles and hand them into the poaching hands of the moneylender. Others had nothing to pledge but their own bodies. The moneylender swallowed everything, and nothing that entered came out, and the house grew and bulged. The moneylenders had already sucked the poor dry of their assets and their sleight-of-hand accounting had left the villagers' principal debt untouched by the repayments, which were marked up against the interest. In the villages where I worked, the moneylenders would survey potential customers with the sleepiness of crocodiles and pose an instant offer with a heavy interest tagged to it, but which appeared a tempting solution to the customer's financial woes. The stratospheric interest rate had doomed several families to permanent debt and bondage.

The village moneylenders have hearts harder than that of the jackal. In every village, moneylenders are reviled, and their business seen as squeezing out the blood of poor farmers. Yet villagers know there is no life without the loan-shark. Farming distress has attracted a new breed of moneylenders. Anyone with some disposable cash—from shopkeepers, government officials and policemen to village teachers—lends in the hope of making a killing. At some time or other, almost all the poor were in their debt. Now the moneylenders lived continually in their Shylock makeup; ostentatiously, their eyes painted to look fierce, their moustaches menacing. Their savage rates of interest were a lifelong nightmare to the poor.

Gunnar Myrdal stresses in his *Asian Drama*,

When the moneylender sees that he can benefit from the default of a debtor he becomes an enemy of the village economy. By charging exorbitant interest rates or by inducing the peasant to accept larger credits than he can manage the moneylender can hasten the process by which the peasant is dispossessed. (1968:1048)

There was a mysterious character in the village who held sway over the people on account of his dominating personality and canny methods. He smoked incessantly, and had an aggressive look in his broad brown face, daring you to interrupt or contradict him when he spoke. He spoke without using his hands: no expressions, and no gestures. He had a hacking smoker's cough, and in the middle of a severe bout, was usually bent double, holding up a warning hand to caution his listeners not to interject or change the subject: he hadn't finished speaking. "Let me talk", he would urge when he was able to straighten up, and breathlessly, sometimes gasping, he would carry on. Clad in a dingy beige turban, a patched beige tweed coat, crumpled white pyjama pants and drip-dry shirt, he would speak incessantly of the promises unfulfilled by the political leaders. I always got the feeling that this village was still shaking off the torpor of the fading socialist dreams of the Shetkari Sanghatana (Farmers' Federation), the right wing political party that held sway in the region in the first half of the1990s.

Then there was an old man, a comedian of sorts, with a frail and comical moustache and a great fuzzy aureole of white hair swirling in a dervish spin, who carried out ecological projects with tremendous zeal. He wore a band of purple feathers and leaves around his forehead like some pygmy tribesman. Sometimes he would drape a row of cowrie shells or discarded military badges around his chest. He could enliven even the blandest group of people. He might have been a court jester performing his part, but he could sting if his low status was scorned or mocked.

As usual, there was the local astrologer whose opinions carried great weight and who drew enormous respect as there was heavy demand for his benedictions. Paunchy and greying at the temples, he was a withered lemon of a man in a bright orange outfit. Silver dreadlocked hair, so long it snaked around his waist like a chastity belt, spilled out from under an even brighter orange turban. A blob of yellow turmeric remained smeared between his eyes, a long staff clasped between hands held in beatific gesture. He would draw an astrological chart on the ground and use cowries (the coins of our forefathers) to read the writing on the, well, ground. He tossed and flung eight cowries on the chart several times and came up with an answer to his customers' questions. He sat in the shadow of the widely canopied tree that had long, coiled trellises, giving the appearance of matted hair dangling from the wizened head of a sage.

Our village was also notorious for game breeders who raised roosters for cockfighting. Where cockfighting is illegal, it has naturally gone underground, or rather on the back roads and into dusty fighting pits in corrugated iron sheds. There, two gamecocks, often drugged, and armed with razor-sharp gaffs, are placed in a pit to attack each other while spectators gamble on the outcome. One bird is usually killed, sometimes both are.

The biggest festival of a village is Holi. Holi, the Hindu festival of spring, believed to date from prehistoric fertility rites, is accompanied by lewd songs, a clang of horns, drums and cymbals, and the throwing of brightly coloured dyes and powders. Villagers prepare by singing folk songs reflecting the Hindu mixture of sacred and erotic. Wearing tunics, billowing loin cloths and turbans, groups of villagers gather in the evening, listening as the men, sitting on the ground and smoking marijuana, sing lustily. The next night, on the eve of Holi itself, hundreds of villagers set off huge bonfires celebrating the myth of the demoness Holika. The blazing stacks of grass, twigs and cow dung send flames and sparks into the night. Villagers thrust newly-harvested sheaves of wheat stalks into the flames. The following morning, swarms of men and children roam the main pathways with bags of coloured powder and bottles or spray guns of coloured water, spraying, smearing and drenching each other with colour in a humorous rite of spring. It is a sort of go-crazy day in which throwing powdered dyes and water balloons on complete strangers and recreational marijuana use by pretty much everyone is acceptable. Markets teem with wooden carts piled with powdered dye. At some point it all explodes in a countrywide colour bomb and water fight.

Baby Fakira Sidame *is an ASHA worker, or frontline health worker in villages in the Yavatmal district of Maharashtra. Chosen by her village as their health representative,* Baby *mobilizes her community to bring their children for routine immunizations, and provides counselling to pregnant women and new mothers about breastfeeding, vaccinations, hand-washing, and other basic health needs. She also runs a day care centre for young children in the community, providing basic education and lunch.*

"Drastic changes have occurred. No one used to do family planning. Many children suffered from polio, many of whom died or were not able to walk. But over the last five years that I have been working, I have been able to reach out to these families through home visits, through meeting them and informing them about better health practices and vaccination. Now there are a lot of changes happening in these communities. People are adopting family planning and coming for vaccination and keeping good hygiene practices. We are trying to do our best and continue to improve our results. Immunization is very important. It is like holy water. It will save children from polio, diphtheria, pertussis, tetanus, and measles. If a child gets immunized, then my community becomes healthier.

"And similarly, my country will also become healthy. When a hungry child gets fed at my centre, I take great pleasure in seeing that that child is full. Also when a child comes to my centre and gets a vaccination on time. Seeing those cheers on the faces of the children brings me great happiness. That's what motivates me," says Baby. A highly laudable vision.

An ASHA (Accredited Social Health Activist) is a community worker who is appointed under India's National Health Programme to assist pregnant women to avail themselves of their health entitlements. There is one ASHA for every 1,000 women. Her job is to spread awareness about antenatal care, ensure that women go to hospitals for deliveries, and receive proper care during childbirth and the postpartum period. Many ASHAs accompany women to a health facility for antenatal check-ups, delivery and postnatal check-ups.

There is another cadre called *anganwadi sevikas* (assistants at the village kindergarten). These *anganwadi sevikas*(nursery assistants) help in creating awareness about the government's family planning programme in the lower strata of society. They also play an important role in reducing child deaths due to malnutrition. The key task that they perform, she says, is improving the human development index. Without *anganwadi sevikas*, a vast majority of the poor would see no improvement in their living standards. These dedicated female health workers are India's primary tool against the menace of child malnourishment, infant mortality, illiteracy, and preventable diseases. They provide services to villagers, poor families and sick people across the country, helping them access healthcare services, immunization, healthy food, hygiene, and also provide healthy learning environments for infants, toddlers and children.

In every village, the anganwadi workers are the first point of contact for all issues related to women and children. The anganwadi worker at my village, Meerabai Chaudhary, was a caring woman who was highly sensitive to the demands of her role, meticulous and efficient, not to mention well-versed in the nuances of official protocols. She would thread marigolds into garlands and stitch up bouquets made from local flowers. I had bought for her five spindles and various tinted threads, which she used for embellishing their floral presentations.

As a rural bank manager, when I had several regular visitors from both Indian and foreign donor agencies, the local arrangements would be handled by the local women members of Self Help Groups under Meera Chaudhary's supervision. At first the alien culture of the visitors would bewilder them, but soon they learned modern etiquette and would treat visitors with fresh juice of fruits from local orchards—custard apple, guava, musk melon and mango—and dense *lassi*(clarified milk).

I remember we once hosted a very high profile delegation comprising foreign visitors, tenured Indian bureaucrats and local officers. I was planning to have several tea-making teams to cater to the different profiles of guests. When Meerabai heard this, she guffawed with laughter as if I had worked out a naïve strategy. She suggested she would organize a single team which would brew tea without sugar. As the tea was served, a half-teaspoon of sugar would be added for foreign visitors, one teaspoon for Indian VIPs, one and one-half for local officials and two for villagers. Despite it being costly, villagers never compromise on the amount of sugar.

I could never win the support of the most threatening creature in Bina: the village headman, a terrifying gentleman with a fierce cavalry moustache and neatly trimmed beard raffishly dyed with henna. He had a craggy face, a large outcrop of nose, and the corners of his eyes were contoured with laughter lines. Every disgruntled individual was a potential vote spinner for him; the true politician sees a silver lining in every dissenting voice as he can translate it into a vote in the electoral bazaar. The banker is a currency without value in the local market as his name is normally recorded in the electoral records of the town where his family is based. Our village leader was a home-grown economist who studied in a local college; he had acquired a fair knowledge of Gandhian economic philosophy from his father who was a freedom fighter and who had served a term in jail for his part in the revolt against the British. He was also an informal consultant on what he would proudly call a dream route to quick wealth through judicious use of government subsidies. Since he did not overtly commit to any ideology, he would indulge in bellicose talk of all political stripes.

He was a walking manual on information about development programmes and would rattle off the fine-sounding schemes, spilling them out as a cherubic toddler recites in one long breath the full course of nursery rhymes. He had a silver-tongued oratory, hectoring people with speeches, and a wild reputation for turf fights with the financial bureaucracy. He preferred to hold court at home, surrounded by fawning retainers, basking in their solicitude. He would regale them with anecdotes and keep the listeners salivating. He was a hard drinker and a reek of liquor would often come out of his mouth.

In village gatherings, he would gloat over his vice-like control over the bureaucracy, unspooling a 'highlight list' of the signature kills he made in the subsidy jungle for his fellow villagers. He was a born jester and provided wholesome entertainment to the villagers. Lampooning the bureaucrats was his favourite sport. He would keep scrolling through ideas and government programmes rather than actually going into details. That is why the villagers only knew the names of projects without ever knowing their important features.

I can't forget the rally organized to celebrate the headman's election. I had to helplessly endure this painful ordeal for three hours. I was made to sit on the podium with the headman's cronies as the headman unleashed a verbal onslaught against their adversaries. His voice, made metallic by the amplifiers, boomed forth an endless catalogue of litanies. The orator, still gripping the neck of the microphone, his shoulders hunched forward, his free hand clawing at the air, had gone straight on with his speech. One minute more, and the feral roars of rage were again bursting from the crowd.

Bank managers working in villages would tell you how an inefficient legal system has made their job drudgery. The Indian legal system is quite well known for its Dickensian delays. Despite repeated proclamations from the throne of the government and the lofty pedestals of courts for dispensation of inexpensive and timely justice, the legal system continues to be dear and mired in interminable delays. The cost to Indian society of its sclerotic legal system is steep. There is no aspect of our social or national life that remains untouched by this malaise, not least the development sector. Unless all arms of administration—financial, legal, political and economic—are fully geared to move in tandem with each other, development programmes for the poor will continue to move in a long-winding way.

One of India's ancient texts warns its readers of a King Nuga, who was reborn as a lizard because he kept two litigants waiting too long over a cow dispute. There would be many a lizard presiding over India's courtrooms if myth became reality today. The laws are quite often so woolly, and so poorly enforced, that legality really means having the right lawyer, who can interpret the law according to the needs of the client. The finery of law makes even common rules a matter of debate and encourages a display of wits in the art of interpretation.

One of the toughest tasks of a village bank manager is monitoring farm loans. A single officer has to take care of almost a thousand borrowers. It is physically impossible for him to meet each one of them personally. The only recourse, therefore, is to keep writing letters and sending notices, reminding the borrowers whenever the loan instalment becomes overdue. It may be difficult to assess whether the borrowers come back with the instalment out of genuine good intentions or fear of the bank letter. Maybe it is a combination of both. Those clients who consult lawyers may be apt to delay their repayments because there will always be some legal point to whip the banker into granting concessions to the borrower. Lawyers thrive on promises and farmers seem to show greater faith in them than in their bankers.

In the hallway, a diverse crowd of rich, poor and middle-class had begun to gather. I entered the courtroom and sat just below the judge's bench. Four dirty fans, on long stems, circled slowly above my head, with the subdued hum produced by low voltage. Lawyers wearing their traditional black-and-white costumes came and went from the courtroom, bowing according to custom as they entered, filling several rows of chairs behind the front row, where they would wait all day long for their case to be heard. Light green folders and crowded dockets were everywhere—stacked high on the judge's desk, piled on the litigant's table, stuffed into shelves on the wall. A long bulb glowed dimly in the hall, threatening to switch off anytime, casting surreal shadows on the walls.

Meanwhile, as I found my case was listed much lower than the cases being heard now, I walked into the main courtroom where a lady judge presided. The lady judge demonstrated herself to be an incisive legal thinker, both in her written opinions and in her questions from the bench. She was also an excellent communicator with the kind of crisp direct style that made her persuasive not only among her colleagues but also among the court's broader audience.

When I returned to my courtroom, the keeper told me my case was being immediately taken up, much ahead of the listed time because the two previous litigants and their lawyers were not present and the third lawyer had sought an adjournment. My encounter in the witness box left my ideals evaporating. As I took my place in the dock, my lawyer, pulling on his robes, hurried into the court. He saw me and raised his thumb. A dizzying number of exhibits—notices, bank vouchers, signed cheques correspondence—were placed before me as my lawyer and the defendant's lawyer sparred over legal issues.

The lawyer defending the defaulter proceeded to grill me in near-perfect theatrical slang with a cannon fire of questions: "Did the borrower sign in your presence"; "Were the contents of the documents explained to him"; "Can you produce any witnesses in support of your argument?" He tried to play a smart game and questioned every simple line of logic. Painfully aware of how words skate over and around truth, never having quite enough nuance to grasp it completely, I contested him equally forcefully, testifying in blunt terms. At stake was a loan of Rs.25,000 and the lawyers were battling as if the country's sovereignty was at stake. He was gesticulating with ferocious gravitas. He reminded me of the famous aphorism: *If the facts are against you, pound on the law. If the law is against you, pound on the facts. And if both are against you, pound on the table!*

My lawyer couldn't respond suitably. He kept skirting around the law. His usual refrain would be, "Your Lordship, this is a leading question." It appeared his strategy was to wear out the defending lawyer or elicit some favourable response from the Magistrate, who kept on overruling the objections. The judge pronounced: "The court found no violations." Perhaps an individual judge may be biased, I thought at the time, but the judicial system as a whole can't ignore both the law and self-evident facts. My lawyer tried to inject some hysteria in the courtroom in order to impress me. He would keep banging the table while making his point. This is not surprising. The law deals with the same sort of questions as politics.

I tried to reason with the Magistrate that, if I had known that each loan could generate a thriving cottage industry of litigation, I would have moderated my enthusiasm and sense of commitment. I was animated with a passion for helping the poor and now I found that I had become trapped in a multiple helix in chasing this vain chimera. My humble, polite voice chimed oddly amid the thundering perorations of top-rank lawyers. The Magistrate seemed to have been offended by my remark, as if he sat on Vikramaditya's throne and lesser mortals like me dare not use his court for moral philosophizing. In front of me sat the philosopher king, the flag-bearer of the cloistered virtue that is justice, holding the court in its majestic grandeur, and I was a supplicant who had the temerity to dispense his own version of wisdom.

He was conscious of being a deity in his own small kingdom in which he exercised unbridled authority. He appeared quite patronizing, dispensing justice the way a modern saint dispenses benedictions. For him everyone who entered the witness box was someone who was arraigned before his stern tribune of justice. The judge grimaced at my audacity and his mouth was a straight, grim line, as if to say, "We know the law better."The regulations of the judiciary are broad enough to be used punitively by small-minded judges. Earlier in the day, a colleague of mine was hauled up in a similar fashion. It was a field day for the Magistrate, slamming people from the banking fraternity, to the undisguised delight of the chattering lawyers.

The courts continue their trend of sticking closely to the language of the governing statutes and rules and reining in creative efforts by lawyers. Everyone knows that those who won't play ball with the prosecutor are going to be convicted. Their intransigence means they will have to serve their full terms. A litigant shot back a profanity to the judge who deflected it calmly. The litigant cackled as he was led away, his sinister laugh echoing in the courtroom.

Standing in the hallowed precincts of the temple of justice, I shuddered, wondering whether the Magistrate would frame me for lowering the dignity and prestige of the court. Looming in front of me was the lofty majesty of law in whose shadow stood a puny creature. The judiciary should not move into such narrow straits and shallow shoals. St. Luke in the Bible abjured the physician thus—"Physician, heal thyself!"

It was in the 4th century BC that the wise Greek philosopher Socrates named four qualities required in a judge–"to hear courteously, to answer wisely, to consider soberly and to decide impartially". To me it appeared that the magistrate had disdain for philosopher kings and was more at ease with his own crude version of a judge.

The government will need to enhance the legal system and—because public sentiment often runs against bank loan recovery efforts—muster the political will to bolster contract enforcement. At first glance, stronger enforcement would appear to work against disadvantaged consumers, but it would actually improve their access to credit. Banks avoid these consumers in part because they find it difficult to collect debts from them.

A general problem affecting the banking system (both public and private sector banks) is the efficacy of the legal system in enforcing creditor rights. At present, the legal procedure is dilatory, and there are difficulties associated with enforcing recovery through seizure and sale of collateral or through forced liquidation. The basic risk mitigation agency, the justice system, is dysfunctional. No crook who flees with a bank's money can be brought to book under the present system, unless he is small fry. Banks cannot send musclemen to throw acid, take away cars or burn crops as lenders in the informal system do to discipline borrowers.

We are paying a price for our lack of adequate understanding of economic principles within the legal system. There is no point in blaming the judges. Besides, Indian laws in this behalf have not kept pace with changes in technology or international business practices. In his autobiography, Jawaharlal Nehru articulated his legal dilemma:

Even more important are the economic changes that are rapidly taking place the world over. We must realize that the nineteenth-century system has passed away, and has no application to present-day needs. The lawyer's view, so prevalent in India, of proceeding from precedent to precedent is of little use when there are no precedents. We cannot put a bullock-cart on rails and call it a railway-train. It has to give way and be scrapped as obsolescent material.

I am always reminded of the epochal words of the great American judge, Justice Benjamin Cardozo:

Free India has to find its conscience in its rugged realities and no more in alien legal thought. In a larger sense, the insignia of creativity in law as in life is freedom from subtle alien bondage, not a silent spring nor a hothouse flower.

Equally moving are the words of Friedman:

It would be tragic if the law were so petrified so as to be unable to respond to the unending challenges of evolutionary or revolutionary change in society.

We had a wonderful homoeopathic doctor in whose small clinic sick villagers would throng. He would bring out one of the little felt-lined boxes arranged on his shelves and open it to reveal a dozen vials, each filled with tiny pills. He would shake three white pellets into my palm and say "One for the confidence needed in handling defaulting borrowers, second to remove the fears encountered in walking through lightless alleys, and another to sharpen loan-appraising skills."A small board hung inside his clinic which had a quotation in the local language by the great homoeopath, Kent: "The physician must penetrate into the inner recesses of symptoms; the very life of the patient must be opened and laid bare. Learn the fears, instincts, desires and aversions of the patient. The remedy often crops out through the affections."Our doctor appeared to take the advice very sincerely.

Once during his visit to my office, he found me in a sour mood. He dropped a few pellets on my palm. "They're for maintaining a calm and gentle mood in office," he said. I did become calm—whether it was because my customers realized the folly of irritating me or the pellets had worked, I will never know.

Indian rural weddings are, by nature, more involved than the urban ones. They last anywhere from three to seven days, involve multiple religious functions and feature guest lists that can stretch to 5,000 people. They're seen as community—as opposed to strictly family—affairs. As land prices in villages on the periphery of cities have skyrocketed, those social conventions have taken on new extravagance. Most big political leaders are from villages where they continue to perform all major rituals. For an urban visitor, it's easy to scoff at such extravagance, to chalk it up to nouveau-riche impulses given free rein. Certainly, an element of social peacocking does come into play—but that alone does not account for the phenomenon. After all, impressing the neighbours is hardly a uniquely Indian concern, and there are more enduring ways to telegraph your wealth than an ephemeral celebration.

The deeper motivation stems from the country's distinct social customs. While the urban tends to focus on the individual, in rural India the family is of paramount importance, followed closely by one's membership in various ethnic and religious communities. An over-the-top wedding is an opportunity to bring together all these people under one super-size tent and to celebrate the core values that define Indian society. It is an occasion for joy, not just for the bride and groom but for all their closest relatives and friends.

For a young manager, rural India and its vast array of institutions and the people who man and service them and the equally vast number of quaint characters that one encounters in the labyrinths of the hallowed portals of these institutions, it looks more a social laboratory where the primary democracy churns out inputs for the larger national governance agenda.

There are miniature versions of all public institutions with all their heat and drama as the vital ingredients of the national policies are sieved through a vast maze of paper trails. It is an experience that made my later assignments at the national level much easier. With the knowledge of the processes at the lower bureaucracy you can better understand and creatively provide wider and deeper values to the nuances that underpin national policies and programmes.

3

Finance For The Poor

Money is the seed of money, and the first guinea is sometimes more difficult to acquire than the second million.

Jean-Jacques Rousseau

Money, says the proverb, makes money. When you have got a little, it is often easy to get more ;the great difficulty is to get that little

Adam Smith, The Wealth of Nations

To give away money is an easy matter and in any man's power. But to decide to whom to give it, and how large, and when, and for what purpose and how, is neither in every man's power nor an easy matter.

Aristotle

Historians will tell you that an explosion of creativity occurs the moment the world starts complaining that there is nothing left to invent or that the search for solutions to intractable problems has become futile. This explosion is fate's way of reminding us that there is always something just over the horizon of knowledge. Social entrepreneurs are now using their talent to foster social change and bring lasting solutions to the chronic problems confronting us. These wide-ranging problems relate, among other things, to infrastructure, health concerns, education, sanitation, connectivity and food insecurity. These new-age heroes have single-handedly spearheaded large innovations and are transforming lives for millions of common people.

The rise of soloists signals the ultimate atomization of the modern world. It also demonstrates that individual initiatives can be as powerful game-changers as collective efforts. The power and reach of individual creativity has grown in inverse proportion to the shrinking of the global village. The failure of conventional strategies to alleviate the problems that the marginalized face today has set flowing the creative juices of shoals of the younger lot. It has catapulted them to a cutting edge vanguard position. This approach leaves no room for alibis and is highly committed to delivering results. This new generation of innovators, many from Ivy League universities, IITs and IIMs, are former bankers, academics, technocrats, bureaucrats and consultants. They have shown that our time-tested values—hard work and honesty, courage and fair play, humility and modesty, tolerance and curiosity—are as relevant today as they ever were. Their tribe believes in the power of ingenuity and artifice to solve problems and mitigate human suffering. They embrace world-changing entrepreneurship and do not shrink from tinkering with and reforming entrenched systems. They favour open-source solutions that share intellectual property–whether computer code or DNA sequences–so that others can improve and build on their creations.

Finance is one field where we have witnessed significant innovations in recent decades. Earlier, we could only visualise social change in rural India because villages were so deeply mired in caste conflicts. These conflicts had engendered local tyrannies and subverted the social order, resulting in bondage and servitude for significant portions of the population for generations. In the 1970s, the locus of change shifted to other areas, which worked in levelling caste divisions and neutralising feudal overlords. Finance was the pivot of this process of change.

When I began life as a rural banker in the 1970s, outsiders rarely visited the villages. Those who did, other than the occasional anthropologist, government extension officer, family planning staff of the government or census worker, were missionaries of various religions. Over the years, I noticed that the balance shifted from outsiders bringing religion to outsiders bringing finance. Of course, those who lived in the villages already had both. As an ancient Indian proverb has it, a village can be formed wherever there come together a river, a priest, and a moneylender. This gradual change in the profile of visitors and reformers was my first introduction to the then-embryonic revolution in development finance which later grew into the niche of social banking.

With globalisation and liberalization, a shift from the socialist to the capitalist approach was evident. Banks had bled badly in the government-mandated programmes for eradication of poverty. They realised that age-old nostrums of finance could not be compromised; a new way had to be found to engage with the poor. Development finance emerged as the much-touted miracle for combating poverty. The eventual arrival of microfinance further strengthened the efforts of professionals and bankers in pursuing solutions for issues facing the poor.

The Self Help Group model of finance, the oldest and most authentic model of microfinance in India, arrived at a time when the poor villagers were already neck-deep in debt as a result of recurrent droughts throughout vast swathes of the country. For the average Indian farmer, the rain gods had long gone deaf. The hapless farmers had no energy left to appeal to the heavens. Even their tears had gone dry. The banking system needed to prevent bad loans from taking off again.

The moneylenders' sleight-of-hand accounting procedures left the principal debt of the borrowers untouched by their repayments which were mostly marked up against the interest.

Government funds had started drying up and the generous dollops of outside aid were thinning. The losses on account of bad loans were taking a huge bite out of the earnings and cash flow of rural banks. Bankers were looking for strategies to deflate the portfolios of bad loans, so they started retreating from rural areas. This was a regressive development for the village economy as it limited villagers' access to even those basic financial services which alone could provide an economic toehold for villagers looking to get out of the slough of poverty and debt.

The poor performance of development programmes had already debunked the notion that subsidies could play a useful role in hastening development. Political doles had only resulted in a devastated economy and severely restricted commercial opportunities. The people erroneously came to believe that the state had all the answers to their problems. Governments, international financial institutions and non-governmental organizations (NGOs) threw vast amounts of money at credit-based solutions to rural poverty, particularly in the wake of the World Bank's 1990 initiative to put poverty reduction at the head of its development priorities. And yet those responsible for such transfers had, and in many cases continue to have, only the haziest grasp of the unique demands and difficulties of rural banking.

Another dampening development on the macro front was that, amid sizzling growth in cities in the past five years, India's largest institutions grumbled that their smaller, often unprofitable, branches in the poorer parts of the country crimped their ability to deploy adequate manpower and capital to urban operations. Foreign banks, which had little obligation to India's farmers, gained the all-important urban market share.

During this period, the idea took root in many countries that financial services could and should be made widely accessible to low-income people through the formal financial sector. The discrepancy between financial institutions' modes of operation and the economic characteristics and financial needs of low-income households resulted in a lack of access to credit for the poor. For example, commercial lending institutions of the time required that borrowers have a stable source of income out of which principal and interest could be repaid according to the agreed terms, and that they hold collateral with a clear title. Self-employed households rarely had either, and as a result, bankers tended to consider low-income households a bad risk, imposing exceedingly high costs on collecting information on these households. Lenders preferred to deal with small numbers of large loans to minimize administration costs. Bankers working with the poor learned that the reverse was needed.

The bankers who began showing up in villages on their bicycles, motorcycles or jeeps in the 1970s and 1980s were usually employees of local branches of state-owned banks. Their mission, as assigned by their governments and assorted international donors, was to find trustworthy villagers to whom they could provide credit. This, it was thought, would help villagers start small businesses, thereby increasing rural economic growth while at the same time empowering people to climb out of poverty.

The bankers and the missionaries, who shared much of the same client pool, were curiously alike in some ways. Usually outsiders to the local community, members of both groups tended to discover their own preconceptions in the villages, rather than the local realities and dynamics. However, many of them genuinely cared about helping poor people increase their incomes and improve their lives. Some were even quite successful. They came with powerful ideas, found other similarly powerful ideas already present, and often became catalysts for the cross-fertilization of their own ideas of social and economic reforms and the wisdom of the locals.

A unique characteristic of bankers visiting villages was the refreshing change in their academic credentials and their willingness to adapt to the harsh realities of rural life. Most of them were from technical backgrounds, endowed with a vision that focused more on the technical and practical, rather than the financial, aspects of the problems of the poor. This was particularly seen in the innovative practices they fostered in agriculture, dairy and small enterprises and artisanry. Their overarching goal was energisation of the rural economy and promotion of entrepreneurial approaches, and development finance was just one of the many sources into which they dipped.

They brought a range of weaponry to combat poverty and agricultural regress: high-yielding varieties of seeds, new techniques for pest management, a modern range of fertilizers and equipment. The veterinary doctors brought exotic breeds of cattle, a range of new drugs and nutritional supplements to combat mortality and improve cattle health. Artificial insemination techniques built superior breeds of cattle.

Bankers also started leveraging the voluntary sector in the villages for supplementing finance with changes in the social dynamics of the village social order. Several of these new rural development entrepreneurs seamlessly adapted to the local culture and enjoyed enormous trust among the local population. These were people who not only revolutionized the cultural mind-set of the rural societies but also harnessed their creative energies into extraordinary regional social and economic movements.

Access to finance is critical for a country's development—it is as much a part of a country's basic infrastructure as access to roads, or electricityor the internet. Ample evidence indicates that economies with deep financial sectors and well-functioning financial systems perform better. Contrary to common impressions, poor people need and use the same variety of financial services and for the same reasons as wealthier clients: to seize business opportunities, improve their homes, cope with emergencies and other large expenses.

A growing body of evidence confirms that gaining access to finance has a positive impact on household welfare. However, the financial services usually available to the poor are limited in terms of cost, risk, and convenience, requiring the poor to, on occasion, tap into other assets, such as livestock, building materials, and 'cash under the mattress', when the need arises. Cash under the mattress can be stolen or lose value as a result of inflation. A cow cannot be divided and sold in parcels to meet small cash needs. Certain types of credit, particularly those from moneylenders, are extremely expensive. Rotating savings and credit clubs (the international variant of the Indian *bishi*) are risky and don't allow much flexibility in loan amount or in timing of deposits and loans. Deposit accounts of formal financial institutions require minimum amounts and may have inflexible withdrawal rules. Loans from these institutions have collateral requirements that exclude many poor borrowers.

Over the last two decades, however, successful experiences of development banks in providing finance to small entrepreneurs and producers demonstrate that poor people, when given access to responsive and timely financial services, even at market rates, repay their loans as promptly as wealthier clients and use the proceeds to increase their income and assets. This is not surprising since the only realistic alternative for them is borrowing from the informal market at an interest much higher than market rates. Barriers to formal savings are bank fees, lack of convenience in operating savings accounts, and the perception among the bankers that the sums available to these potential customers are too small to deposit.

The financial illiteracy of the poor has exiled them from formal financial institutions, despite the fact that modern banking is more than two centuries old. For decades, balancing one's chequebook has been the cornerstone of personal finance for conscientious adults in the developed world. I remember when I first opened an account of my own in my college days, I received a little booklet, the ubiquitous passbook, in which every deposit and withdrawal was acknowledged by the bank staff. I learned that keeping track of the bank balance was the personal hygiene of finance, like brushing your financial teeth. The implicit message, not just for me, but I think for society at large, was that the bank account was the locus of money management. All one's main financial transactions would pass through the account, and the account would serve as a running financial statement, showing not only income and expenses but also personal solvency. This philosophy, termed 'financial inclusion', has been the cornerstone of personal finance for adults in the developed world. And it is now the key focus of governments in developing countries. Financial institutions are now engaged in a vigorous battle to enlist the poor as their clients, not just for their business but to open a window for the poor which allows the global development winds to touch their lives.

Access to financial services - financial inclusion - implies an absence of obstacles to the use of these services, whether the obstacles are price or nonprice barriers to finance. It is important to distinguish between access to - the possibility to use - and actual use of financial services. Exclusion can be voluntary, where a person or business has access to services but no need to use them, or involuntary, where price barriers or discrimination, for example, bar access. Failure to make this distinction can complicate efforts to define and measure access. Financial market imperfections, such as information asymmetries and transaction costs, are likely to be especially binding on the talented poor and on micro- and small enterprises that lack collateral, credit histories, and connections. Without inclusive financial systems, these individuals and enterprises with promising opportunities are limited to their own savings and earnings. This access dimension of financial development has often been overlooked, mainly because of serious data gaps on who has access to which financial services and a lack of systematic information on the barriers to broader access.

Financial inclusion covers a gamut of financial services that can link the poor to the financial ocean. Formal accounts and savings may help poor people smooth their consumption and weather unexpected events such as unemployment, accidents, illnesses and deaths without resorting to expensive loans which can lock them in debt traps.

Financial inclusion enables poor people to save and to responsibly borrow—allowing them to build their assets, to invest in education and entrepreneurial ventures and to improve their livelihoods. Poor people save, borrow, and make payments throughout their lives, but to use these services to their full potential, to protect their families and improve their lives, they need products well suited to their needs. Bringing this about requires attention to human and institutional issues, such as quality of access, affordability of products, sustainability for the provider of these services, and outreach to the most excluded populations.

But financial inclusion is no new idea or philosophy, it is only that it has been retrieved from the financial backwaters and resurrected. A by-product of the drive towards financial inclusion is the radical idea that the thing people really need, more than business loans, is a safe place to save their money. It's what development expert Robert Vogel calls the "forgotten half of rural finance."

I remember in the early eighties, all of us bankers were part of a financial inclusion revolution that was far more vigorous than the one we see now. The wave of commercialization put the brakes on this enthusiastic journey and a great mission was abandoned and orphaned. The high profit goals spurred bankers to design rabbit holes in which the poor would get trapped and lose their accounts. Introduction of penalties for not maintaining minimum balances and for accounts remaining inoperative (absence of transaction in the account) led to a mass-scale demise of bank accounts of millions of poor account holders. Without informing the poor customers of policy changes, the bankers sheared and denuded the accounts of their bank balances by applying penalties, finally knocking them off the bank ledgers altogether.

Financial inclusion should not end with just opening accounts. The customer must make this account his financial diary and conduct transactions which can grow into a credit history. Or else all these accounts would remain deadweight. What needs to be done is to make more and more of these accounts actually transactional, and actively transactional. Once in a way the subsidy also comes in, so that's the first set of transactions. But after that, [what is important is] getting the customers used to the habit of saving, getting them to use formal channels for the remittance of money and then, through the way the money comes into the account, building some kind of credit analytics and making small loans and micro insurance available to them.

Two decades back, a worldwide initiative was launched by the voluntary sector, later bolstered by commercial investors, to make credit accessible to the hitherto unserved population which remained out of the orbit of the financial planet. This approach was designated 'microcredit.' The concept of microcredit was later enlarged to include savings, insurance and remittance with the entire bouquet of services falling under a common umbrella known by the term 'microfinance'.

What exactly is microfinance? Microfinance refers to a variety of financial services that target low-income clients, particularly women. The institutions which administer and provide microfinance are termed Microfinance Institutions (MFIs), and their services include loans, savings, insurance and remittances. Microloans are given for a variety of purposes, frequently for microenterprise development. The diversity of products and services offered reflects the fact that the financial needs of individuals, households and enterprises can change significantly over time, especially for those who live in poverty. Because of these varied needs, and because of the industry's focus on the poor, microfinance institutions often use non-traditional methodologies, such as group lending or other forms of collateral not employed by the formal financial sector.

Although microfinance has been around in various forms for years, its modern incarnation is most closely tied to Mohammed Yunus, the founder of the Grameen Bank. In his autobiography, he describes how, as a professor in Bangladesh, he came to understand the importance of finance for the poor. Horrified by the consequences of a famine, he left the sheltered walls of the university to find out how the poor made a living. When he started making small loans to local villagers in the 1970s, it was unclear where the idea would go. Around the world, scores of state-run banks had already tried to provide loans to poor households, and they had left a legacy of inefficiency, corruption and squandered subsidies running into millions of dollars. Economic theory also provided ample cautions against lending to low-income households that lacked collateral to secure their loans. Yunus vowed to one day make profits—and he argued that his poor clients would pay back the loans reliably. Yunus was one of the early visionaries who believed in the idea of poor people as viable, worthy and attractive clients for loans. That simple notion has put in motion a huge range of imitators and innovators who have taken that idea and run with it, improved on it, expanded it.

In an episode that has now passed into the folklore of microfinance, Yunus encountered a woman who made bamboo stools, Sufiya Begum. The raw materials she needed to make one stool cost only twenty-two American cents, but she made a pitiful two American cents on every stool; because she had no capital, she had to borrow money from middlemen in order to purchase supplies, and sell the stools back to them to repay the loans. Yunus was appalled: 'I watched as she set to work again, her small brown hands plaiting the strands of bamboo as they had every day for months and years on end. How would her children break the cycle of poverty she had started? How could they go to school when the income Sufiya earned was barely enough to feed her alone, let alone shelter her family and clothe them properly?'

Yunus paid off the money she and other villagers owed to loan sharks. To his surprise, the borrowers paid him back in full. He discovered that while the credit market was the scene of the most brutal exploitation of the poor with high interest rates leading to persistent indebtedness ending in forced sale of assets and subsequent destitution, it was also the arena in which interventions to break the cycle of poverty were easiest. His pilot programme has now become a movement for both financial and social empowerment–particularly for poor rural women.

It was the start of the microcredit revolution. Traditionally, banks shunned the poorest as bad credit risks, since they have no collateral for loans. But with a series of increasingly ambitious experiments–initially with himself as guarantor for bank loans–Yunus established that many of the poorest could be good borrowers: they knew a line of credit was their only chance to break out of indigence.

Yunus emphasises: "If you go out into the real world, you cannot miss seeing that the poor are poor not because they are untrained or illiterate but because they cannot retain the returns of their labour. They have no control over capital, and it is the ability to control capital that gives people the power to rise out of poverty."

When Yunus formalized this loan-making arrangement as the Grameen Bank in 1983, the bank adopted its signature innovation: making borrowers take out loans in groups of five, with each borrower guaranteeing the others' debts. Thus, in place of the hold banks had on wealthier borrowers who did not pay their debts—foreclosure and a low credit rating—Grameen depended on an incentive at least as powerful for poor villagers: the threat of being shamed before neighbours and relatives. Since traditional credit ratings and past credit histories were unavailable for most microfinance borrowers, repayment of the loans was guaranteed through a process known as "building and placing reliance on social capital". The collateral created through the process of joint liability through group lending is termed as "social collateral" or "moral collateral". With individual financial histories having been built over the years and the borrowers realising the importance of making their loan repayments on time so that others are not starved of credit by their default, and to keep up their reputation as honest borrowers for getting easy access to credit in future, the Grameen Bank has now moved to individual loans, with the individual reputation of borrowers replacing the group guarantee.

The model of microfinance in Bangladesh, as it originated at Grameen Bank, involved tiny loans with fixed terms and amounts to women, group liability, weekly meetings, forced payments into a group savings account, and a set of 16 social pledges chanted each week while standing at attention. Yet the great revolution that fetched Yunus international acclaim angered politicians in his own country. Like all great reformers, he has himself become a target of a political vendetta in his country. The government of Bangladesh has played its trump card in its long-running campaign against Grameen Bank and Muhammad Yunus: legislators passed a law that effectively nationalizes the bank, by wresting control of it from the millions of women who controlled it as a cooperative and divested Yunus of his position in the institution which he'd cradled since its inception.

The Joint Liability Group (JLG) system, the basic unit of microfinance in Bangladesh, was, in its classical avatar, an operationally intensive model with strong emphasis on adherence to simple yet well designed processes. A group of borrowers get together and form the basic unit–the Joint Liability Group; five is the most common number of members but membership can range from four to ten. Coming from the same neighbourhood, they know each other well enough to understand the cash flows and requirements of the members' households and have insight into the ability and willingness of members to repay. This model helps financial institutions to overcome the difficulties involved in screening individual borrowers. The borrowers are poor women who have absolutely nothing that could be repossessed. They have no credit record, little education, no formal employment history. The costs of checking the creditworthiness of these potential clients and servicing their loans would be an astronomical percentage of the tiny amount they would borrow.

Before any one group member obtained a loan, the entire group had to undergo a training session, spanning one to two weeks, to learn the bank's strictly enforced rules and procedures and to help members develop their business skills. After the initial training period, each group member attended weekly group meetings with an officer of the bank. Up to ten groups of borrowers in one area federated into a "centre" and elected a centre chief and deputy centre chief. Several centres in turn formed a branch. Each group formulated and considered loan requests which were reviewed and approved by the centre chief, a bank worker, a programme officer, and finally the bank's branch and zone manager.

All loan requests were discussed candidly at group meetings; transactions between the bank and individual members of each group did not remain confidential. The group scrutinized each member's prospective enterprises and business proposals, ensuring that they were well thought out and therefore more likely to make a profit from which the loan recipients could repay the loan. Group members strove to keep business ideas that were not feasible from being approved and to share ideas to make businesses more profitable. Moreover, in forming their groups, members screened out prospective borrowers deemed unlikely to repay a loan. Once the Bank approved a loan, group members monitored how the money was used. This ensured that borrowers were more likely to operate their business properly since they would frequently be examined by their peers.

Peer pressure was also sustained by the sequence of loans. Say, for example, that one member of a newly formed group received a loan. The other four members were ineligible for loans until the initial borrower demonstrated regular payment of the weekly instalment. Each JLG thus had an incentive to encourage a delinquent member to make her payments, or it could resort to making the missed payments as a group. Second loans were not approved for any one member until the accounts of all members were settled. In other words, the group ensured mutual accountability and served as a form of moral or social collateral. By relying on the borrowers themselves to monitor loans and guarantee repayment, the bank was able to forego close analysis of individual loan applications, thereby lowering the high transaction costs that discouraged individual loans to small businesses. And by grouping borrowers, the bank staff could service more loans with fewer contacts required by the bank staff.

Two other factors also contributed to loan repayment success. First, most loans were for shorter periods. Borrowers initially received a small loan, so as not to overwhelm them with cash. Once the borrower repaid the first loan, subsequent loans could be larger and have a longer repayment period. This incremental lending technique provided incentives to the borrower and minimized the risk to the bank. The Grameen model was embraced by most countries and became an international model, albeit with tweaks relevant to each country. One weakness of Grameen replications was an emphasis on loans at the cost of fostering savings habits, which was the key ingredient in the original

Grameen model. In several countries, this deficiency wrote the obituary of microfinance.

The initial motivation for microfinance was, to a great extent, gender neutral. It emerged, however, that women entrepreneurs invested the profits from their businesses in ways that had a longer-lasting, more profound impact on the lives of their families and communities. This unassailable truism became a fundamental premise of the microfinance business model and the success of microfinance as a poverty alleviation tool. It also forced the realization that the close knowledge of clients' lives and financial needs—traditionally a hallmark of microfinance—may have become secondary to the push for greater numbers of clients.

The Indian version of microfinance, baptized "Self Help Group", is quite different from Bangladesh's "Joint Liability Group". The most important distinction between the two is that the former lays greater emphasis on financial literacy, building of social capital, empowerment and capacity building of members. These are secondary concerns in the Joint Liability Group model, which focuses more on financial metrics in contrast to the social ones. Self Help Groups were initially the basic constituent units of the microfinance system in India. It was much later that the original Grameen model was introduced in its classical form in India but the Self Help Group model remained as the most authentic indigenous form of microfinance.

The basis of Self Help Groups existed in rural society prior to rural planners' formulation of this concept. A common bond—most commonly caste or sub-caste, but also community, occupation and place of origin or activity—links affinity groups. Since these groups provide monetary as well as moral support to individual members in times of difficulties, they are also called "solidarity groups". The agency that undertakes the task of forming these groups must try to identify these groups on the basis of their existing natural bonds

The two models intersected at the point of the belief in extending credit to the unserved and underserved. However, the international Joint Liability Group model and the Indian Self Help Group model have fundamental divergences in the business models. Whereas in most countries Joint Liability Groups are formed in order to obtain credit, Self Help Groups invariably have a savings component, which precedes credit. It is only when the group matures and savings habits are firmly ingrained among the members that credit can be considered. Secondly, while Joint Liability Groups are just credit groups, serving as conduits of finance for the poor, the Indian Self Help Group includes capacity-building, awareness-raising, and exposing the poor women to a variety of social, economic and health issues confront them and imparting skills for solving their personal and family problems at the group level. They are also taught the skills to manage conflicts within the group.

The Self Help Group-led microcredit approach in India first evolved as the Self Help Affinity Groups facilitated by the Mysore Resettlement and Development Agency (MYRADA) in 1985, and was adapted by the National Bank of Agricultural and Rural Development for implementation by commercial banks. The adapted version, which underwent modifications to suit the needs of formal financial laws, started in 1992 as a pilot project and was upgraded to a regular banking program in 1996.

A Self Help Group is a group of a few individuals—usually poor and often women—who pool their savings into a fund from which they can borrow as and when necessary. Such a group is linked with a bank—a rural, cooperative, or commercial bank—where they maintain a group account. For a period of time in the beginning, the women only save money. They deposit a small sum, ranging from Rs 20 to Rs 50 each month. After six months, the women are eligible to take small loans. These loans can either come from the group savings account or through the bank. The group helps determine if the loan is appropriate for each member and serves as a screening point for the bank. Because the liability of the loan is shared among the group, it is in each member's interest to ensure that all other members are capable of paying back a loan on time.

Loans are then given out to individual members from these funds upon application and unanimous resolution drawn at a group meeting. The bank permits withdrawal from the group account on the basis of such resolutions. Such loans, fully funded out of the savings generated by the group members themselves, are called 'interloans', and have a short repayment period, usually three to six months.

After recording regular loan issuance and repayment for a minimum period of six months, the bank begins to lend to the group as a unit, without collateral, relying on self-monitoring and peer pressure within the group for repayment of these loans. The maximum loan amount is a multiple (usually 4:1) of the total funds in the group account.

Once the group matures, and graduates to business enterprise, the financing is more need-based and is directly linked with the capital needs of the business.

I began my first experiment with Self Help Groups in the late eighties during my assignment as manager of a small two-man unit in Bina near Nagpur. We were running a small pilot program borrowed from Thailand. It was a wild and risky adventure because state-run banks still had not approved the model.

Although my experiment in Bina was not a complete success, I was able to draw on my learning to refine the model. Warora was to be the first test of this learning curve. Mobilising the villagers, particularly the women, was a tightrope walk of promoting Self Help Groups. Initial spadework consisted of informal visits to our bank's clients, particularly those who were illiterate in matters of finance, to create awareness about the actual role of a banker in the rural economy. My staff would emphasise that a bank loan was a scarce commodity which had to be recycled. The people had such Stone Age notions of banking that many of them believed bankers had cash printing machines with which they generated as much cash as they needed. The bank manager was supposed to be the owner of the cash in the vault, as he held its keys.

Initially, we avoided broaching the subject of SHG. We told the villagers that the purpose of our visit was mainly to know the banking needs of the villagers. We had to ingratiate ourselves with them; they had become used to cheap subsidised credit under government programmes, and would not accept any initiative which would not promise or deliver quick benefits. This was an unfortunate legacy of unimaginative politicians who throve on the gullibility of the people. Money and promises are powerful allurements on Election Day: when people were declined loans because their families had been bracketed as defaulters, they promptly sought help from their political patrons, who encouraged them to boycott loan repayments altogether.

When I began the task of promoting Self Help Groups in Chandrapur district in Maharashtra, the local villagers were leery about our intentions. They could not tolerate our direct interaction with their womenfolk. Their rancour and bitterness manifested in their intemperate language and intimidating tactics. I tried every textbook model to thwart the attempts of these leaders to sabotage my agenda and I did succeed in weakening their bases and demolishing some of their bastions.

Yet the leaders continued to foment trouble but I remained unfazed. With the use of homilies, anecdotes and tales from local mythologies, we tried to purge deeply entrenched misperceptions of both banking and bankers. Though the people knew that bankers were much gentler and kinder, more civilised people than moneylenders, the animus they had harboured against moneylenders extended to bankers when they found that, unlike moneylenders, the doors of banks were closed to the poor. Our project in Warora appeared to be in limbo as these elements remained intractable. With their strident rhetoric, the local leaders would try to arouse the passion of the villagers against us. There was no way we could bypass the men folk, particularly the hardliners. It was only after we managed to build bridges of understanding with a small group of local leaders that we began the actual process of forming Self Help Groups and providing loans.

Most of our senior bosses were sitting ducks. They refused to face the reality of the socio-economic dynamics of the rural areas of our country. All too often they believed these goons, who had been holding us hostages, to be social victims who had suffered years of subjugation in the caste-driven village dynamics. The senior management wasn't keen on poverty alleviation programmes but the banks were under the compulsion of government diktats to accept it. The senior management clearly saw that these loans were unviable for banks and were likely to be abused by politicians for obliging their buddies. The history of cooperative banking bore out this fact and was largely responsible for the failure of cooperative banking in India In trying to demonstrate a veiled acceptance of the government directive, they issued coded communication without asserting their commitment to these poverty alleviation loans. These loans, in fact, went against the philosophy of robust banking. The bankers have never been keen about these development programmes because most of them have eroded the viability of the banking system. Clients have misunderstood these developmental loans as government doles.

The women of Warora were the first to hear the overtures of us bank officials. So many fly-by-night savings schemes had burnt their hard-won savings that they had grown cynical of outside agencies flogging savings and insurance policies. Many of the charlatans selling financial plans did so while juggling other jobs, from driving auto rickshaws to running electric repair shops. These agents sold the raciest products they could, and encouraged the villagers to churn policies rather than renewing policies and therefore avoiding a succession of new policy charges. Some of the women had even the gall to question our integrity.

Bankers' initial discourses on microfinance had set off an avalanche of consternation and protest among the menfolk. We patiently tried to allay their fears and doubts about the new programme. I would break bread with low caste villagers. To the men folk who thought that we were using their women as guinea pigs for our banking experiments, we promised that time would demonstrate all our efforts were aimed at uplifting not just women but the entire village.

The enthusiasm of my boys would flag in the face of the politicians' broadsides and the torrents of vituperation, and the slovenly postures of village leaders. But the frequent altercations with villagers steeled us in our efforts, and we developed confidence to face up to threats from those with a vested interest in the failure of our programme. Apart from inexhaustible energy, this project needed craft, diplomacy, persuasion and only occasionally the sternness of rules and laws. it also called for something greater that all these–what I can only call an earnest, transparent sincerity, born not out of years of encountering intrigues and turbulence but the ideals that one brings from one's formative years—the atmosphere in which one grew in one's family, and the conditioning that was an almost unconscious part of one's time in school and college.

We had to tiptoe through a political minefield. It was a vibrant universe of fast-hatching leaders of a rich diversity of stripes and hues. In fact, trying to patch up with these groups is like building relations between a wolf and a sheep. I had to play dumb on several occasions so that leaders didn't get irritated, because on previous occasions, they'd created a big ruckus in the village the evening after I'd sent them packing out of my office. The burly moustachioed worthies who stalked me were really ferocious and required diplomacy of a high order to pin them in their tracks. The temperature of the political rhetoric kept heating up. Bleeding the banks to aggrandize the rich farmers had become a favourite sport of the politicians, who had been using banks as cash dispensers for populist programmes. Most rural branches were hobbled by a legacy of political interference. The greater part of the last decade of the twentieth century was spent by banks in cleaning their branches of the avalanche of bad loans in which they had been buried. The years of sloppy lending had left a vast hole in the balance sheets of rural banks.

We persevered and the villagers' resistance was whittled down by our persuasive approach. It was necessary to purge people's minds of the disease of loan defaults before we could build awareness of our new programme, which was based on zero tolerance for loan defaults. The default syndrome had mutated into an epidemic which had engulfed entire villages. We had to make clear that loan waivers were not a solution to their financial problems, but were at best a bandage, covering the wound that would continue festering underneath. The new programme was aimed at building sustainable self-reliant institutions which would not depend on outside grants. The womenfolk were doubtful, asking us countless questions, the most perplexing being, "Of all places and people, why have you chosen us?" Or also, "Please do not give it to me. I am scared to death looking at money; I have never touched money in my life." Some would say, "Give it to my husband because he is the one who handles money." Yet others explained their reluctance saying, "You know, my mother said when she died, 'My daughter, no matter what happens in life never borrow from anybody.'" Well, I would try to flatter them by saying there was something special about them that had brought us to them. We worked hard to convince them that there was nothing inherently fearsome or shameful in taking a loan to increase their earning capacities. I worked hammer and tongs to get people interested in the concept. The local leaders urged people to renege on their loans, making delicate local political ecosystems crackle with hate and anger. I judged it best to navigate political shoals without tying myself into ideological knots, but these issues were blunted by the women's coming to believe our intentions were good.

The challenge of establishing even a minimal level of trust with the women of these groups showed itself in all my meetings with female Self Help Groups. My guide, Asha, a passionate and indefatigable dynamo who had recently graduated in social sciences and had joined a voluntary agency, emphasized to me throughout that the major challenge of any development initiative was to cultivate the mindset of the villagers. Some women and men took initiative in mobilizing their village to undertake development projects and climb out of poverty. Regardless, there was a great empathy among the majority that could be the catalyst for a major change in the livelihoods of the entire population of the village.

The importance of group solidarity and mutual self-help would be theatrically explained by my field animators. "I'll tell you what to do," cut in Asha. She held up a twig in what was perhaps the first lesson they were receiving in the strengths of collective power. "As one person with a complaint, I can be ignored or broken," she said, snapping the twig in two. "Even if there are two of us, we can be ignored, divided or broken." she said, again snapping the pair of twigs. "But if we are more in number, a group together," she held the twigs together and failed to snap them even with a tough twist, "nothing can break us and we can get what we want."

The first step in building a group is identifying women who can work as a homogenous unit and who enjoy each other's trust. The process of group formation can take five to six months. A change in membership is not unusual in the first few meetings. It is necessary at this stage to allow a free and unrestrained flow of the inner feelings of these women. The purpose of these meetings is to ground the concept of self-help in the minds of these women. Any unresolved conflict will, in the long run, manifest itself in the form of cleavages that can tear the group apart.

Questions are common in the early stages of the process. I remember at the first meeting in a village called Charurkhati in the Chandrapur district of Maharashtra in 1993, an elderly woman queried: "I am more than 60 years old. Suppose I happen to die next year, what will be the benefit for me from your programme?" Others ask what would happen to unmarried girls' savings should they marry persons outside the village, or inquire, "Sir/madam, you are asking us to contribute our money. How much are you contributing for the group? Why should we save if you are not contributing anything?" or "Do you get any commission for this work?"

In any Self Help Group, once a core set of members has been established, a leader must be selected along with two deputies. These three women have to be accepted by all members and will share the duties of running the group and keeping the accounts. The group leader keeps the minutes, the savings and loan register, the weekly register and the members' passbooks, as proper documentation of the activities, especially of the internal lending, will help the approval process from the bank.

A number of grievances start erupting at this stage. It is better not to proceed with the formation of a group until these conflicts have been resolved because the group will always be sailing in choppy waters. Even small frictions may rock the boat enough to capsize it. As in any new group, it is the individual with initiative and drive who has to shoulder most of the responsibilities in the initial stages. The *sanghatika* (group leader) often protests about her responsibilities, saying things like, "Members may not come to meetings punctually and regularly so why should I alone be responsible for maintaining the records of the group? All the members should share the work." These members have to be handled with tact. The leader must be made to understand that having been chosen to be the leader is indicative of the group's faith in her leadership qualities.

The motto of the Self Help Group becomes "Savings First—Credit later." The women are taught that the savings habit is crucial for climbing out of poverty. They are also exhorted to save from sources other than surplus income, such as reductions of essential expenses. In other words savings must rise and consumption be brought down. The Self Help Group process is oriented towards building new capabilities for budgeting and managing the cash flow. The primary goal is that the individual members must become economically independent and acquire basic skills in handling small business and familiarity with local investment avenues.

Collective responsibility and group pressure act as social collateral. Towards this end, the process has three essential steps: 1. Learn to save. 2. Learn to lend what you have saved. 3. Learn to borrow responsibly. As loans are repaid, usually within six months to one year, the money will be re-loaned to either existing borrowers or new ones. This cycle of investment and reinvestment multiplies the value of each rupee loaned. The vast majority of the loans go to women because studies have shown that women are more likely to reinvest their earnings in the business for the betterment of their families. As families move above the poverty line, their businesses start building steam. Entire communities stand to benefit from this expansion. Jobs are created, know-how is shared, civic participation increases, and women get their due recognition as valuable members of their families and communities.

Self Help Groups are encouraged to practice transparency and accountability. Accountability is often thought of in its vertical relationship, as something citizens seek from power-holders. However, this project focuses on the horizontal, developing women's sense of accountability to themselves and as well as to their community. First, accountability is learned through intensive initial training. Community resource people (women who are seasoned, successful members of the Self Help Groups themselves) train new members about the importance of working together to achieve common goals. New members are taught that their own well-being is interconnected with that of other members in the group.

Traditional wisdom has always held the household as the female domain and the world outside as the domain of the male. This is more pronounced in the rural areas where women–even though they work in the fields–are inextricably associated with the kitchen, the inside, the private. "Women were thought to be incapable of understanding what went on outside the domestic walls," writes sociologist MN Shrinivas. However, there is overwhelming evidence that women-run SHGs are the best managed, with women showing a much greater sense of responsibility and also a commitment to human development objectives such as health and education of their families. Self Help Groups help inculcate the banking habit in rural women, and running them is a great lesson in governance, teaching the value of discipline, both procedural and financial. They broaden the horizons and expand the capabilities of members who must interact with banks, government departments and NGOs. Well-run SHGs are subject to external audits that enforce prudence. Since most SHGs are women's groups, the potential for women's empowerment is huge. There are reports of SHG office-bearers being elected to *gram panchayats* (village councils) and becoming more effective leaders in panchayat institutions. In a nutshell, it is not merely financial uplift but empowerment that is potentially achieved in good SHGs.

The collective has to go through phases of 'forming', 'brainstorming', 'norming' and 'performing'. Even if the process is slow, the process of training, retraining and making the group cohesive must be done. This edifice can continue to serve the poor and the marginalized on an auto-pilot basis once it stabilizes. Once this happens, the poor can not only take control of their resources, but can hire professional help to manage their resources. This transformation does not happen overnight, but through a long process of community intervention. It took me almost a year to form and nurture thirty Self Help Groups but all of them have survived and are now in their eighteenth year of existence. All of them have their own cash reserves and can service their own financial needs conveniently even if they drop the bank credit line.

The Self Help Group concept has attracted the attention of behavioural scientists who are trying to leverage the social capital to enhance the women's self-esteem and develop them into community leaders. A new technique in this area is a design meeting where women undergo various phases of personality development. A typical design meeting with the members of a Self Help Group starts with the consultant showing them a picture of a woman with a sad face, and asking an open-ended question as to why the members think the woman is sad. This leads to a flurry of statements by the women, primarily based on their own experiences. Then another picture is shown of the same woman but with a neutral face, and the leader asks what changes might have happened in the woman's life. After giving some time for responses, the next picture of a happy woman is shown and the question repeated.

This is a reflective process for the women, who use their personal experiences as reference points. The responses they give for the sad or happy states in the life of this woman are their own stories. For instance, in one village, one of the major reasons given for the sad face was the pressure to have sons. In another village, it was sorcery: branding women as witches. Indicators of women's empowerment were distilled from such discussions.

Self Help Groups are thus more than a window of financial support for women. They also provide access to information as a means of improved livelihood choices, as well as enhanced perspectives. Group members as well as their families and community leaders perceive access to information as a critical value of the Self Help Group membership. Members belong to a collective that can negotiate, resolve problems, and ensures a place for them in community life and public spheres.

However, the process is not without concerns. While efforts have focused on the vulnerable, there is evidence that savings groups tend to exclude the most vulnerable or impoverished because they are migratory or unable to attend meetings due to their being agricultural or casual wage labourers. A number of Self Help Groups also report that a few women had left the groups due to their inability to contribute the required savings. While groups are enabled to manage their own financial affairs, this leads to another set of dynamics with which groups are now grappling: the dominance of the literate, who are invariably from a better-off section of the community, with others having to depend on their skills and goodwill.

Microfinance had generated considerable enthusiasm, not just in the development community but also at political levels. Inevitably, there was some over-advertising. Microfinance is not a magic solution that will propel all of its clients out of poverty. However, serious impact studies are demonstrating that microfinance produces real benefits for poor households. Of course, the microfinance model of the past two decades has its own limitations. Most MFIs started as not-for-profit, non-governmental organizations delivering loans. For some time, it seemed that development objectives and commercial profitability could be accomplished without friction, but microfinance soon suffered a mission drift and profit maximization replaced poverty reduction as the main agenda.

One pitfall of the agenda of the new microfinance players who use the JLG model is their belief that credit is the most vital need of the marginalized. They feel that credit can unlock the entrepreneurial spirit, which, as it matures through a process of exposure to market economics, could help in generating indigenous solutions for the problems that have prevented the poor and the marginalized from moving up the economic ladder–problems that include illiteracy, malnourishment, chronic illness and food insecurity. In the name of sustainability, outreach and reliability, the new microfinance is destroying a culture of social trust and a vast reservoir of social capital built by the painstaking effort of a cadre of committed and motivated volunteers who sacrificed personal comfort, social life and, in many cases, risked their life and career as part of the normal hazards that go with a rural assignment.

Also, some of the leading microfinance institutions (MFI) have shifted their focus from building livelihoods to consumer lending, asking how much of the poor family's purse or wallet they can gain by providing loans and consumer goods. What India now needs are some game-changers in microfinance, not more or bigger loan dispensers, fuelled by external funding. These game-changers can learn from SEWA Bank and BASIX and scale up some of the positive lessons of these grassroots organisations.

The international MFI model, as against the India's bank led Self Help Group model, is a different ballgame altogether. Here the sponsor is a profit-oriented venture capitalist, who sees the rural credit market as a fresh business opportunity. The MFI apparently brings great professionalism, innovation and technology to its enterprise of venturing to provide loans that banks do not. Yet MFIs form no groups engaged in governance functions, unlike Self Help Groups. Even when they operate through NGOs, MFIs are primarily concerned with lending and recovering what they lend to cohorts of people, at times at very high rates of interest.

While the mainstream microfinance institution model built on the Joint Liability Group methodology turned out to be both unsustainable and detrimental to a large number of poor, the Self Help Group approach has the potential to make a decisive impact on the security and empowerment of the most disadvantaged in the current context of farmers' suicides. It may also be critical in positively influencing profitability of banks in remote rural areas.

I am a diehard supporter of the Self Help Group movement but I must frankly concede that some of the microfinance institutions have also done remarkable service in the field of financial inclusion. How do you explain poor women in remote villages without any collateral getting loans of R.1 lac to acquire plots of land? In a remote village in Wardha, a woman named Anu approached me for a loan for constructing a house. I tried to convince her to take a small loan and repair her old home, thinking she wouldn't be able to repay a larger loan. I was stunned when she showed me her file containing records that she had previously repaid a loan of Rs. 75,000 from a microfinance institution at 24 per cent interest before the scheduled end of the repayment schedule. Where I had been hesitant of lending her Rs. 25,000, I sanctioned a loan of Rs. 100,000 and felt satisfied that I had done justice to the poor, hardworking woman who had an impeccable credential of financial integrity.

I admit that in my new role as a designer of programmes for housing loans for low-income segments, credit histories built up by microfinance institutions are the only authentic guides for the track records of the borrowers. I once believed that banks alone could provide financial inclusion. I now realise that, despite huge resources both in terms of capital, manpower and technology, banks' lack of staff commitment and poor human resource policies have ensured that financial inclusion will remain a vain chimera for them. Most banks have ramped up their rural banking outfits but these efforts are mere drops in the bucket.

Few poor households have access to formal insurance against risks such as the death of a family breadwinner, severe or chronic illness, or loss of an asset including livestock and housing. These shocks are particularly damaging for poor households which are less able to absorb the financial consequences of such an event. Given the high cost of risk and the limitation of the insurance from informal solidarity networks, one must wonder why the poor do not have more access to formal insurance, that is, insurance supplied by an insurance company. Health insurance, insurance against bad weather, and against the death of livestock, which are standard products in the lives of farmers in rich countries, are all but absent in the developing world.

My hopes for the Self Help Group model for microfinance, which I consider to be the most authentic and women-focused, have been only partially fulfilled. More than half of our borrowers have not experienced continuous development. Many made progress only to slip back into poverty. We need to understand why they go on and on taking small loans. Some of the poorest villagers whom I knew as malnourished children have, against the odds, grown into adulthood, married and had children of their own. I marvelled at their endurance and resilience. According to observers, these changes are in sharp contrast to the previous marked absence of women in public spaces and the despondency, dependency, and at times apathy that defined the Vidarbha region in Maharashtra. These changes have not occurred overnight and the process involved has not been simple. Women, eager to share their experiences and accomplishments, unanimously attribute the source of their transformation to their new-found access to 'mahiti' (information) and a subsequent growing awareness of and ability to act on their rights. Further, they also assert that they derive their primary strength from their emergence as a collective based on their enhanced economic status. Be it the Self Help Group meetings in Madheli, an informal gathering in Ashi, a discussion with the federation members of Warora or the cluster meeting in Nandra, the presence of women in public spaces and their coming into their own voice, accompanied by decision-making and action, is hard to ignore.

The linkages between different approaches towards development, poverty reduction and empowerment must be considered. It is not enough to address the economic indicators of poverty. While incomes have to be augmented through livelihood generation interventions, for which credit is an important component, determinants of human poverty in terms of health and education requirements require attention. Likewise, social poverty, which manifests in corrosive evils like caste taboos, norms of dowry and adherence to vices such as alcohol and drugs, has to be woven into empowerment programmes.

In nearly three decades of academic work and grassroots involvement as an administrator of financial programmes in local rural development, my experience is that microfinance programmes that are run on the principle of building huge returns for investors most often spell the death of the local economy. Put simply, to the extent that local savings are intermediated through microfinance institutions, that country or region or locality will be left behind in a state of poverty and under-development. This is an 'iron' law of microfinance. Focusing on isolated cases of microenterprise success simply does not add up to economic development. Support for microfinance in India is overwhelmingly political and ideological—the economic rationale is simply not present.

Microfinance institutions were meant to free villagers and urban slum dwellers from the moneylenders' grip. But lack of regulatory oversight, unbridled political cynicism and the myopic herd-like mentality of the private sector combined to threaten pushing India's poor in the arms of the moneylenders again. Microfinance institutions have to rejig their agenda: moderate profit, re-infuse the spirit of social responsibility and restrain their greedy impulses. They still enjoy enormous client support and if their mission remains clear and they remain true to it, no politician can dare challenge them. The electorate has demonstrated that it can't be swayed by populism and sloganeering. It wants development and transparency in administration. We are a vibrant democracy with a sense of maturity and robust common sense even amongst the poor. Had it not been for this, the poor would not have been able to bring such a powerful microfinance lobby, with international support, to its feet.

The narrow idea that capitalism is only about creating value for shareholders, that business is only about profits and the excesses to which the story has led around the world, is badly broken. Adam Smith, the father of capitalism, understood that capitalism works only when people tell the truth and have a sense of justice. Ethics and business go together at the core of capitalism. "Business is a very beautiful mechanism to solve problems, but we never use it for that purpose. We only use it to make money. It satisfies our selfish interest but not our collective interest," states Muhammad Yunus. "I'm not against making money, but I am saying we can do both. We have designed a capitalist system wrong. We assume human beings are one-dimensional—all they do is make money—so we've created a money-centric world. Money commands everything because that's our interpretation of capitalism ... what kind of world is that? It's a very uncomfortable interpretation of a human being. We have been turned into robots. Yes we are selfish, but also selfless, but we don't allow that to be brought out."

Two decades back when I first joined the pilot project of NABARD for the promotion of Self Help Groups, I was sceptical about the success of the initiative. Several questions kept nagging at me. Would the village women talk to us? Would their husband not dissuade them from meeting us? Would they trust us, given their past record of having been misled by outsiders? How would we communicate with these illiterate women? Should we really experiment with them and in case we fail, make them suffer the wrath of local interests?

The connectivity to the villages was atrocious. Bovine trails doubled up as roads and there were no mobile phones. I still vividly remember several remote villages dimly lit with hurricane lanterns. Poorly paid animators (village women volunteers who double up as social initiators and money collectors} would spend endless painstaking hours imparting financial literacy to poor, illiterate women. The financial institutions were amazed as these Self Help Groups that clocked one hundred per cent repayment began spawning at a time when public sector banks were almost groaning under the weight of dud loans. They found it a wonderful opportunity for using the model to bolster the quality of their portfolios.

Poor women's struggle for empowerment and participation in India's economic growth has been a revolutionary saga. Surprisingly, the media and the public intellectuals, who have been so strongly and convincingly gunning for transparency at the higher levels, missed the enormous grassroots movement that is not only reducing the trust deficit but imbuing the grassroots public institutions with greater transparency and stronger governance. For poor women, it is a journey towards the second Freedom or the real Freedom, as Mahatma Gandhi said when he talked of the unfinished agenda at the time of independence.

Through the Self Help Groups, these women are transforming their own lives and that of their communities; the sisterhood is so close knit and persuasive that women have begun to think of themselves in a different way. I'm told that you can see the same kinds of eye-popping changes even in surrounding villages. For example, I burst out laughing when told that woman now had so much respect for themselves that they decline to be photographed with politicians in search of publicity, who are themselves disgusted at being rebuffed.

Of late, economists have begun to realise that banking isn't just extending soft loans to the poor. More importantly, it is a safe haven for savings. The primary requirements of low-income households go beyond simple savings vehicles. Many households are looking for a way to manage their money or cash flow, but for these consumers, money management differs from pure long-term savings or credit in that its principal focus is balancing times of cash surplus and cash deficits over a typical salary cycle—for example, 30 days.

Many people get into debt stress at some points in their lives. They scrimp on groceries for a couple of weeks to have the cash for next month's loan payment. Or they miss loan payments because a lingering illness keeps them away from their business. That's *acute* over-indebtedness. While acute debt stress can be serious, some temporary over-indebtedness is a normal part of the ups and downs of life and might not mean that a person has borrowed too much.

As bankers who strive to bring about wholesome development, we have to remember that all women, regardless of their marital status, need access to education, good jobs, and support for domestic duties. Both widows and married women deserve freedom from culturally entrenched marital practices that degrade and commodify them, as well as legal protection from their husbands' debts. Although transforming long-held laws, beliefs and practices may be difficult, it is the only way to keep price tags off women and ensure that they have dignity as well as true economic agency. It has been said that women who are closest to the world's most pressing issues are best placed to solve them. In many countries, women are adjusting to large-scale economic changes through community-based grassroots organizing efforts. But can women be expected to use local solutions to clean up and compensate for larger economic problems without also being allowed to influence larger decisions?

The idea that small loans enable millions of poor people to pull themselves up by their bootstraps has captivated liberals and conservatives alike. Yet no one should be lulled by this livelihood finance boom into believing that it is a cure-all for global poverty. The problem is that not everyone is ready or able to take on debt. Some people struggling to feed their families require more basic help and financial training.

Low-income persons live in risky environments, vulnerable to numerous perils, including illness, accidental death and disability, loss of property due to theft or fire, agricultural losses and disasters of both the natural and manmade varieties. The poor are more vulnerable to many of these risks than the rest of the population, and they are the least able to cope when a crisis does occur. In my experience, fate is likelier to provide the greater quota of calamities for the poor, who suffer the most on account of the cruel bureaucracy of nature. Poverty and vulnerability reinforce each other in an escalating downward spiral. Not only does exposure to these risks result in substantial financial losses, but vulnerable households also suffer from the ongoing uncertainty about whether and when a loss might occur. Because of this perpetual apprehension, the poor are less likely to take advantage of income-generating opportunities that might reduce poverty.

In contrast with many for-profit models, which line the pockets of those aiming to exploit the poor, SHG interest is always reinvested into the community. The Self Help Group is not a static institution; it grows on the resources and management skills of its members and their increasing confidence in getting involved in issues and programmes in the public and private spheres. It is a very effective means of empowering the poor women. Empowering, in this context, implies the personal capacity for action in channelling society so as to affect the flow of resources and control of the spheres affecting their lives. Few development ideas have been so buoyed by high expectations in recent decades, and few have been so buffeted by difficulties in recent years. Images of microfinance lifting people out of poverty now compete with ones of the poor driven by debt to suicide. Where does the truth lie? Research studies find insubstantial evidence that small loans lift people out of poverty en masse but argue that financial services, like clean water and electricity, are essential to a modern life. The practical question is not whether microfinance should continue, but how it can play to its strengths, which lie in providing useful services to millions of poor people in a business-like way.

Microfinance has come under increasing scrutiny in recent months. Stories of astronomical interest rates driving the poor deeper into poverty, compounded by tales of malicious moneylenders intimidating borrowers to the point of suicide, have recently come to light in the international press, exposing fundamental flaws in the design of institutional for-profit microfinance. Not only are borrowers often innumerate, illiterate and unfamiliar with interest rate calculations, but they frequently have little or no awareness of local demand for goods and services. Consequently, they often fail to establish successful income-generating ventures and therefore cannot repay their loans. Despite the current criticism, for many years the enthusiasm for microfinance left little space for nuance. One lesson is clear: when you set the bar so high: there is a long and likely fall from grace.

The biggest problem with the international JLG model of microfinance is that people who get these small loans usually start or expand a very simple business. The most common business for microfinance is simple retail - selling groceries - where there are often too many people, fierce competition, and where they don't really earn enough money to get out of poverty. We need to create more jobs, and microfinance does not help to do that yet. The debt trap is an under-reported problem. Quite a few people invest money, their business does not make money and goes under, and they are stuck with the debt. The interest rate on this debt, even with a microfinance loan, is quite high, so some are never able to repay it. Another reason why they get into a debt trap is that, in theory, you should take a microloan to invest in the business. But in practice a lot of people use microloans for a wedding, festival, or to buy something. A lot of these people don't know how to use debt. Even people in rich countries often don't know how to use debt. They think that once you have a credit card, you can buy anything. If you get microloans, it doesn't necessarily mean you can buy things you couldn't afford before. Indeed, one of those who have thoroughly studied the phenomenon, Thomas Dichter, says that the idea that microfinance allows its recipients to graduate from poverty to entrepreneurship is inflated. He sketches out the dynamics of microcredit: "It emerges that the clients with the most experience got started using their own resources, and though they have not progressed very far--they cannot because the market is just too limited--they have enough turnover to keep buying and selling, and probably would have with or without the microcredit. For them the loans are often diverted to consumption since they can use the relatively large lump sum of the loan, a luxury they do not come by in their daily turnover." He concludes: "Definitely, microfinance has not done what the majority of microfinance enthusiasts claim it can do--function as capital aimed at increasing the returns to a business activity."

The growth in coverage of microfinance is limited to pockets, and MFIs across the country have developed a tendency to congregate in select areas. It is very common to find urban and peri-urban settlements to have between 10-20 microfinance institutions operating within a small geography. This has led to the problem of multiple lending, which has raised the issue of client over indebtedness, default and strong arm recovery tactics. On occasions, charges have also been made of client suicide because of repayment pressures, but this appears to be more a figment of the imagination of the vernacular press than corroborated by any evidence on the ground. Hence, multiple lending is a well known phenomenon and the sector has continued with an ostrich-like attitude to the problem. Despite evidence from across the globe, no efforts have been made to address the short-comings of the group-based lending product and collection methodology, which remains almost exactly as it was when imported in the late 1980s.

Hence, the role of private sector microfinance whether in 'for-profit' or 'not-for-profit' formats will remain. However, any business which forgets its client cannot have a bright future. In the desire to grow at double digit (and even triple digit!) rates, the microfinance sector may have forgotten the raison d'etre for its existence - its clients. Adopting a client responsive approach, coupled with ethics-based transparency, could take this sector to greater heights.

In some ways the microfinance that is seen is not recognisable as the one that was there in the initial days. The sector must change with passage of time. While products and processes can change (hopefully for the better), can the concern for the customer change? MFIs justified their entry on the argument that banks do not finance the poorest and are not empathetic to their requirements. Is the MFI sector better able to deal with poor customers today than the banks? Many MFIs started financing the poor but somewhere they lost the customer focus and along with that the mission too. The goals do not any more seem to be making credit access affordable; nor is it accompanying the livelihoods of people. It is no more about improving income generation in the hands of the customers. Book value multiples, price to earnings ratios and enterprise valuations dominate the discussion. High interest rates are justified as necessary to find more mainstream funds for further growth.

The biggest disadvantage of the MFI model however is that it is less participatory and empowering, since the "banking" functions and procedures are taken care of entirely by field staff of the MFI, who disburse and collect loans. In the SHG model million of poor women deal with the banks and do their own accounting and cash handling. However, some MFIs argue that this is actually a disadvantage of the SHG programme (because most women do not want to get involved in the banking function), and that it is more efficient to focus on achieving one objective effectively, which in the case of "minimalist MFIs" (the vast majority) is delivering financial services. Also they point out that given the millions of poor women in SHGs who have to be trained in book keeping and accounting, the training requirements of the MFI model are a little less daunting.

It may appear that the naysayers are ready to sound the bugle and shout out "The king is dead, long live the king", that microfinance may once more redefine itself and in its new avatar be a leaner, more modest business with lesser interest rates and moderate profit that yet continue to be profitable. Only time will tell.

4

A Livelihood Of Her Own

If you want something said, ask a man; if you want something done, ask a woman

Margaret Thatcher

Pride and dignity would belong to women if only men would leave them alone.

Egyptian Proverb

A feminist is anyone who recognizes the equality and full humanity of women and men.

Gloria Steinem

In the early hours, when the sun is still a brown moon, a lovely landscape stretches along both sides of the highway connecting Nagpur and Chandrapur, important cities in Central India's heartland. The countryside does not betray its hand to the traveller between Nagpur and the epicentre of the Baba Amte's acclaimed social and environmental laboratory, *Anandwan* (Forest of Bliss). But it's the dawn that makes the journey worth it. It was a radiant autumn morning. Nowhere was it wholly deserted: there was someone somewhere in every frame of vision—a solitary man behind a plough, a boy washing a buffalo in a pond, a frieze of women waiting at a well. Sleek cars juddered past us, giving sheen to the highway.

The houses were of clay brick the colour of the earth. Occasionally, we passed the fat, tapering chimneys of brick kilns. Many trees had shed their winter foliage and had fresh, light green leaves sprouting on their branches. Juicy cantaloupes and watermelons were piled up in mountainous heaps in grocers' shops at highway villages.

We turned off the highway onto a secondary road, and the car clattered through an area whose squat, brightly painted houses sprouted metallic rebars from the tops of their walls in hope of growing a storey or two taller in a more prosperous and elegant future. We left the vehicle near the kerb and decided to walk through the village. Shadowed eyes watched us negotiate the puddles like trespassers. We saw women walking through the cotton fields to collect water at the mud-muddled river, a slow river, practically asleep.

As we ventured deeper into the village, I noticed women drawing water at a well. When they saw us approaching, they hastened hauling their metal jerricans up by rope. Other women squatting on the flat platform sprang to their feet and slipped into their houses and closed their doors. "These are loan recovery officers," a young man yelped to his friend as they rode past on bicycles, careful to avoid the deep ruts carved by the steady traffic of bullock carts. Tiny clusters of houses huddled beside the road, and when an automobile approached, naked children cowered in fright, and then invariably darted into the car's path as panicky chickens do.

I attended my first major meeting in Charurkhati, a village in Chandrapur, on a Sunday. Charurkhati was one of the larger villages in which I spend a major time during my three decades of development finance and it provided the bulk of my education in rural society. It propelled me to become a good ethnographer if not an accomplished anthropologist.

On our way, we had passed a government school in which the teaching staff had not arrived. I was told that most public schools in the region suffered from pervasive corruption. By the grass shacks, handmade dung-cakes were stacked in geometric perfection, drying for fuel. Already the wheat fields enveloping this jumble of low brick-and-mud houses were well past waist high, undulating waves of green-gold that lapped into the distance, a gentle barrier fencing off the villages from the main road.

The sun was low but the air still hot when we arrived at the tall ceremonial gate; arbours of palms and mango leaves had been erected for us to walk through. The women waved at us with hectic energy. Chanda's girls ran up and locked elbows with mine, singing their welcome song as they escorted me over a flagstone path through a maze of homes made of mud with roofs of straw. Chanda Buradkar was an effervescent volunteer who had established her reputation as a community organizer displaying rare finesse. She would relieve me of a number of ordinary chores, such as sending errand boys to mobilise women, and organise logistics for the meeting. The village leaders clustered around us, greeting us. The courtyard was filled with women and children who regarded us as if we were envoys from another planet. A huddle of children followed. Chanda daubed greetings of sticky purple rice to our foreheads, beamed and wandered off.

A kindly gaggle of women waited for us, sitting under the dappled shade of the banyan tree outside a simple stucco house as if attending a classroom, although this was their monthly meeting. Some members had walked hours to attend the meeting; they had to show up if they wanted their loans. The women ranged in age from their twenties to their fifties; many had small children with them, who played nearby or sat solemnly on their mothers' laps. These women were affable neighbours with a common mission of transforming their own lives and that of their communities by joining peer groups, so strong and close-knit and persuasive that they had begun to think of themselves in a different way. They were members of a cluster of Self Help Groups in the village.

Before we were ushered into the meeting room, we were asked to stand on small, low-ended stools. The elder women, in keeping with the local tradition of welcoming a guest, sluiced water over our heels and toes, dislodging the last clinging grains of sand. A coloured poster on family planning, too large for indoor display, had been tacked to the otherwise bald wall. I slumped down a fraction to avoid breaking my head against a scraggy scar of flaking concrete as we went inside. The women were soon herded into the meeting room, where they sat cross-legged on the patched *dari* (coarse carpet), made of fertilizer bags stitched together, elatedly swapping household news. My urban muscles weren't supple enough to adopt the cross-legged lotus position, however. After a few more minutes of chattering in groups, loudly calling out for the ones who had not yet arrived, and asking the younger ones to settle down, the meeting started.

This month's meeting was taking place at Kamal's house; it was her turn by the rotational order. Kamal Mhaski was financially well-placed and could afford to host these meetings; she came from a prominent political family of the village and owned a large parcel of land. In Kamal's house, her elderly father- in-law was the presiding patriarch; his sagging charpoy stood in the corner. He had a stubby, emaciated, sunken-eyed look. The room was partially illuminated by a fluorescent light covered with years of accumulated dirt The portraits of divinities jostled for space on a worn-out shelf with fading photographs of departed ancestors, all stained by ash scattered from the incense burned daily.

The meeting started with a traditional group song, in husky melodious expression with a staccato rhythm. Though my Marathi was rusty and the village women's dialect was different from what I was used to, I could discern the theme of the song: unity, self-help, trust and the poor banding together to help each other. It was very touching and an apt beginning for the group meeting. One of the verses of the song went like this: "Nothing is stronger, or more embedded in the marrow of our bones than the need to save for a rainy day. It is not written in words, it is written in our hearts." Another telling verse described how the poor women drove out a merciless moneylender from their village. The soft, frail voices soared out of the courtyard, chasing away the stillness of the long summer afternoon, and then they trailed off. For a moment, the women seemed lost in thought, as if they were penitents invoking their lord's mercy and guidance. It was a way of expressing thanks for being given a permanent parole out of the prison of poverty.

It was a delight watching the group meeting. "Sirrrrr", someone said, rolling the rs, and then everyone started saying it, laughing. The women conversed together with great animation and all at once. A tiny lissom lady with a sparkling face interjected, "Hullo, what part of the country are you coming from?" This inevitable question came point-blank, with a smile. "I am from Nagpur but have come as a migrant worker to Warora," I said. It was the accepted introduction. A new visitor is a momentary prize. A village gathering will always welcome him with more unaffected warmth than would a city one. The interest will not be simulated nor the greetings faked.

About fifty women filled the tiny room, spilling over and sitting in one another's laps. The floor was of freshly swept mud mixed with cow dung, the roof of weathered tiles with grass sprouting from the seams. A few women stifled yawns. Others poked the snoozing companions awake. I asked them what they had learned. How was the Self Help Group helping them, beyond just providing money? The women flushed with pride. They all pulled out their passbooks, where their loans and weekly repayments were recorded, and pointed to the spot where they signed their name each week. In rural India, where literacy often hovered below fifty percent and most women received little or no education, these signatures were evidence of the power they felt. Many told me that within their homes they were the only family member to achieve this level of literacy. It was ample proof of the success of our literacy campaign in the villages.

I complimented the group leaders and told the members that the number of thumbprints should go down every month so that the village would become eligible for the government award for a hundred percent literate village. The group leader assured me that in the next three months they would require ink pads no longer, only pens; there would be no more need for thumbprints. A few months later, when I revisited the group and asked how many women had kept the promise of learning a proper signature, every hand in the room shot up.

A few pleasantries later, the women got down to the crux of the meeting. The group leader called out "One". On her command, the women stood up in unison, though with a few poorly suppressed sighs; as they did, the air was pierced by the sound of dozens of knee joints cracking. There was a patter of handclaps. Bowing my head, I said hello: "*Namaskar",* meaning "fine." Faces lit up and sparkled. In unison, they responded "*Namaskar*". One or two began talking to me in Marathi. Any small effort to communicate on my part elicited similar gracious appreciation. They would gleefully lap up any Marathi word thrown at them in an Anglicized accent.

I noticed that close to half of the women in attendance had their backs partially or fully turned to me, and at least ten were partially veiled. Most were too shy to speak in the beginning, especially since the men, alerted to my presence, had gathered nearby to keep tabs on the proceedings. Some of the women were attending the meeting clandestinely. The women were giggling and whispering to each other throughout, casting nervous glances to see if there were any men folk outside the room observing the meeting through the windows. I hinted to Kamal, the meeting organizer, to ensure that these men did not loiter any longer. This done, I could see the women's confidence rise a few notches and we commenced the meeting. Minakshi said kindly, softly, "Here, women won't look someone in the eye, won't talk to someone they don't know. You have to accept it."Minakshi was the only matriculate in this women's commune.

As the interview went on, and I told them about myself, they began to open up, with many removing their veils and turning to face me. Some of the local grandees present at the meeting endorsed my credentials, mentioning that I belonged to a reputed bank and I was a known sympathizer of the poor. At this point, I asked the women how they reacted to the presence of moneylenders now that they had access to bank finance. When Kamal assured them my mission was to help rid them of moneylenders, the room erupted with a volcano's blistering lava of rage against the local moneylender community. But some felt it difficult to totally avoid the moneylender because of the time and complicated paperwork involved in securing a loan from a bank.

Walking into a women's Self Help Group, one will be amazed at the professionalism and efficiency with which financial transactions are handled. The women gather each month at the appointed time, usually at the end of a long day labouring in the fields. Each woman arrives, passbook in hand, with the idea for her next loan in her head. Despite the tired faces, the energy in the room is bubbling as the women know they are accomplishing something big, something that will help lead them and their families towards a better future. Tucked somewhere in their saris are rumpled currency notes representing their loan repayments, interest and savings. The women share a community bond—a bond these periodical meetings are designed to strengthen.

The group leader took charge as she roared for quiet at the top of her voice. Like a crescendo, the stories rose and fell, filling the room with a pervasive energy. Like a seasoned driver, the group leader steered clear of all these excuses. One woman asked whether it was necessary to save in order to become eligible for loans. This was a new voice, crisper than the others: Pushpa's voice. She was standing at the back of the crowd. Kamal's face wrinkled, pinkened and seemed to swell slightly. "Hang it all. What do you want to know that for!" she snapped. "Either save or shut up. Bite your tongue, you evil lady. Take your words back!" In the midst of the unexpected commotion and venting of pent up anger, Kamal and I lost the thread of the argument. Pushpa scrunched up her pinched face and launched into an angry speech which flustered Kamal. I had to use all my persuasive skills to restore peace. Kamal then proceeded to upbraid a defaulter who was her neighbour. The lady squirmed when Kamal waggled her finger at her and demanded, "What are you doing with the earnings from your cows?"

"There are so many expenses at my house; I can't cope with the loan" moaned Lata Buradkar.

There came a tart retort, "Why did you eat chicken yesterday? Why did you send your son to a movie? Why are you making plans for the wedding of your daughter? My daughter manages with two sets of school dress. Why did you buy a third set for your daughter?"

As the meeting went on, women, craving gossip, broke out into conversation. At Kamal's call to order, the murmuring subsided. Grandmothers, mothers, and aunts rocked restive children on their laps and thumped their foreheads to put them to sleep. The children, conditioned to the numbing jolts, grew groggy and their eyes became unfocussed. A debate about going over-budget had Kamal's mellow voice sharpen into an I-mean-business tone.

"Up-to-date accounts are very important. Even if you spend one rupee, there must be a record. I think this is a genetic obsession with every woman; she must know where every rupee comes from and where every rupee goes," she smirked slyly. She possessed a phenomenal degree of control over each and every muscle in her face. Some sniggered; some choked, trying to suppress their laughter. One by one, she cleared the doubts like a glow-worm lighting misty nooks. Initially, Kamal confided in my ear, one could observe only a ruffle of heads and a babble of affirmatives. But with time, women had started questioning the group on a number of issues. The meetings had, of late, grown quite interactive.

When one villager asked why she couldn't borrow more money, the answer came straight from Kamal: "It is like when a new bride comes into her husband's home. The mother-in-law won't give her all the keys of the house until she trusts the girl." A wave of understanding rippled through. I made everyone comfortable, asking them to share their doubts and difficulties with ease and without fear. "We will sit as long as your doubts remain unclarified. If you don't share your problems, you will not get solutions."The women nodded and whispering started among the small crowd.

There were moments of hilarity as I struggled for the right vernacular vocabulary. When all the preliminary computing was complete, Neeta Dhote, the village animator representing the local voluntary agency, did a series of crosschecks to make sure the figures and the cash she had collected tallied. (Were she to fall short once she arrived at the office, she would have to make up the difference from her own meagre salary.)When that sum came out to Rs. 16,300, the total in the day's collection register, the accounting was finished. I turned my attention to the women sitting in the last row. Throughout the meeting, they had remained quiet, and had not forwarded any passbooks or money; this last group was still in its training period.

One group leader stood up and said that she had problems tallying the account book after applying interest to the loans. Kamal told her we would straighten out the problems after the meeting. Lalita, the most confident and mature of the lot, raised her hand, but when she saw a senior group leader also raising her hand, immediately brought her own down. When she was asked to speak, she said she would take her turn after the latter had spoken. All of a sudden, two elderly women rose up and said the leader was not totally impartial in dispensing loans and they felt slighted. Taken aback, Kamal turned to me and rolled her eyes comically and said, "What do you think you would have done in such a situation?" This, her first direct question, put me in a quandary. Until now, I had been mostly a listener. I told the two women to take up the leadership of the group if they felt they could run it better. They withdrew, realizing their gaffe.

As I watched Kamal conduct the proceedings, I marvelled at her ability to connect with and explain things to village women. She understood how to reach the women who most needed reaching: illiterate, poor village women. She knew how they thought and lived because she was one of them. Her power and grace seemed to emanate from something she had made contact with, deep within the emotional psyche of her sisterhood. When her job was done, I asked the treasurer of the group to assist me in reviewing the group's accounts, and went through the books more thoroughly than I had during the previous visit. This was necessary to understand the financial health of the group and how it managed money. It was a sort of audit in which we could detect financial discrepancies and counsel the group members, particularly the accountant. Lata, dressed in a patterned pink sari, with piercing eyes and a skinny face highlighted by a facial expression that wandered between anger and hilarity, handled the session with great aplomb. She swatted away irrelevant questions with toughness. It was finally my turn to chair the meeting. I regaled the women with some of my amusing experiences with other Self Help Groups, to strike a chord with them. I then prodded them to share their own experiences. Like a musical crescendo and diminuendo, the stories began to rise and fall, filling the room with energy that was strong and pervasive. Money had started working magic for these women. Small money, not big money. A borrower who lost her husband inherited a family of seven dependents. Because of famine, she had few remaining means of survival. Yet, through perseverance, she was able to create a web of entrepreneurial activities—from trading in baskets and food grains to animal raising and managing her own kiosk—that allowed her to send all the children to school and to clothe and feed them. How did she do this? Through microloans, through steady savings, even in times when saving was difficult, and by buying her way. Most animal raising loans are for goattery as they do not require any veterinary knowledge or skills. Most villagers also hire a kiosk at the nearby town and sell vegetables grown in their villages. It fetches them a good profit margin.

Painful stories started dribbling out when women got a chance to 'uncrate' their anxieties. Some gut-wrenchingly sad, some viscerally moving, some riotously funny. One elderly woman began to weep and the weeping unpicked a deeper vein of grief—such a terrible groan issued between the whimpers. It was a typical tale of a villager being badly fleeced by the moneylender, stripped of both money and dignity.

Towards the end of the meeting, a woman sneaked into the room and, avoiding looking at us, quietly took a place behind a corpulent lady to avoid our sight. Kamal immediately glared in rage and hectored the woman "We all have work to do with the harvest, but this meeting is only one hour a week. What excuse could you have for being late, tell me. I'm never late to these meetings, ever! I live further away than any of you. Why should have I to round up members and keep bothering myself? Shouldn't you show up voluntarily?"

Narrowing her eyes, jabbing her finger, Kamal croaked out her favourite argument, "Saving money is not an obligation to the group. It is for the member's welfare. Attending a meeting is not a favour to me. If you are not interested, you are free to leave the group. Members may come and members may go— but the group shall go on." The offending borrower took it in her stride, staring straight ahead with a blank expression during the outburst. Sounds came from the back row as if a dozen women were choking back their laughter. Suddenly two women came pelting into the room and stood by the door, wiping the rain from their hair and shaking it off their saris.

Kalpana's brisk description of her group at work struck me as exactly right. She was herself a matriculate and wife of a senior school teacher and she could gauge the real usefulness of the SHG for women.

These meetings, according to her, were not social events, nor were they occasions for planning peasant revolution or female emancipation. They were awareness building meetings, concerned with learning saving habits, getting and repaying loans, keeping proper records of money, learning about better schooling and health for their children and becoming aware of developments both in the village and elsewhere. The rigmarole of preparing for the meetings and the daily genie of homework needed to be appeased and this meant rigorous discipline.

For the thirty years she had been working in the area, Shankuntala was like a saint to the locals. Shakuntala's face always had a calm resolute expression. When she spoke, it was with cold assertiveness. At Shakuntala's prodding, the villagers went to work with their spades, and before long there were wells dug and 1,000 eucalyptuses planted. A pond was dug. Away from the glare of the world, she had become a part of local folklore. Her word was treated as a command and women volunteered to work every Sunday for two years to lay the roads. The wells took months. The pond took a couple of years. But no one complained. Before departing, we told the women they must observe the discipline of punctuality. I emphasized that we had travelled to this remote village only to conduct this meeting, and members should understand the labour and time involved in monitoring just a few groups. The leader of the group, a sensitive lady, soothed my temper, saying that they were aware of the work involved, but that the village woman had many domestic chores and needed to get their husbands' permission.

"May I have permission to end the meeting, Sir," Sangita asked in a firm but respectful voice. The sun was just above the curving line of trees on the slope, mellow and tired after a long day's work. As the sunlight thinned and the cold breeze picked up, a farewell *bhajan* was sung in a soulful chorus emphasizing the solidarity of the group and the primacy of thrift. The singing conjured up worlds of lament and forbearance as the babies started digging their fists into their sleepy eyes. The plaintive sound of the song mimed the sunset wind.

The Indian village woman is pliant and adaptable, just like the clay that the woman potters knead and give myriad shapes and forms. Bury her and she is steadfast as the earth. Burn her and she will ride the flames. Women know which emotional button to press. They are not seducers;

they are mind experts. There's a brave practicality in the face of the steep nastiness of life and yes, along with all this there is also a lot of heart. The women are not lost, just temporarily obscured like stars that cannot be seen in mid-afternoon. Perhaps Self Help Groups are those intimate spaces that have enabled rural women to experience that freedom. The confidence these women have gained through training and through the solidarity of the Self Help Group allow them to counter criticism at the individual level. "Even if someone opposes me, I can reply with confidence," says Vimalbai, who comes from a Self Help Group and was now the village headman (*sarpanch*). She herself only recently experienced false accusations by her predecessor, a male, in an attempt to cover his own mismanagement.

The progress of this kind is hard to quantify—and easily lost in the grand reconstruction schemes being bandied about. We could see in the new cultural patterns the strides taken by women. The demure graduates swathed in colourful saris, the sloe-eyed Mangalas and smock-clad Latas in their ceaseless pursuit of redefining the contours of their life. The Self Help Group model has shown women are creditworthy clients because it debunks and defangs so many of the prejudices and stereotypes that unfairly hold women back, such as the notion that woman cannot be the primary breadwinners of the family.

As women have gained new skills and knowledge, their feeling of self-worth has increased, and they have gained the necessary confidence to take a more vocal stand at the household level. As Sunita Ledange explained, "In the beginning, we didn't know anything. Before we organized ourselves into a Self Help Group we used to believe everything and agreed with everything our men told us. Now we have learned to express our opinions and views and now our men even ask us what we think." Though male family members continue to choose a suitable match for the family's sons, many women report having the final word in decisions on their daughter's' marriage partners, a position which was previously unthinkable.

As Ranibai Meshram and Nirmala Wansinghe put it, their greatest pleasure is that they have won their freedom, at last, from a bondage which was only theirs to be felt, which none saw. They fraternize within the village, do not need to seek permission from their tyrant husbands, caste differences forgotten. They even squat and demonstrate at the local BDO's office whenever their grievances remain unheeded. Development practitioners are now pinning their hopes on Self Help Groups to bring about a rural revolution.

Sheela Gulhane remembers a time just two years back when drunken husbands would come to the SHG meetings convened by bank officials, and create a ruckus so that the bank officials couldn't interact with the women. When the women returned home from the meeting, the husbands would vent their spleen upon their spouses. These women have remained married for years to philandering addicts because they feared losing guardianship of their children.

Shobha is a slender, dark-skinned mother with haunting sable eyes and a fine figure that the loose folds of her ragged sari could not disguise. Her mother recounts, "Two years ago, Shobha had become a mental wreck. Her husband's behaviour took a toll, leaving her mired in abject poverty and anguish. She wept in the lonely confines of her house, deliriously mumbling in despair, before bank officials convinced her to join the local Self Help Group to overcome her trauma." But a two-year association with the group has transformed her. A flash of pain shoots through her eyes when she remembers the tragic days. Her husband has also now recoiled from his old habits of abuse after Shobha engaged him in gruelling counselling sessions, indicating the extent of transformation in him as well as Shobha's own abilities as a counsellor. Shobha's association with the NGO and her visits to various workshops and training centres where she attended weeklong programmes on social psychology had made her a keen psychologist.

Commerce has a profound ability to make people put aside their differences and interact with each other. "Before the Self Help Group came on the scene, I was zero," Kamla told us as she sat down to finger through her ten year-old daughter's hair for lice, another daily chore. Her teenage son swept the courtyard beside them. "We were share-croppers. We could not find food to feed our children or clothes to dress them. Now we can buy food and lease land and send our children to school. I have repaid Rs. 5,000 for the loan I was given by my Self Help Group. I have money left over from which I want to buy a goat."

When asked whether these loans have created indebtedness and consequent stress, the women claim they feel liberated, not subjugated. They have entered a new world; the old world may slowly become extinct.

During one of the visits of the bank staff, the men asked the women to consider their case for being enrolled in Self Help Groups. The timid women murmured their opinions to the ones next to them, and the information was passed to the leaders like a game of Chinese Whispers. The leaders then spoke on behalf of their groups: the answer was still 'no', because the men were loath to save and prone to frittering away their earnings. Why should they want men to share the fruits of their labour?

"No, but let them have a different group," a woman suggested. "They wouldn't be on the same wavelength," another said. A young, soft-spoken woman said, "There is machismo involved here. When there is not enough income, men are dipping into their savings. The men are not allowing us enough time for meetings. With men joining, the male group meeting will acquire priority." Did their husbands know about their savings? "No!" they responded at once. "If they knew we managed to save," one said, "they would give us no money for the house." Everybody broke into wild laughter.

Lata was a regular figure at our meetings and training programmes held periodically in Charurkhati for the cluster of five villages. She imbibed the values of thrift and hard work assiduously. One morning, I joined Lata on the long ride home to her village. As we approached, hordes of curious youngsters swarmed around us. She steered me into her home, a simple cement structure, with a tiny shrine built into a wall. She twirled her finger, tinkling her metal bracelets, as she gestured to her mother. Her mother daubed my forehead with purple rice. As the whole family squeezed inside, Lata lopped the top off a fresh coconut, popped in a straw and offered it to me. After I had finished and handed over the rind, she hacked it open with a scythe and gathered the cotton-white cream in a steel bowl and was keen that I not only taste it but consume the entire bowl.

When it was time for me to leave, she wished me *namaste,* then grabbed my hand in hers and gave it a tight squeeze. In a barely audible whisper, she said, "I am grateful to you for introducing me to this programme...Now I am on my third loan—Rs. 20,000. My husband does not take even a rupee from my shop. He pays for our food and clothing from his shop while I have bought things for the house—tape, TV; I have paid to get my son trained as a carpenter in Nagpur; I have bought my husband a wheelchair from Chandrapur which he can manage himself. I am not interested in raising cows or anything. I am busy enough with my shop."

I was completely blown as I listened to the stories of these tenacious women. They have sophisticated credit algorithms: "Does the woman own a buffalo? Some chickens? Does she have a toilet in her home? What kind of roofing material does her home have? Does she bring a shawl to the village meeting? Does she come barefoot to the meeting, or does she wear slippers? Do her children come to the school properly washed and dressed?"

If you go to Charurkhati today, you will find that life in the village quite different from what it was a few years ago. Not substantially richer, because there is still drought, no industry save rain-fed agriculture—but the overall quality of life is better. There's a bank, a school, biogas plants; farmers drive around on motorcycles. Women are out of the house and working on village improvement projects such as sanitation systems and vegetable gardens. They have started small businesses. The fields are heavy with grain. People eat more nutritious foods, use toilets instead of the woods, and wash their hands and bodies with the clean water now piped into their backyard. They know how to prevent the diseases that kill poor people. They use mosquito nets and repellents to ward off mosquitoes. They know they must boil water for drinking to protect the family from water-borne diseases. Even more remarkable is the social transformation that the movement has wrought. No one drinks. Only a handful smoke. There hasn't been a crime here in years. Even the practice of untouchability has weakened. Dalits suffer far less discrimination than before, as do women and girls. The village is brisk and prosperous. Signs of rural modernity abound. As Muhammad Yunus himself says, "When a destitute mother starts earning an income, her dreams of success invariably center on her children. A woman's second priority is the household. She wants to buy utensils, build a stronger roof, or find a bed for herself and her family. A man has an entirely different set of priorities. When a destitute father earns extra income, he focuses more attention on himself. Thus money entering a household through a woman brings more benefits to the family as a whole."(*Banker to the Poor).*

Women producers lack the contacts to reach better markets. A small grower of tomatoes has to sell her produce at the village level to traders at half the price that she could command in the city. An embroiderer has to sell her exquisite fabric to a trader at one-tenth the price it finally fetches in the larger venues. A small salt producer cannot hire a railway car to reach the wholesale market and has to dispose of her salt at a fraction of the real price. The handloom weaver buys scarce yarn at double the price that a factory pays. The leather worker has to give up her trade as all raw leather in the area has been exported. Similarly for capital: a small vendor borrows at 15 per cent per month from the moneylender, while banks lend to businesses at the same rate per year. A marginal farmer mortgages her land—and all rights to produce on it—during a lean year, as she cannot access cheaper sources of credit. Seeds are borrowed in the sowing season, to be returned with 250 percent interest at harvest.

The first loan that I sanctioned to a village woman gave me a unique experience. Women entrepreneurs will shy away from loans, having personally witnessed the shame women in their village suffered at the hands of moneylenders. Villagers would dissuade me, saying a woman would hand the money over to her husband who would fritter it away. Even our staff said, "Let us forget about this project because we cannot compel them if their husbands have reservations. If they are not willing, why are you forcing them to avail these loans?"

I emphasized to my staff that when these women say no, it is not their own voice. It is the voice of their history, the way they were treated, that took away all their confidence. One day, after we coax off the crust of fear that grew around them, one or two of them take a loan, and others feel encouraged to follow suit. Nevertheless, it took me six years to bring about that increase in awareness and ambition.

There is an internal wrestling in the mind of the borrower. She quakes, fumbles and sleeps poorly, fretting. She agrees with great hesitation. She spends a sleepless night, tossing and turning, debating whether she should go through with it. One nagging thought keeps arising: "What will become of my parents and family if I cannot repay the loan? My mother has toiled so hard to guard her reputation." The woman has created problems for the family already, just by being a girl, being a woman. She doesn't want to create more by borrowing what she cannot repay. In the morning, her friends come over and encourage her because they have all decided to go through with it, and if she drops out, everything collapses. "Don't worry, we all will support each other;

we have to take a chance, otherwise our fate will never change," counsels a fellow member.

Godavari Uikey was a fifty-two-year-old illiterate woman, who was a member of one of the oldest groups in the village but since the group did not have a credit line with the bank and had a low cash base, her loan requirements could not be entertained at the group level. Because of drought, she had few remaining means of survival. Married at 18, she had three children, all daughters, and she was the sole breadwinner. She had an alcoholic husband whose habit she funded out of her wages and who beat her if she answered back. Godavari's life consisted of cooking meals, taking care of her children and staying quiet. Always required to ask her husband's permission to leave the house, and these requests usually denied, she described herself back then, in a breathy, weak-lunged voice, as "sad and alone", with a body work-hunched and wiry. Her neighbours confided that she was a tear factory even on good days. While struggling to survive on her family's meagre income, she did not think she had the authority to tell her husband to stop spending thirty percent of their earnings on liquor. Fear of poverty and respect for society kept her locked in a bad marriage, as did the prospect of losing custody of their children. The glassy stare in her eyes revealed some of the despair.

One day, Godavari's neighbour, Vimal Dahule, told her about the programme that helped women pool their own savings—sometimes as little as Rs. 20 a month—and then provide loans to each other. Defying her husband and leaving the house without permission, Godavari and some women in her community went to learn more about the programme, and decided to start their own village savings and loan group. Godavari was excited about what the bank and its manager might mean for them, but her husband tried to dispel what he considered her silly notions that any bank would actually help them."I don't want to have anything to do with the bank," he said at first, with a dismissive toss of his hands to his wife who he felt was being taken for a ride by a charlatan banker.

When I first proffered the loan, Godavari stuttered with fright and her honest face crumpled in despair. Clenching and unclenching her fists, she drank a full glass of water from a battered aluminium jug. I assured her that if she made a serious attempt at properly investing the loan and yet failed in generating surplus, we would not divest her of her bare belongings in the way of a moneylender. Godavari scratched her head, did quick mental math and decided to give the loan a try. There was nothing to lose. When I placed the envelope in her astonished hands, her eyes grew large and lambent, and they darted at the cheque book lying on the table and then back at me. She signed the receipt in a hurried, untidy scrawl.

She screamed in delight as she saw what was inside the envelope. She trembled. Tears rolled down her cheeks. With help from us and with the combined resources of her new business partners, Godavari bought a cow for around Rs. 4,000 which continues to produce daily dividends—more than three pints of milk that she sells to the upper-caste landowners in the neighbouring village. Recently, the cow gave birth to a calf. Godavari was already engaged in dairying as a wage labour and her dream of having her own independent unit was realised.

The experience reinforced our belief: you can't just give a woman a loan and then send her on her way—you have to accompany her as she struggles to make her way out of poverty. Godavari's business took off quickly, and she began earning enough income to provide for her family, send her daughters to school, and pay for her husband's medical bills. She gained some of the respect she deserved from her husband, who allowed her more freedom and even began to help her with her business ventures.

Godavari is now seen by her community as a 'husband-tamer' and a smart businesswoman. Since joining the programme, Godavari has not only become an inspiration for other women in her community, but she serves as a prime example of how economic security can provide the right kind of aid for women and their children and even have a positive effect on marriages.

Though illiterate, her skills at financial arithmetic are phenomenal. She and the thirty other women of the village Self Help Group even managed to chase the local liquor shop out of their village. They walk about proudly in their uniforms—identical saris that they bought out of the money they pooled from their precious savings. Contrast them with their appearance just a few years ago—a group in discoloured rags. She remembers standing for hours at the local water pump—which she could not touch—waiting for a higher caste woman to take pity on her and fill her bucket. She was so poor, she washed her hair with mud and owned a single sari. When she laundered it, she had to stay in the river until it dried. She herself says, "When I started, I had no support from anyone, no education, no money. I was like a stone with no soul. When I joined the Self Help Group, it gave me shape, life. I learned courage and boldness. I became a human being." Now an infectious smile seemed to have dug a permanent home in her face. Other women in this village got tiny loans to invest in miniature businesses.

None had made better use of the cash than Renuka Mahalle, a shrewd, flinty young mother who put her profits from four loans into cows, goats, land, a sturdy house and private tutors for her daughter. "I can make money out of anything," she boasted in her wheezy voice, a flower-shaped gold stud glinting in her nose. Her house was made of mud, dirt, and cow dung with a thatched roof. In the yard, bricks were stacked up, clothes were slung over a line, and small fire pits held twigs for cooking sorghum flatbread. A brown cow lay contentedly in the shade. When the dynamic Renuka got her first loan, for Rs. 5000, she already had Rs.2000 saved from working as a cook and raising chickens, the family trade. She invested her savings in a cow she later sold for Rs. 10,000. Her next Rs. 10,000 she invested in a thresher machine. It takes care of her own farming requirements, and when it is not in use at her farm, she rents it out. The villagers are also happy that they don't have to hire one from an outsider.

Sushila's story tumbled out in a gruff voice. She had a wonderful childhood despite a poor home and dreamt of lending some of her effervescence to the new home. An abusive husband shattered her dreams of a peaceful family life into a hundred tales of suffering. She worked twelve hours daily, six days a week. She held up her chafed hands as evidence and we squatted by the fires, hearing the notes of the hounds dying out in the countryside, watching a small temple, shaded by a hallowed *pipal* tree, slowly fill up with worshippers.

When she was starving, her neighbours helped as best they could, she recalls; but the woman who helped most was her friend who brought her to the Self Help Group. She had to save a certain amount before qualifying for a loan—as do all members—so she took in laundry to supplement her tenant farming. Her bruised dream of happiness and prosperity slowly started healing. We had brought back some of the gloss of her dream.

When Laxmi, in a depleted village in Chandrapur, had first held Rs. 500 in her hands, they had trembled. It was money that gave strength to her hands, changed her life, and that of thirty other women in the village who had been rooted to a patch of soybean that glowed like emerald and scorched their bare feet. Laxmi's eyes filled with tears while telling us that, as a widow, she couldn't provide her four children with enough to eat. Today, although finances are tight, Laxmi and her family are getting back on their feet. "I've always wanted a better life but didn't know what to do, but now I have this mushroom-growing skill and can support my family. Why didn't you people come three years earlier?" she asks playfully.

The local panchayat leader, Ashabai, comes from a village of five hundred people. "My village has no lights, no water, and no road. The women got together because of the *bishi* (an Indian *ROSCA*, Rotating Savings and Credit Association)." Ashabai was made of sterner stuff; but being alone, her patience would run out. An exposure to the groups has honed her patience and built resilience. Initially, she attended the meeting with her husband in tow. A few months back, the husband was shoved away. Since then Asha is on her own. She knows she will be debarred from the group if the husband continues to accompany her and if she remains totally dependent on him. One of the cardinal goals of group membership is that the women must be encouraged to gather enough self-confidence to no longer need male chaperones. When first speaking on stage about her experience, she could mumble and splutter only a few sentences. Today she is a refined, confident public speaker.

Rekha Asutkar, who now is an organizer for her saving group, used to reside in a tiny, rickety house that could no longer withstand the fury of the monsoon. She was in a dilemma whether to invest her meagre savings in business or to construct a small sturdy room. When the bank agreed to give her a loan to start up a business, she constructed a *pucca* house and utilized the bank loan to set up a grocery store. Today she has a decent house and a small but flourishing grocery shop. She proudly proclaims that in Andhra Pradesh, Self Help Group women have turned into celebrities and in Rajasthan, they have catapulted to the silver screen. She is confident that the day is not too far when a woman from Warora will grace the cover page of a women's magazine. The women snap pictures of various celebrations in their group as a matter of record for posterity.

Vimalbai was a fiercely independent woman, who was endowed with the gift of logic and love for mainstream participation. Her rasping voice and tough demeanour marked her out for a leadership role. She wanted to understand and then break all notions of male exclusiveness in local political decision-making. Her husband was a drunkard who used to beat her. She invited us into her hut, where it was dim and cool. She lit up the small *chulha* (stove) to brew tea as she recounted how membership in the Self Help Group helped her rebuild her confidence and her life.

Manda had already taken a loan for the construction of a house and was not eligible for a business loan which she desperately needed. She was a reputed tailor of the village but her sewing machine had broken beyond repair. Because of drought, she had few remaining means of survival. She managed to raise half the amount and the rest she took from the moneylender. During one of my visits to her house, I saw a strange creature at her doorstep. Manda opened her steel almirah and took out a bag containing loose notes. She was stealthily counting them, trying to avoid my gaze. I could sense it was all about a moneylender's loan. I took out my wallet and gave her Rs. 1,000 with an assurance that I would assist her further if she shunned moneylenders. Manda resisted, saying my money was equally hard earned, but took it hesitatingly, saying that she would repay the whole amount as early as possible. I told her that I was not worried about my money being returned (I was not going to accept repayment) and my anxiety was the continued dependence of the women on moneylenders.

Each of these women began with not a scintilla of hope. "I had nothing, nobody," said Mina, who worked as a maid for payment in rice after her husband abandoned her. "I was scared to become a member of the group. I was too poor to repay a loan. But now that I'm getting goats at reasonably priced loans, I'm interested."

"The village men would flare up at me if they found me talking to the male staff of the bank," recalls Savitri with a giggle. She remembers the *pradhan* (headman) asking her, 'Why were you talking to the bank staff alone?'I told him, 'I am talking to you alone right now. Is that any different?'He sputtered for a while, but that shut him up."

Bayabai still lives in a windowless hut, sleeps on a mat on the floor, and cooks outside over a twig fire, but the programme has made her rich in other ways. When it's dark inside the shack she strikes a match, lights a kerosene lantern, and turns the flame up by twiddling the metal hoop at its side. An amber glow seeps through the sooty glass panels, a dull, flickering light, and shadows spill across the room."When I came to Charurkhati, I was like a stone with no soul," said Bayabai. "People would sneeringly comment "See her, the dirty skin-and-bones. Is she a woman or a muddy stick?"The bankers gave me shape and life, courage and boldness. I became a human being." Her face was worn and her skin weathered, but her eyes were alight with purpose.

Attests Sanjay Modak, the *upsarpanch* (deputy headman), the strongman of the village: "It is only when the *mahila mandals* (women clubs) emerged that life changed in our village. Our women would not even sit with us, let alone talk with us. Now, they tell us what to eat, how to function better in the fields. My mother's position in society depended on how many children she had. Her children consumed her energy. She had no time to think of the village or other women. My wife now works more outside than in the home. She not only runs her home but also helps other women run theirs. Our women now question, and know their own worth."

A Self Help Group also offers its members housing loans and provides them with useful items at cost price: seedlings and seeds for the vegetable garden, alum to purify drinking water, iodized salt to combat goitre. Bank employees hold workshops to educate borrowers, who have established village elementary schools, paying for them through their own contributions. Many eat more nutritious food than before and now plan their families. Tellingly, the dowry custom is under siege.

We trained some women as village health workers. The quality these women had was not the mechanical ability to store information but the ability to recognize needs, relate to them and communicate what they had learnt. Beginning in the benign area of health, the women slowly gained confidence and moved on to other social areas. They began asking for change from the bus conductor, demanded the presence of a school teacher and expected proper services from local village officials". The women's hands have now blossomed into fists," says Suvarnarekha Patil an NGO activist in the vanguard of the Self Help Group movement. "From birth, a woman is doomed in these parts. She is cursed and deprived—first of a mother's love, then of a husband's love. She is not really married to a man but to his whole family. The only way she proves herself is by bearing children. They lend her prestige, become her security. A woman may have five daughters and one son. If you ask her how many children she has, she says one. She does not count the girls. That has begun to change."

Why this focus on women?

The woman is the centre of these initiatives because she is the fulcrum around which the village poverty economy revolves. From the early dawn, the woman is up and around, working about the house, taking care of the family and catering to the whims of her husband. Millions of such women are also wage-earners, working all day in the farm. Back home in the evening, it is back to cooking and more chores. Yet these women match their male folk, nay surpass them, in everything—hard work, initiative, patience and adjustment. At the lower end of the economic strata, women are saddled with husbands who only drink and help produce children, but the women still work from dusk to dawn, providing succour to their families, including a drinking allowance to errant husbands. While the village woman cooks, she may breastfeed one child and watch over three others. If she fails in any of these tasks, or performs them too slowly, her husband often feels it is his prerogative to beat her. And yet invariably she considers her husband a god. At the well at dawn, in the hearth at dark, ploughing, sowing, harvesting, threshing, milling, the women are constantly on their toes. As Muhammad Yunus himself says, "When a destitute mother starts earning an income, her dreams of success invariably center around her children. A woman's second priority is the household. She wants to buy utensils, build a stronger roof, or find a bed for herself and her family. A man has an entirely different set of priorities. When a destitute father earns extra income, he focuses more attention on himself. Thus money entering a household through a woman brings more benefits to the family as a whole."

Allowing women direct access to financial services might improve their possibilities to become entrepreneurs, thus increasing their individual incomes, their chances to become more independent, and their participation in family and community decision making. There is also an important insurance effect: better access to credit, savings, or insurance services reduces the need to use child labor as a buffer in the case of seasonal income fluctuations and transitory income shocks and allows consumption smoothing. In the case of transitory income reductions resulting from health shocks, it also allows faster attention to health problems. Finally, there *is* an aggregate infrastructure effect, with more efficient financial institutions and markets allowing more private and public investment in the construction of schools and health facilities.

Consequently, the vast majority of microloans go to women because experience has shown that women are more likely to reinvest their earnings in the business for the betterment of their families. As families cross the poverty line and micro-businesses expand, entire communities will stand to benefit. Jobs are created, know-how is shared, civic participation increases, and women stand to get their due recognition as valuable members of their families and communities.

Women traditionally face greater access barriers to formal banking services than even the poorest men and are thus also credit-constrained to a greater extent than men. In some countries, women are legally barred from opening accounts or applying for credit. In most of the developing world, women would not be deemed credit-worthy since they do not hold formal sector jobs or the titles to their houses. Interestingly, women's lower opportunities if they do not hold formal sector jobs, makes them more likely to pay the high interest rates required for sustainable microfinance.

Second, experience has shown that repayment is higher among female borrowers, mostly due to their more conservative investments and lower moral hazard risk. Given that moral hazard seems to be the constraining factor in outreach to low-income households, women might therefore be the more attractive clients. While adverse selection might be more problematic among women, the joint-liability technique helps control this risk.

Last, but not least, one of the often articulated rationales for supporting livelihood finance and the targeting of women through Self Help Groups is that these groups are an effective entry point for empowering women. Given an opportunity to fight hunger and poverty, a poor woman turns out to be a better fighter than a poor man. It has been our experience that poor women have the intense drive to move up; they are hardworking, concerned about their human dignity, concerned about their children's present and future, and willing to make personal sacrifices for the well-being of their children. In order for a woman to be empowered, she needs access to the material, human, and social resources necessary to make strategic choices in her life. Not only have women been historically disadvantaged in access to material resources like credit, property and money, but they have also been excluded from social resources like education. By putting financial resources in the hands of women, banks help level the playing field and promote gender equality. I was awed by the resilience and strength of the women I met. Given a chance to improve their lives through economic activity, they showed a remarkable ability to grasp the nuances of business. They disproved the myth that all villagers are perpetually trapped in the sloth of poverty. I was always inspired by Gandhiji's words in *Harijan:*

In the case of the Indian villagers an age-old culture is hidden under an encrustment of crudeness. Take away the encrustation, remove his chronic poverty and his illiteracy and you have the finest specimen of what a cultured, cultivated free citizen should be.

But even as the self-help philosophy grew and the movement spread, the slow response from banks showed that large swathes of women continued to remain unserved. At one of my meetings I discovered that none of the poverty-stricken women who attended had ever dared to apply for a microloan. One woman's pierced nose was empty because she had already been forced to sell her gold stud for money. Another's nine-year-old son pedalled a rickshaw for Rs 20 a day to keep the family fed. But they eagerly joined our new programme—and were pleased to see their goats multiply. They were still so poor that their bodies seemed little more than collections of bones beneath worn saris, but their new assets offered hope.

By the time I left Warora for my new assignment elsewhere, the roots of the self-help movement had penetrated the nooks and corners of Warora's hinterland. The momentum was too vivid to wear off immediately. During one of my recent visits, I found that women had hollowed the male-dominated power-grid in villages. Like termites, they had mined the out the male bastions.

I remember there was a woman who started out with a mud hut. When I came back after three years on a personal holiday, she had a three-room house with a cement floor, and the goats were stabled in the hut in which she had stayed before. When her group of women first came for loans, they sat hunched, looking down into their laps. They would take the small pile of pastel and white notes they got as part of a loan and fold it into a hairpin behind their ears. They were looking so frightened because, they said, they were afraid they couldn't pay it back.

One of them was so dazed that she wanted to know the name of the person who had recommended her for the loan. Some of them even suggested taking only a part of the loan. For the remaining they said they would consult their husbands and then come back. Two or three years later, these same women were running businesses, and were often involved in politics in their village. Does everyone succeed? No—but it is the same in the investment business. You don't want to take a lot of risk? Buy some hens. The less risk-averse borrowers will pool their loans and buy a baby water buffalo and rent it to men for farming. And then there are those who blow right past livestock and build a brick factory.

As individuals, women are insecure and indecisive, but when serried into groups they blossom into creative efflorescence. I visited a village a month away from the rainy season. The villagers were getting their fields ready. Equipped with agricultural tools, the women who were trained measured the fields and estimated the quantities of fertilizers, insecticides and weed-killers that were needed. Others observed and got trained on the job. "Our objective is to gain perfect mastery of all the basic agricultural techniques," said Sunanda, a dynamic new farmer. Accounts were maintained meticulously and the cash value of all borrowed inputs was calculated and paid up later. Each shareholder had an individual account and loans taken were noted down. "This way, we are sure not to find ourselves with inflated bills after the harvests," Sunanda explained, adding, "We make it a matter of principle to pay back the money that was lent to us to the last penny. We do not want to discourage those who trusted us." The village men were unanimous in their admiration. "We have been surprised by their rigorous management and the output of their fields," they remarked. In their determination to become self-reliant, the women had collected savings, which, complemented by a small government loan, was to help them set up a bore well equipped with a pump. This would irrigate seedlings before the first rains fell, and also augment the drinking water supply to the village. Taking advantage of this, the women could sell their harvest in the market before the other farmers, and at better prices. These earnings, as they said, would "help improve the menus at home, help with purchase of medicines and clothes for the family." This year, part of the profit had been used for the creation of a ten hectare vegetable garden, which produced tomatoes, cabbages, onions, lettuce and potatoes. Some of these were consumed locally, the rest were sold at weekly markets. Despite the success of their enterprise, the women still have several hurdles to cross, not least the traditional prejudices against women's independence. For instance, most organisations giving agricultural loans prefer to give them to men. As the leader of the women farmers confided, "Till now we didn't even have our own plough to work. We had to borrow it from the men. Sometimes we had to postpone the dates of ploughing." The-women had therefore decided that the profits from the next harvest of the vegetable garden would-be used to buy ploughs. In the meantime, they did the work with their hands.

Rupali was so excited that she could barely stop talking about her experiences. "I used to be so ignorant—I barely stepped out of my house—but now I know where the BDO sits and where the Collector's Office is located. If the village *sarpanch* (headman)does not listen to our problems, I do not hesitate to go straight to the higher officials to lodge my protest." Her confidence stems from her involvement with the literacy programme operating in her village for over five years. The women explain how they discovered their inner strength since their involvement with the Self Help Groups. It is no longer possible for anybody to short-change them by paying them less wages. "Now we are armed with information. We know what the minimum wage is and demand it without hesitation," says Malabai. Earlier, the sarpanch would bring in cheap labour from neighbouring villages to work on government projects. "This is absolutely illegal. We fought against it and battled it out to ensure that the work was allotted to our villagers and that they were paid their rightful wage." The real benefits, the women say, cannot be measured in rupees—a lesson for anyone who believes that the poor are motivated simply by material needs and not the desire for respect, community and recognition. A vital part of the entire programme is the fellowship they share with their sisters. The Self Help Groups have become astringents for soaking up the pain of their individual members.

If you visit Warora today, you will find that life is far different from what it was a few years ago. Not substantially richer, no—there is still drought, no industry, only rain-dependent agriculture—but better. Warora's villages have clean water, and many have pipes carrying that water to a pump in every backyard. Most houses have soak pits, a simple and cheap drainage system dug outside every house that eliminates standing wastewater; they are moving on to toilets. In an area nearly barren of trees, Warora's villages have planted millions. The government's afforestation plans supported by dollops of aid have given a fillip to the greening of barren lands, and helped in restoring the health of the environment. There are several incidental benefits, better rainfall patterns, improvement in the quality of soils and food security. Dalits are less oppressed and upper caste women are free to leave the confines of their homes. Women are better educated and more interested in educating their girls. The fact that most credit being given is used for consumption and not for income-generation purposes is not necessarily an indictment of development finance. Consumption can go overboard if the credit is taken to finance a lavish wedding. But a lot of micro-borrowing goes into paying school fees because the borrower can't afford the lump sum fees, paying for medical services, etc. Offering timely credit to a poor woman whose son needs medical attention is an important benefit in terms of the livelihood that is created.

The biggest drain on a villager's finance is a health problem. Also every day of sickness means loss of a day's wages. It is necessary that villagers get timely medical care so that ill health doesn't compel them to skip off labour. Studies show that the effect of micro-credit is not only income enhancing but more importantly, income smoothing, enabling the purchase of goods or services otherwise unaffordable. Self Help Groups have formed federations, leveraged their finances and influence, and even delivered insurance, ambulance services, and other commercial and government services. The loss of income due to sickness and incapacitation of a borrower or a family member, and the high cost of health treatment, are detrimental to individuals and families in the developing world. Therefore, it is not surprising that illness and death of family members are among the most common reasons why livelihood finance participants remain mired in poverty, default on their loans and/ or drop out of a livelihood finance programme. This is a strong reason why institutions think of providing micro insurance to women of Self Help Groups. My personal experience is that villagers can themselves set up, administer and manage an insurance fund pooled out of their monthly savings; the school teacher or the postmaster could serve as ombudspersons. This could do both for health insurance and cattle insurance.

If you want to see the credibility of poor women borrowers, you must visit villages in the suicide-prone Yavatmal district of Maharashtra, where banks had to plough dud agricultural loans like a mountain of rotten potatoes. My experiences during the last few years in Yavatmal have made these convictions indelible. I was leading a credit camp for my company, engaged in housing finance through Self Help Groups in the interior tribal villages in Kelapur block. I was struck by the plight of a family whose tin roof had blown away. I offered a Rs. 5,000 loan to the women. To my great surprise, she refused, saying she would not be able to repay it. I tried to convince her to accept it and to get the interest rate further reduced by my company, but she remained unmoved. Her daughter, who was observing our interaction, told me that the mother would never take a loan, as the last time she had taken one she was already under great moral stress and had to donate blood at least two times at the nearest hospital to meet her loan instalment commitment.

In Sakhra, deep into the forest belt infested by tigers and other wildlife, lies an island of incredible honesty. In a village called Nagezari, almost twenty kilometres deep in that belt, a group of twenty tribal women told me that they had repaid the bank loan despite assurances from political leaders that the loans had been waived by the government. They went all the way to the bank office to check with the manager if loans had actually been waived. He told them that this was incorrect and the loans of agriculturists alone had been waived.

Sakhra is a unique example of totally illiterate backward women ensuring the rights they have been guaranteed by the law by virtue of their being forest tribals and also the protection under the laws for displaced people. Sakhra is a resettlement village in which villagers uprooted by a development project have been rehabilitated. Seventy households led by Anusaya, lovingly called Amma, have fought their way on their own. They demonstrated before the local administration for days to get a barely motorable road constructed. Each family owns six acres of irrigated land, and at least a pair of bullocks, two cows and a few goats. Six enterprising young boys own premium brand motorcycles. A few weeks back, a tiger had mauled a resident beyond recognition. Now the villagers have set up bamboo fences around the courtyards of their houses. Ammai was a wonderful host and served a sumptuous meal to our entire group. I offered a token donation for village welfare after we had a sumptuous meal at her place. Ammai was up in arms. "Feeding guests is a fulfilment of God's obligation. How dare you do that? If I visit your house, will you charge me for hospitality?" I was put to shame as I realized that as we grow prosperous, our hearts grow narrower. These women are now star clients, who can make the best of financial intuitions blush. For example, after support from her husband in the initial phase of establishing a cluster hatchery in the village of Khairgaon, Ranibai now manages the hatchery on her own. Another hatchery, belonging to Manisha Meshram, is now the family's most important source of income, as her husband is too old to work. This economic dependence, she says, has altered her family's internal structure, with particular implications for decision-making. Her two sons, who are also contributing to the family's portfolio, now come to her in order to debate relevant issues and make joint decisions.

Four women in Maya's group in Bina village in Nagpur district had used their loan capital to buy the expensive thread needed for weaving fishing nets. Before joining the bank, they were forced to weave nets on a contract basis for others, arrangements under which they earned next to nothing for their efforts. Manda, the only tribal in the group, invested her Rs. 5,000 in a grocery store she ran from her home. When her group had been formed six years earlier, the four original members wanted no part of Manda, until the branch manager told them sternly, "The bank was created for people like Manda, the dirt poor. If you do not take her, there will be no group here."

However large or small their income gains, poor women find empowerment through access to livelihood loans. According to the World Bank, for instance, livelihood finance empowers women by giving them more control over household assets and resources, more autonomy and decision-making power, and greater access to participation in public life. This defence of microcredit—more particularly livelihood finance—stands or falls with individual success stories featuring women using their loans to start some sort of small-scale enterprise, perhaps renting a stall in the local market or buying a sewing machine to assemble piece goods. There is no doubt that, when they succeed, women and their families are better off than they were before they became micro-debtors, and have solved numerous community problems through grassroots measures. They have created ways for other women and themselves to earn a living, especially when traditional agriculture, mining and factory jobs are no longer available. Leaders of these projects recognize that income alone is not enough to alleviate poverty, so they often pair skills training with education, particularly in basic and financial literacy, and give women information about their legal rights and social issues, including protection against violence and exploitation. Women farmers face a variety of obstacles, including a lack of access to information technology, agricultural training, financial services, and support networks like co-operatives or trade unions. Without these services, women cannot develop resilience to withstand political, economic, social or environmental upheaval, and remain dependent on their male family members. However, despite the structural problems and widespread despair, female entrepreneurs such as Godavari Uikey are finding creative ways to carve out a place for themselves in the marketplace, boosting the economy as well as their confidence and independence. Today, she Godavari has repaid the first loan and gotten another, doubled her merchandise, and gained a new sense of independence as the family breadwinner. Poor people show inspirational courage and ability to transform the little that the deck has dealt them into livelihoods for their families and their communities. They already have skills, are politically conscious, and are aware of the need for schooling their children and taking care of their health. But their lack of income makes using what skills they have impossible. Providing investment capital for additional income generation can unlock the capacity of poor people to solve many, if not all, of the manifestations of poverty that affect their lives.

I recently decided that it would be a good moment to go back to the villages in Maharashtra to find out what local people had to say about our twenty years' of work among them. I went to uncover memories of the early days of the social mobilization work. After more than a decade and a half of it, I wondered what the villagers would have to say. Would there be the same story of initial enthusiasm and hope worn down by a string of disappointments, as had been the fate of the social actions programme before me? Did villages still suffer much poverty? Where were all these empowered women and their successful microenterprises? I was interested in these questions because I had detected a new mood at the corporate offices of banks and microfinance institutions: a growing sense that another change in direction was needed, and could not be long delayed. On a walk through the quiet lanes in October, past herds of snoozing water buffalo and carts pulled by teams of oxen, in Nandra, Swati pointed to the village hand pump she had gotten fixed. She showed off the new brick lanes, electrical poles and street lights installed on her watch and checked on the progress of a new community hall, being built for Rs 90,000. I found that the villagers had now put a premium on educating girls. This was in contrast to the trail of unkempt, unwashed children who would circle me during my stay in the village. I overheard a group of children in school singing a series of what sounded like nursery rhymes. On closer listening they turned out to be catchphrases from popular television commercials. The women's bright clothes were flashy symbols of their newfound prosperity and some had jazzed up their houses. Irrigation previously had consisted of asking the gods for the rainbow. I now found sprinklers spouting rainbow streams of water into the fields. In one village, a new deep well replaced the old inadequate shallow one. A large pond had been dug to catch rainwater and provide for aquaculture. Irrigation stretched from the pond to fields planted with grains, quick-growing rice and potatoes. There was watershed management to stop erosion off the steep slopes. There was a light shining in the villagers' eyes when they talked about the transformation of their village economy. Hope had begun coursing through communities once shackled by fatalism and low expectations. For a world where people live on less than an American dollar a day, this is an important step. Women previously diffident and withdrawn are stepping out of the confines of their homes to acquire an identity of their own. They have learnt the art of properly presenting themselves in the assembly of men, whittling down emotion to its barest expression. Most of the one million women elected over the years at the panchayat level came out of the Self Help Groups. The women are not asking for hand-outs. They are simply asking for an opportunity. The world's poor now probably have a greater say over their lives than at any other time in history. Though not dramatic, not a headline grabber, the change is a slow and quiet transformation underway in even the most far-flung villages. Almost everywhere I went I found local campaigns to share basic resources like land and water, to build democratic school boards, trading co-operatives and credit movements, and to make the government accountable at the highest and lowest levels. These are the small revolutions that are changing the world. But the revolution is not yet complete. Now is the time to move beyond livelihood finance to create broader economic opportunities for women, situating them as central and pivotal players in the 'macroeconomy'. Only then will we bring our revolution full circle. In the words and expressions of these unlettered people I found the bliss and flavour of quotidian wisdom worn humbly and lightly. In the lives of these tenacious women I found the story not of a country's doom but a story of a country's will to survive.

This may not be a revolution but at the very least this is a revolution in the making.

5

Shaping Their Destinies

Women are the real architects of society.

Harriet Beecher Stowe

When a woman rises up in glory, her energy is magnetic and her sense of possibility contagious.

Marianne Williamson, Woman's Worth

A woman is the full circle. Within her is the power to create, nurture, and transform.

Diane Mariechild

Nandra is connected to the nearest motorable road by a three-kilometre stretch of dust that masquerades as a road. During the rains, this path would be a treacherous morass. Someone intent on finding new passages across the bush might drive through, on the red and rutted track that is the only thoroughfare, without pause. But a marooned traveller, perhaps someone whose motorcycle has broken down among herds of cattle and thickets of thorn, might stop here and glimpse, for a moment, lives remote from the towns. With fewer than one hundred residents, Nandra's small children seemed to outnumber adults and wandering poultry the people.

We sped through the dust bowl of an expanse of khaki fields with stubbles of harvested wheat and neat squares of sunflower glowing under the sunlight. From each side of our speeding car, the broad fields of paddy, flat as a man's hand, ran down to a horizon so distant it seemed the edge of the world. Much of the countryside surrounding the fields was unfertile-looking scrub, with only the occasional village, with its gaggle of bullocks. Traffic warnings distilled into single sentences by some poetic bureaucrat and painted on boards for public nourishment were visible along the road: "Lane driving is sane driving", "If married, don't flirt with speed", "No hurry no worry", "Risk taker is accident maker", "Better late than never", "Drinking whisky is risky". My companion and I made a game of spying them first and reading them out: *Road signs are signs of life. Highway is not a way to get high.* And on a bridge over a river, the mysterious *Please don't beep down.*

It was extremely dry, so there were long stretches of dusty roads, yellowed brush and withered and knotty trees. The earth in some areas was a deep red colour, rich in iron. Tiny villages dotted the landscape, and rutted dirt roads snaked off into the odd copse of trees.

We finally arrived at the village where I was to implement on an intensive scale the lessons I had gleaned from my earlier experiences as a development banker. The focus was to be a development strategy owned and driven by the local people. I was convinced, after my limited exposure to development banking programmes in my earlier assignments, that those toiling at the bottom of the pyramid need all the levers they can get to climb their way out of the sunken depths of poverty.

The 'bottom up' approach is about living and working with the poor, listening to them with humility to gain their confidence and trust. Their trust cannot be bought outright or manipulated with money, or by grafting urban assumptions of development onto existing rural practices, which in fact may destroy existing workable structures. We must first understand their economy at a granular level and, most important, thoroughly understand their local culture. That approach is a welcome contrast to the grandiose foreign-aid schemes that do more harm than good. Experiences show that governments too often derail the money intended to help the poor to pad the pockets of civil servants instead. Mired in bureaucracy and corruption, the benefits rarely reach those who needed them the most.

The bottom-up approach means that local actors participate in decision-making about the strategy and in the selection of the priorities to be pursued in their local area. Experience has shown that the bottom-up approach should not be considered as alternative or opposed to top down approaches from national and/or regional authorities, but rather as combining and interacting with them, in order to achieve better overall results.

Rural policies following this approach should be designed and implemented in the way best adapted to the needs of the communities they serve. One way to ensure this is to invite local stakeholders to take the lead and participate. The involvement of local actors includes the population at large, economic and social interest groups and representative public and private institutions. Capacity building is an essential component of the bottom-up approach, involving:

- awareness raising, training, participation and mobilisation of the local population to identify the strengths and weakness of the area (analysis);
- participation of different interest groups in drawing up a local development strategy;
- establishment of clear criteria for selection at local level of appropriate actions (projects) to deliver the strategy.

Participation should not be limited to the initial phase but should extend throughout the implementation process, contributing to the strategy, the accomplishment of the selected projects and in stocktaking and learning for the future. There are also important issues of transparency which need to be addressed in the mobilisation and consultation procedures in order to reach consensus through dialogue and negotiation among participating actors.

Too often the way in which outside aid has been given displaces or discourages local resource contributions, resulting in total aid that is zero-sum, or worse, negative-sum. The constant presence of poverty and despair on your doorstep imparts an oppressive sense of guilt and frustration to life here which no amount of benevolent paternalism ever fully removes. When poor communities think at the human level, all their goals are interconnected. But under the top-down model, in the absence of a global grass-roots movement partnering with the communities, the goals have been compartmentalized to suit donors and governments. In fact, rural development involves integration of its subsystems into an organic whole.

The buzzwords *empowerment, participation, partnership, ownership, transparency* and *accountability* all imply changes in power and relationships, but these are contradicted especially in aid by top down standardised demands and the mindset that goes with 'delivery' Reputed consultancy firms now use the "curveball" technique during training to put consultants in situations where they need to think fast and solve problems on the fly. The aim is to see how they respond and whether they can think on their feet. Modern education means that younger consultants are better prepared for this than more senior staff, because students today are encouraged to discuss and question, rather than just being told what to think.

During the last 40 years, Third World governments, backed by international aid organisations, have poured billions of dollars into cheap-credit programmes for the poor, particularly in the wake of the World Bank's 1990 initiative to put poverty reduction at the head of its development priorities. And yet those responsible for such transfers had, and in many cases continue to have, only the haziest of ideas of what they achieved, and how their intervention could be redesigned to improve matters. Studies done by microfinance institutions (MFIs) tended to look at their chosen institution alone, and often to idealise it, leaving readers unclear which of the new ideas might work in which environments.

In many places, those programmes have become essential buffers against drought and landlessness, but they also have been plagued by waste and corruption, a record cited by those who argue that a nationwide employment programme would funnel more money, not to the poor, but rather to corrupt politicians, bureaucrats and local power brokers. Now, a number of organisations have shown that such projects can work, that grass-roots capitalism is one of the best routes out of poverty.

It is now almost an item of faith with me that the poor act rationally, however straitened their circumstances. If their undertakings are too small, or their efforts too thinly spread, to be efficient, it is not because they have miscalculated, but because the markets for land, credit or insurance have failed them. Good management of even the smallest asset can be crucial to very poor people, who live in precarious conditions, threatened by lack of income, shelter and food. Importing expensive, unworkable ideas, equipment and consultants from the North simply destroys the capacity of communities to help themselves. Any goal that is driven from the top by international donors and governments not accountable to the communities served and without financial transparency is doomed to fail.

Although imported programmes have the benefit of supplying 'pre-tested' models, they are inherently risky because they may not take root in the local culture when transplanted. Home-grown models have greater chances of success. The hundreds of millions of households who constitute the rural poor are a potential source of great wealth and creativity who, under present institutional, cultural and policy conditions, must seek first and foremost their own survival. Their poverty deprives not only them but also the rest of us of the greater value they could produce under more conducive circumstances. The people who pioneered the world's most successful development programmes recognized this potential and always sought to evoke it. The results have been miraculous.

We need to bring in the poor to the conversation. Interventions that take the end user into account almost always have better success rates than top-down decision-making. But many social enterprises are still not talking enough to their poor customers to find out what they really want, and too often policy makers have no idea what their end beneficiaries really need. I hope that the expanding use of technology across all segments of society will help to create platforms for exchange of ideas, so that people can better express their needs.

The poor are yet to find their voice, even as the media (for that matter, the entire establishment) have become the megaphone of the classes that are prospering. The preference for growth over social justice, indeed, the argument that economic growth is the road to social justice, is advocated over and above increased spending, is required for accelerated growth to translate into inclusive growth? The answer, I fervently believe, lies in inclusive governance. In the absence of Inclusive governance, the people at the grassroots, that is, the intended beneficiaries of poverty alleviation programmes, are left abjectly dependent on a bureaucratic delivery mechanism over which they have no effective control. The alternative system would be participatory development, where the people themselves are enabled to build their own future through elected representatives responsible to the local community and, therefore, responsive to their needs.

Not only is responsive bureaucratic administration almost a contradiction in terms, the Indian experience of the last six decades would appear to confirm that bureaucratic delivery mechanisms absorb a disproportionately high share of the earmarked expenditure: up to 85 paise in the rupee, said Rajiv Gandhi; perhaps 85 paise says the Planning Commission in a recent evaluation; not quite so high, says the Prime Minister. We can leave it to experts to argue how many angels can dance on the head of a pin; for our purposes, it is enough to note that 75% to 85% of expenditure on poverty alleviation schemes is absorbed by the delivery mechanism itself. No wonder outcomes are so derisory. In India, over a hundred schemes are delivered to the same set of beneficiaries through mutually insulated administrative silos, set up by Central government ministries intent on jealously guarding their respective fiefdoms. Thereby, convergence of schemes at the delivery point becomes virtually impossible, thus depriving beneficiaries of the multiplier effect that would operate if the beneficiaries themselves, through their locally elected leaders, were to have the authority to plan and implement the utilisation of these resources in keeping with their own respective priorities. So far, I am on well-trodden ground. But the argument for a systemic reordering of the delivery mechanism to shift from bureaucratic delivery to participatory development runs much deeper.

Top managers, academics and consultants live in a planet of their own—in a total disconnect with the average citizen—dominated by summits, conclaves and conferences- each one considered an important saloon for designing some unique and path breaking solutions. The same big names on podiums, with lofty aspirations and oversized ambitions, preening and drooling the same set of figures, the same weary phrases reverberating the halls. and the same denizens chewing on the same cud amidst the usual fanfare that marks such events as the latter day emperors—presidents, prime ministers, plutocrats, puppets, dictators, heads of scientific bodies and development organizations and barons of finance parade in their pinstripe suits, labour in their ivory towers and ride in their personal jets as poor people continue to suffer the pangs of poverty. The glitz of advertisements, posters, brochures, campaigns, publicity material and the fancy talks overflows with verbiage and rhetorical grandeur that give an impression that a mountain is going into labour. And what we get at the end is just a mouse. The speakers exult in long winded commentaries, without savouring life itself. They are like someone who stand on the bank of a river, taking it as the ultimate destination, while the poet plunges into deep waters, for isn't that the only way to taste the flavour of the water midstream? We live in an age when noisy posturing too often substitutes for reasoned debate and brash opinion trumps hard facts. The thread of the argument often disappears in a blizzard of gee-whiz statistics, acronyms, and catch phrases in interviews with eminent folks of all kinds. Yet the words used to describe them—inclusive growth, environmental sustainability, poverty eradication-are rendered meaningless by overuse. They will quibble over how to fix responsibility, they will fight over words in long documents, they will challenge evidence presented as proof of the crisis, and they will negotiate percentages and deadlines for reducing poverty levels.

ꕥ

During my assignments in rural India I witnessed how seemingly simple knowledge can have a big impact on farming communities. I have been puzzled ever since why information-driven initiatives have not flourished. Many of the Self Help Groups I worked with struggled to come together to save Rs. 20 per month, never mind to become the catalysts of change in their communities. Their struggle was not due to lack of ability, but merely a lack of willingness. My boss had emphasized this point many times, but I did not truly believe him until I witnessed the construction of a community well and installation of a hand pump, the money for which came as voluntary contributions from women. Without any external assistance or prompting, the villagers convened and decided to take up the challenge.

At the site, there was a high level of organization. Records were being kept on how much each family had contributed and worked. Men and women were working diligently together hauling stones up the hill. The entire project was scheduled to be completed within a month. And yet this was the same village whose SHGs could not manage to meet together once a month to save Rs. 20. If only they could be convinced that building the foundations for development, such as constructing water-harvesting structures, or investing in good breed animals for future dairy profits, was of equal importance to that of building the a community well, then rapid changes in the livelihoods of the people could happen.

The project was a watershed. It showed us the potential for collective action that lay beneath the villagers' apparently passive exterior and paved the way for the building of the village centre. Villagers worked together, stitching banners, painting posters, erecting flagstaffs on the roofs, and stringing wires across the street for the reception of government officials who came to visit. They marvelled at this voluntary initiative of the local community. It was a major lesson even for them.

I saw villages that enjoyed a dramatic increase in crop yield and incomes after agricultural scientists advised farmers on watershed techniques—a fancy term for digging ditches so good that soil is not washed away. While it will not solve India's deep-rooted agriculture problems, better information can significantly boost food production and rural incomes. Although there is much discussion in public forums of involving stakeholders for appropriate development of the society in which the poor live, poor people rarely get the opportunity to develop their own agenda and vision or set terms for the involvement of outsiders. The entire participatory paradigm illustrates that people are participating in plans and programs that we—outsiders—have designed. Not only is there little opportunity for them to articulate their ideas, there is also seldom an institutional space where their ingenuity and creativity in solving their own problems can be recognized, respected and rewarded. The situation of the proverbial cart having been placed before the horse. Any such project requires meticulous planning and careful implementation, involving complete and accurate information on all the important variables to be dealt with: socio-cultural, environmental, and economical aspects.

One of the things that can happen as you go into a community to serve it is a subtle dehumanization of the people there. It's not intentional, but it happens, especially when you roll into a village with projects already formulated. There is a difference between being invited into town to live and learn where you can help with the endogenous development process already underway, and arriving with ready-made solutions to problems you haven't yet encountered, but assume (or hope) exist. It's as if you've got a hammer and are looking for nails. This approach shifts the people in your new community from the subject to the object of development. If the inhabitants have not yet given you their trust, and shown you the social topography of the community, the people may even seem like obstacles! You think "If it weren't for these damn people and their baffling behaviour, I'd have had these women's projects finished long ago!"

Tackling poverty requires an approach that must start with the people themselves and encourages the initiative, creativity and drive from below. The strategy must be at the core of any transformatory exercise if the results are to be lasting and enduring. I had the privilege of watching the village women acquire a sense of dignity once they were given tools for self-sufficiency. And I learned, maybe most importantly, to listen with my heart and not just my head. Are poor clients last in the long list of our objectives?

Villagers no longer trust the elite. In this, their instincts are right. The *gram panchayat* (village council) members are also handicapped. On their backs ride the brokers of power and influence, who dispense patronage to convert a mass movement into a feudal oligarchy. They are self-perpetuating cliques who thrive by invoking the slogans of caste and religion and by enmeshing the living body of the panchayat in their net of avarice. For such persons, the masses do not count. The lifestyles of such persons, their thinking—or lack of it—their self-aggrandisement, their corrupt ways, their linkages with the vested interests in society, and their sanctimonious posturing are wholly incompatible with work among the people. They are reducing the panchayat organisation to a shell from which the spirit of service and sacrifice has been drained.

The panchayat leaders and block officials and the local elite show no sensitivity to the poor people's problems during their visits to villages. They strut through arrogantly, treating others like *prajas* (subjects), which anyone of consequence of India usually does. It requires a temperament honed in the company of individuals steeped in noble values to endow oneself with charm, grace and ability to mix easily with all ranks. The villagers consistently speak to visitors scathingly of the snobberies of the elite.

That paradoxical nature of India is a cliché, which has worn its usage rather well, due to the truth embedded in it. The paradox is rooted in the attempted imposition of a modern democratic ethos on an entrenched feudal culture, which articulates itself in various ways. The dominance of a feudal mind-set in India has been overlaid by centuries of Brahmanism which privileges birth over all other attainments, thus preventing the maturing of democracy in the country. Political choices are made not on the basis of merit, but rather on family or other primordial ties. The affirmative action programmes are now aggressively realigning the caste calculus. No one wishes to harm powerful interest groups.

This, however, is not to diminish the role of professional outsiders who have successfully entered into the conditions and outlooks of rural people in order to fashion programmes from the inside out, so to speak, by showing deep respect for the capabilities of the people whose lives they hope to improve and being persistent as well as patient (being impatiently patient, one might say). We must try to relate to our clients as people and not as some mathematical abstraction, some algebraic alphabets. What is now needed is that development managers work with people at the lowest level of the economic ladder rather than dealing them as statistics in a file. We need people with perceptive minds and receptive hearts.

The determinants of poverty reduction are policy instruments that benefit the dominant coalition of political power but also benefit poverty reduction. If a set of instruments harms the interests of the dominant coalition, it will not be implemented, even if it is known to be a determinant of poverty reduction. Advocacy for poverty reduction must mean not only advocacy for instruments that we know will lead to this outcome, but also for a realignment of the dominant coalition in a way that will orient it to the interests of the poor. Specifically, this means that we should advocate for empowerment of the poor so that they can indeed challenge the dominant interests, to shift alliances in a way that will make possible policies and interventions for poverty reduction.

As far as policy matters are concerned, there is a strong concern at the senior levels of banks for reforming the rural credit delivery system and making it more effective. This may be explained by the heightened interest in Self Help Groups among top executives who have participated in seminars or workshops organised by foundations, universities and the government. In fact seminars are also used for business purposes where the institutions sponsoring the show showcase their achievements. These seminars resonate with buzzwords and end in copious policy statements. Participants arrange discussions and seminars over glitzy parties at swanky hotels. I had a quick eye for vanity and I would perceive the frequent incongruities between the way people talked and the realities of the situation.

It must nevertheless be admitted that in most banks, successful development finance programmes are more individual- than institution-driven. Most senior managers are thrifty in the matter of praising juniors. The time has come when we must institutionalize the best practices through recognition of individuals who have innovated them. Recognition is a way of not only indicating an organization's endorsement and appreciation of an individual's work but also bringing it to the notice of those who can replicate it with necessary modification based on the local culture.

Any debate about the economic policy for the poor is usually tortuous, long-winded and insular. Without poverty to eradicate, there will not be anti-poverty programmes from which funds could be siphoned off for private use. Without laws, there will not be opportunities to extort side payments for their violations. A vast number of papers are required to complete even a small piece of work, which then meander through several sections before they can yield any fruitful action. To cut through the fog, we have to lend our ear to the voice of the people who are the stakeholders.

What we need today are innovative solutions that can take into account the peculiarities of the people at the bottom of the pyramid. Social innovation is taking place at multiple levels, driven by passion to make a difference.

Financial institutions have till recently focussed on scaled down versions of their conventional products. They realised very late that the rural society has its own peculiarities and it required exclusive products appropriate to its needs. The poor have different requirements than the urban clients and hence research will have to be conducted on financial versus consumer products to see the feasibility of the product. For example, documentation. Electricity and telephone bills are easily available in cities, but villagers often do not have those amenities. Some villages are plagued by power breakdowns, and so have solar powered or battery powered refrigerators. Therefore, alternative documentation will have to be worked out. A monthly saving scheme is good for city dwellers, but villagers will love to have a daily collection scheme because constraints prevent them from accumulating money over the course of a month.

Thinking about novel uses of existing products, such as mobile phones, is another source of solutions. The mobile phone is being integrated into various business processes, from poor farmers gaining access to commodity prices to providing vital health information to rural families, to paying for water. Since the majority of these farmers are women, this means not only overcoming decades of neglect of smallholder farmers in general, but also overturning generations of entrenched gender inequality, during which women have had less access to the essential elements of farming: land ownership, seed and fertilizer, capital and credit, education and training.

My experience of working with poor women emphasises the fact that work is their foremost priority. Most poor women in villages are intelligent, hard-working and have nerves of titanium. They know that if they do not work, their families do not eat. All manner of self-employment—sewing, delivering small items, making handicrafts—could be facilitated with a small amount of capital for a sewing machine, a bicycle, or tools. Availability of decent loans is far more important to them than shaving a few points off the interest rates of those loans.

Over years of wandering the villages, I have been compelled to revise much of my received wisdom about what our rural priorities should be. We must be challenged to see the reality of poverty and vulnerability through the eyes of a particular individual, typically a woman, and to understand how that person strives to overcome it. This way we can get a feeling of her daily worries and needs and develop solutions that have relevance to her needs.

It's crucial to help people shift their thinking so they believe they can do the job. Role models matter more than words. Mentors are more important than formal training. To that end, we must introduce bank clients to people like themselves who are succeeding in the kind of environment in which they themselves will need to succeed. The tacit knowledge that senior executives have accumulated over the years must be passed on face-to-face, revealing culture in action.

Consider, for example, the remoteness of our professional lives as bankers from our villages. In the village, each successive generation is born into the rigidity of caste; each generation must bear the rapacity of the moneylender and the merchant and the random cruelty of nature: floods, famines and pestilence. And yet the majority survive and adapt. In other words, there is in the villages some collective wisdom for which the professional's knowledge is not a substitute. This is why the divide between the professionals and the villages is so serious; now if we do go to the villages, it is to study them, to do good for them—but not to become *of* them.

You must not volunteer for work where you 'educate' the community about its problems, in which you generate plans and then get 'buy-in' from the community, and in which the priority is the development product (latrines, health centre, church building) rather than the people, for which you bring in the capacity rather than help build it within the community. This kind of 'help' is likely to stunt development because it creates dependency, conflict and feelings of helplessness. If you are already inside such an organization, do what you can to help colleagues realize that development is an ongoing, endogenous process. It cannot simply lurch along, dependent on outsiders arriving with solutions and resources.

Instead of mapping problems from needs through external solutions, we must help the community identify its values and then map these through local resources to develop a vision and action plan. Intervention may still be called for and appropriate strategies devised, but the kind of intervention that gets them over a bump in the road, not the kind that builds the road, provides the car, petrol and driver, buckles the seatbelts and pays the tolls.

What is required is sympathetic but hard-headed leadership, operating from a variety of institutional bases (government agencies, NGOs, banks). It should make common cause with rural people, learning with and from them how to make desired and sustainable improvements in the customers' conditions of life. NGOs that carry out developmental work in the field are stuck within programmes specified by planners in far-removed developmental agencies and donor institutions. Creative plans that run counter to the conventional wisdom at the core of most programmes seldom qualify for funding. Thus, project proposals are prepared to reflect the requirements set by these far-removed planners in terms of methodology and outcomes. Demonstrating compliance on paper ends up more important than getting the job done. As a result, recipients of developmental funds spend significant time preparing reports that will find approval with the planners to qualify for continued funding, and less time worrying about what actually benefits the poor.

I feel that approaches to rural development that respect the inherent capabilities, intelligence and responsibility of rural people and systematically build on their experience have a reasonable chance of making significant advances in improving those people's lives. The real challenge for development practitioners lies in finding tools that are aligned with local capabilities.

If, therefore, nearly fifty years later, it has been found necessary to re-emphasise the need to ensure that social justice accompanies economic growth, it is not because we were not conscious of that need from the start, but because we only now have come to realise that, however high its rate, economic growth does not automatically generate a proportionate rise in economic status.

During my career as a development journalist, I always travelled with a camera. I had a morning college curricula and spent evenings working with a newspaper. Photo-journalism was a specialized field by itself and I had developed enough expertise to get bylines for my pictures. During my rural assignment, this skill further helped me ingratiate myself to the villagers. Whether digging the bed of an irrigation canal or repairing a road at the height of summer, or transplanting rice seedlings in the wind and rain of July, all enthusiastically posed for me. Somebody had spread the myth that the photographs would be shown abroad, and this added to the pleasure of being photographed. My experience as a travel writer had honed my photography skills and I was aware of the entire process from taking a photo to processing and printing it.

The photography also broke the monotony of their work. The camera enabled me even to cross barriers imposed by my bachelorhood. Some months after I had moved into the village, wealthy landowners invited me home to take pictures of their wives, daughters and daughters-in-law. The fact that I did not accept money for taking pictures and that I was taking them all the time added to my reputation for prodigality. In short, the camera became a passport every place. Many a villager knew me as the cameraman.

One of the basic requirements of a bank account is a photograph. Every individual was required to submit three copies of a photograph for opening a bank account. I found this requirement the biggest bottleneck for villagers, particularly women. They would incur not only the expense of the studio photograph itself, but that of travelling not once but twice, often ten kilometres, to the town in which the studio lay, first to have the photograph taken, then back to collect the photographs after the three days it took to process and print the photographs. Dairy farmers were in a worse plight. When an animal died, the insurance company required a close-up photo of the dead animal in a pose that displayed the insurance tag latched to the earlobe. At times, the borrower would surrender his claim if he was not in a position to shell out the required amount for the photograph.

Colour photography had just been introduced in India, and it was a great novelty. Previously, colour photo rolls had been sent to Mumbai for printing, but a lab had recently opened at Nagpur and it was offering a substantial inaugural discount to attract customers. The printing process had a technique that produced four passport-size prints on a single postcard-sized sheet. The cost was therefore kept to the barest minimum. We retained three copies for the bank's use and returned the extra copy to the customer as a complimentary memento. My staff also visited the farms to photograph dead animals for insurance claims; this token service won us a lot of laurels. The bank already had a provision in its operations manual for reimbursement of the expenses of such photographs. We used this provision to purchase photo rolls and defray the expenses of the processing lab.

Since we were regular clients providing both business and publicity to the photo lab, the lab gave us one complimentary roll with a one-time free print of the entire roll as part of a new promotion campaign. We arranged close-up portraits of thirty-five of the poorest households in the village, photographing them against the backdrop of their mud hovels and cattle. We gave them these printouts mounted in attractive frames donated by the lab as a gift on the occasion of the commemoration of Independence Day. This grainy memento still adorns the houses of many families, renewing their memories of their association with the bank.

The reality of village life as experienced by the poor living on the margin of existence is often different from the assumptions made by the administrator who has no ground view and whose understanding is based on secondary sources. These assumptions may also be coloured by past biases and prejudice. It is difficult for us to understand the fears, the hesitancy, the pain and the labour with which the poor live and which therefore separates the project from its implementation, or what is easy or difficult for the rural poor.

As Robert Chambers has pointed out, the rich, the powerful and the urban-based professionals are at the core of the development process while the poor, the weak and the rural people are at the peripheries, leading to a systematic bias in terms of rural poverty. Any attempt at economic reform or better governance cannot succeed without addressing the needs of the poor. Gandhi had this advice for policy makers: 'Recall the face of the poorest and the weakest man whom you may have seen, and ask yourself if the step you contemplate is going to be of any use to him.'

Then there is the new phenomenon of rural development tourism—brief visits which may be part of a CSR initiative of corporate houses who plant saplings in a few villages and then spend a fortune to run massive banner lines tomtomming their commitment to Rural India. Roadside tarmac meetings with the more influential people in rural areas, asking the predetermined questions. Car convoys with the entourage zooming through a crowd of villagers awed by the grand peacockry, as often American expatriates are dispatched who require SUVs. Vehicles are a classic expense because donor agencies love to have cars which can dazzle people and draw attention. These projects really require grassroots workers who can stay a few days at the centre and get full insights into the problems and the needs of the villagers.

The aid structure often involves top-down decisions, incredible bureaucracy and paperwork. Most development practitioners will tend to agree with me that aid personnel normally interact little with the project beneficiaries, and are more interested in the documentation of the partner agency than confirming whether it is practicing what it has documented.

Lack of time eliminates the open-ended question; fact checking is impossible, and prudent, hopeful, or otherwise self-serving lies become accepted as truth. Refugees in a rural camp said of government officials that "They come, and they sign the book, and they go", and "They only talk to the buildings. We have to crane our necks in the caustic heat just to see them, forget about talking with them." "They slouch in grimy plastic chairs under a nearby tree. Or else they plonk themselves down where they can and start beavering away."

The visitor sets out late, delayed by last minute business, by subordinates or superiors anxious for decisions, by breakfast delayed at his wife's eagerness to pack some sandwiches for the husband lest he might have to take a nibble of the unhygienic outside food; there could be a last-minute cable or telephone call from an upcountry colleague. Or delays might come from mechanical or administrative problems with vehicles, or by urban traffic jams. Even if the way is not lost, and there is enough fuel and there are no breakdowns, the programme usually still slips behind schedule. The visitor is ensconced in the luxury of the Land Rover seeking a temporary escape from the rigours of an imposed rural visit through music on headphones.

As the entourage arrives, accompanied with a haversack of sandwiches and soda-water bottles, there is a gala welcome, a tribal dance by girls, women in traditional attire daubing vermilion on the foreheads of the temporary gods, dignitaries warming hands on flickers of holy fire, local notables (headmen, chairmen of village committees, village accountants, progressive farmers) waiting obsequiously for a *darshan* (view) of the dignitaries. Whatever their private feelings, the poor have been told earlier that they should give their children an early bath and dress them in their best clothes. The school teachers have been helping the girls rehearse the welcome dance for the dignitary. All are mouthing slogans that will portray the visitor as a great saviour.

Buntings have been hung; the villagers had kept awake overnight cleaning the entire village. Girls had got up early to deck their front yards with colourful *rangoli* (ornate patterns drawn with coloured chalk powder). As the dignitary's car zooms in, you have the village official in his pinstripe suit chasing the car with impeccable etiquette to be the one privileged to open the door and usher the visitor into a new world.

A day before the visit, the local host is provided with an assortment of high-end brand-name accessories: Bombay Dyeing bed sheets, pillows covers, towels, napkins, toiletries and more. A complete set of Italian crockery in the car of the hostesses will precede the visitor's arrival. They will manage the high tea exercise. The entire consignment of assorted biscuits and choicest dry fruits will be provided. There will be a wide variety of welcome drinks such as coconut milk, Coca-Cola, coffee, tea or milk; at least one should exactly fit the visitors' tastes.

The traditional turban is strung around the dignitary's head along with garlands. Speeches are made. School children sing or clap. Photographs are taken. Buildings, machines, construction works, new crops, exotic animals, the clinic, the school, the new road—all are inspected. Some special group—the Self Help Committee or the women's handicraft group, its members dressed in their best clothes, is seen and spoken to. A small demonstration of manufacture of cottage cheese being done by a girl entrepreneur, a knitting salon by a group of girls and a display of traditional sweetmeats prepared by women are put on display. The guest tastes a few sweetmeats. The elderly woman gets a whole pack nicely wrapped and passes it on to the driver to be delivered to the dignitary on reaching home base.

They nervously respond in ways which they hope will bring benefits and avoid penalties. As the day wears on and heats up, the visitor becomes less inquisitive, asks fewer questions and is finally glad, exhausted and bemused, to retire to the rest house, the host official's residence or back to an urban home or hotel. Before returning, he asks his deputy to write remarks in the Visitors Book using the most fulsome adjectives and he mechanically signs off without bothering to read the remarks. Villagers suggest they have prepared a special meal for the dignitary, putting their culinary skill to the best use. A few offer packs of custard apples and exotic local varieties of vegetables which are mechanically directed to the driver for safekeeping. They are politely told that the dignitary has a restricted diet and prefers to stick to it. After the dignitary's departure, the village swiftly returns to normal, no longer wearing its special face. These people have no time for piffling sentimentality when there's living to be done.

For government staff, there are similar pressures and patterns. On the first appointment, inexperienced technical or administrative officers are posted to the poorer, geographically more remote, and politically less significant areas. Those who are less able, less noticed, or less influential, remain in those outposts longer, if not permanently. The more able and visible, and those who ingratiate themselves to bosses or who have friends in headquarters, are soon transferred to more accessible or prosperous rural areas, or to urban peripheral areas which continue to be classified as rural areas, thanks to certain inept yardsticks set by government authorities. With promotion, contact with rural areas, especially the more remote districts, recedes.

If a serious error is committed, or a powerful politician offended, the officer may earn a 'penal posting', to serve out punishment time in some place with poor facilities—a remote area, hot and healthy, inadequately connected to the nearest town, without proper infrastructure, distant from the capital—in short, a place where poorer people will be found. The pull of urban life will remain: children's education, medical treatment for the family, chances of promotion, congenial company, consumer goods, cinemas, libraries, hospitals, and quite simply power, all drawing bureaucrats away from rural areas and towards the major urban and administrative centres.

Once established in offices in the capital or in regional or provincial headquarters, bureaucrats and bankers quickly become over-committed in terms of their time, unless they are idle and incompetent, or exceptionally able and well-supported. They are tied down by meetings, committees, sub-committees, memoranda, reports, programme notes and urgent papers; vendors trying to get their air conditioners, furniture, computers, taxi and travel booking services organisation-approved;

going daily through the dossier of newspaper cuttings, staff recruitment, training programmes for staff, workshops for themselves; finalising tour itineraries with personal secretaries, discussing weekend recreation plans with liaison staff, disciplinary enquiries, and far too many investment experts with alluring investment options and opportunities. There are times of the year, during the budget cycle, performance review, preparing and approving business plans, supervising proper juxtaposition of figures on the spreadsheet, when they cannot contemplate leaving their desks. The very emphasis on agricultural and rural development creates work, which further restricts them in their offices.

If the head of the department or organisation is inactive, he may be relatively free. But the more he tries to drive his goals and introduce new management techniques that he picks up from the occasional seminars that are part of his professional circuit, the busier is our official. Post-seminar and -workshop organisation consumes further precious time: business cards sorted, emails sent to important participants with brief but pithy sentences praising their ideas, and acknowledging with appreciation emails from participants who have similarly eulogised him.

By then it will be time for the next seminar. The same formalities have to be completed again. Registration, travel and hotel bookings, a short background paper prepared by the subject expert in the organisation. The circuit continues and the networking process keeps sprawling, spawning a planet of its own. So the more paperwork is generated, the more coordination and integration are called for, the more reports have to be written and read, and the more inter-departmental coordination and liaison committees set up.

The more important these committees become, the more members they have, the longer their meetings take, and the longer their minutes grow. The demands of aid agencies are a final straw, requiring data, justifications, reports, evaluations, visits by missions, and meetings with ministers. Each member is on so many committees that it is hard to ensure that he at least marks his attendance even though he may be mentally occupied with the agenda of another meeting. The staff has to spend overtime processing data, finding logical conclusions and marshalling arguments to support their assumptions. A whole battery of staff is immersed in designing flip charts and preparing Powerpoint presentations, embellishing them with illustrations, charts and tables and drafting executive summaries of committee reports. The grip of the urban offices, capital traps and elite activities has tightened for government, aid agency and NGO staff alike: more and more emails, meetings, negotiations, reports, often with fewer staff. Participation has risen in the pandemic of incestuous workshops, many of them about poverty, consuming even more precious time.

When poor communities think at the human level, all their goals are interconnected. But under the internationally conceived top-down model absent a global grass-roots movement with the communities as equal partners, the goals have been compartmentalized into project mode, to suit donors and governments. Where possible, I think it's much better to support local groups rather than those international organizations, as the locals cost much less than foreigners and they usually have a much better idea of what people need. Outside aid prevents people from searching for their own solutions, while corrupting and undermining local institutions and creating a self-perpetuating lobby of aid agencies.

The urge to reduce the poor to a set of clichés has been with us for as long as there has been poverty. The poor appear in social theory as much as in literature, by turns lazy or enterprising, noble or thievish, angry or passive, helpless or self-sufficient. Even journalists who feign such deep interest in the lives of the poor struggle to get even a single fact straight. When people talk about fighting poverty, they talk about making agriculture more productive, educating girls, passing laws to prohibit discrimination, building roads, fighting traditional superstitions about health, equalizing the balance of trade between countries—there are endless solutions, because poverty is endlessly complicated.

The international poverty industry is worth tens of billions of US dollars a year. It's bursting with experts and consultants. There is a surfeit of studies, reports, books, PhD grants, loans, consultancies. Rural development is now becoming an old-fashioned cause. Rural reform has become the policy bandwagon everybody is clambering on, and every progressive politician across the country wants a piece of the rural development pie. What the new bandwagon implies is rural reform, a new way of developing the villages. Changing their mindset from a charity-oriented approach to an opportunity-oriented one. To bring a new novelty to their appellation, writers and journalists have added the new professional label of 'activist'. This double-barrelled appellation is a lethal combination, with the country's judicial system also moving in as an important stakeholder. The political leaders too have their share of acrobatics in the development 'circus', with minions projecting themselves as missionaries leading the crusade to redeem the wretched.

Indian development finance experts have come into their own and, after mystics and godmen, they occupy a good position in the global space. Poverty does not catch their attention, but poverty stalks their arguments in metaphorical guise; what it refers to remains vague. The language used to describe the poor is the purplest of late Victorian prose, while the actual existence of poverty was proven by the simple expedient of citing the observations of British administrators about the conditions of the Indian poor: terms are used that the poor themselves can make no sense of. Figures are tabled, graphed and charted, and invariably used to compare India with other countries, but not Indians with Indians.

I recall the days when my idealism for the Bhoodan movement was fierce enough to blind me to the difficulties of rural reforms. I realize now that the greatness of a rural reformer lies not in ideology but in natural human qualities that can inspire faith and fervour in people.

The important thing is not the number of years you've worked in the field or your educational background—what is important is whether you are committed. To create a cadre of visionary rural programme leaders, organizations need to send people out irrespective of whether they're from a local college or an elite institution, a college graduate or an MBA, to discover India, spend time in villages to better understand rural culture and the ecosystem. You have to be an anthropologist first and second a financial manager second.

During my engagement with NGOs, I found some of them very possessive of their staff and clients. To consider the poor as a permanent source of income is outright commercialization, which strongly militates against the basic mission of a civil society—ensuring that people don't remain pawns in the hands of their leaders. Civil society has lost a great deal of its credibility by trying to keep the stakeholders it represents as captives and hostages; it holds a moral responsibility to develop the capabilities of the poor such that they become sole arbiters of their destiny.

Today, in the absence of any legal definition, a voluntary organization comprises a wide range of civil society and interest groups, which are also called Non-Governmental Organizations (NGOs) and non-profit associations. The people associated with them are generally human rights or social activists, academics, intellectuals, celebrities, high-profile journalists, think-tank hirelings, retired bureaucrats, jurists, lawyers, environmentalists and so on. They espouse a range of cultural, political, economic, security and philanthropic considerations.

In terms of resources and expertise, some of these NGOs are sometimes as strong, if not stronger, than some smaller sovereign states and international bodies. They have the capacity and capability to breed new ideas, advocate protests, mobilise support, both within and across the borders, provide goods and services, shape, implement and enforce national and international commitments. Their vast network, crossing territorial boundaries, offers the civil society groups an unprecedented reach and extent of influence. Some NGO leaders have influenced the decision-making process of the government from within by being part of government delegations.

The members of civil society must understand the great personal risks and hazards that those in positions of authority have to face. They must remember that loans are given out of public deposits, not out of State money, and represent the hard-earned precious savings of the poor. Bankers are the custodians of this money, and civil society members have a responsibility to educate the people about the sanctity of loan repayments. Then there are cases where officials lose their promotions and even sometimes their jobs when forced by deceitful borrowers into actions which are later labelled negligent acts by the institutions. The civil society space has begun to be dominated by groups with questionable credentials. Civil society activists must be made to undergo competency tests from independent authorities to qualify as legitimate activists. The government is equally clever in patronizing those groups owing allegiance to its ideology. Civil society should show the same zeal and commitment in cleaning its own house the way it wants to clean the stables of the establishments.

Despite positive contributions, NGOs have not been involved in developmental undertakings intended to create large employment and wide income generation through sustainable businesses. This is attributable to their lacking good managerial skills and the organizational structure necessary to take up business ventures. Further, donor funds are usually restricted to narrowly defined projects. Consequently, NGOs are best suited to play the role of support to projects funded by governments and international agencies, or those limited initiatives approved by private donors.

Unfortunately, those NGOs that carry out developmental work in the field are circumscribed within programmes specified by planners in developmental agencies and donor institutions. New ideas that deviate from those already specified by planners seldom qualify for any funding. Thus, project proposals are prepared to reflect the requirements set by these planners in terms of methodology and outcomes. Demonstrating compliance on paper trumps actually getting the job done effectively. As a result, recipients of developmental funds spend significant time preparing reports for the planners to qualify for continued funding rather than conducting the projects for which they are seeking funding.

Civil society has failed Bharat, not India, compromising the very spirit of volunteerism. They do not know what sacrifice means. They have not managed to set an example of simplicity, of compassion, of humility, of courage (as Hemingway defined it, 'grace under pressure'). Civil society has no role models to offer. All we see is greed and materialism surrounding us and there is nothing that sets civil society apart. The only sign of success is how much money you make or how big your business is.

Rural poverty alleviation is not a matter of resources; it's about designing policies that will actually work on the ground. We design something while sitting in government offices with some experts but we never try things out. We never admit failure. We never suggest returning to NREGA and take what worked and dump what didn't.

Skill development for wage employment is perhaps most crucial to long-term alleviation of poverty. However, much thought needs to be devoted to evolving the right training method. It should focus on learning by doing rather than in the classroom. A range of entrepreneurs in the fields of construction, textiles, leather, gems and jewellery, and so on will have to be brought in, and candidates will need to work as apprentices. A better approach to eliminate poverty, however, would be to make the environment conducive to increased flow of credit to the poor, leaving micro-level credit management to financial institutions, and transferring the subsidy from the individual level to the community level for human capital formation of the poor and developing physical infrastructure useful to them. The government's involvement must be confined to macro affairs such as policy formulation, framing incentive mechanisms for both banks and the bureaucracy to make poverty reduction a priority.

There is growing evidence and recognition that serving poor people requires intentional outreach to those living below a nation's poverty line. However, matching intent with action requires strong commitment from businesses' management to improving the lives of poor people through better incentives, leadership, communication, and culture. It also requires effective use of information systems—electronic or manual methods of systematically collecting, analysing and acting on information in a timely manner.

I often wondered why was it that when there were so many government programmes for the welfare of the rural poor that poverty was yet so endemic. Either the nets were not cast sufficiently wide or too many holes were blown in them. But money, as a senior programme officer told me, is irrelevant. "What is the point of putting more water into a bucket already leaking badly? The problem is not lack of money. It is lack of accountability of those who spend it." Even the government feels that 85% of development spending does not reach the poor, being either sponged up by the 'delivery mechanism'—the consultants, advisers, their equipment or studies—or simply pocketed outright. This has become a touchstone for all government programmes and is now parroted in all Indian development literature.

In many cases, Western aid is running down bureaucratic rat holes. Fortunately, civil societies are training local leaders to serve as watchdogs by using the audacious Right to Information Act. The aim is not to directly blame or indict per se—bare-knuckled confrontation would alienate the government—but to remind public servants that someone is watching them, and that the negligent will be named and shamed.

A critical success factor is creating organisational capabilities at the local level that can mobilise and manage resources effectively to benefit the many intended recipients. We need plans, systems, mutual accountability and financing mechanisms. And even before we have all of that apparatus in place—what I call the economic plumbing—we must first understand more concretely what such a strategy means to the people who can be helped. Capacity building at the village level is crucial to making them aware of the entire development process, including the aid structure, so that they are in a position to monitor it effectively.

In a small project, everyone can participate in decision-making. Practical advantages of participation for project effectiveness and sustainability weigh heavily in favour of same: participation can reduce waste of project resources and lead to recurrent cost recovery. Most important, it gives people a stake in the project resources and thus makes them willing to support it. The negatives of participation are that it is difficult, time-consuming, and tricky; it can permit elites or freeloaders to get more than their share; it can stir up conflicts that society and culture have traditionally been able to keep under wraps; it can alienate governments; and so on.

The success will depend on the charisma and the personal commitment of the project leader who inspires the team and lets their creative aquifers charge back to life. Although there is much discussion in public forums of the appropriate development of the society in which the poor live, poor people rarely get the opportunity to develop their own agenda or set terms for the involvement of outsiders. The entire participatory paradigm illustrates that poor people are participating in plans and programmes that we—outsiders—have designed. Not only is there little opportunity for them to articulate their ideas, there is also seldom an institutional space in which their ingenuity and creativity in solving their own problems can be recognized, respected and rewarded.

Financial development through public participation enables individuals to make the most of their potential and represents a tool for expanding financial democracy. We have made historic strides toward the consolidation of political democracy, revolutionizing governance in India's rural hinterland, but these have not been accompanied by the democratization of means and opportunities. Financial democracy is fundamental for achieving greater inclusiveness, improving social cohesion, and generating broad-based growth. It is therefore crucial for economic dynamism and political stability; the lack of financial democracy prevents people from gaining access to resources that would enable them to make the most of the opportunities that they have!

True development involves a transformation of the state of a human being. However, such a transformation must have the active involvement and participation of those being affected by it. True development is one that transforms groups without destroying their culture, traditions, environment, livelihood and social patterns, which must be preserved and protected because they are central to the very life of the people. The forests around them provide food, medicine, and livelihood, a sustainable solution to the triple whammy of food security, healthcare and employment which the state is ill-equipped to address. True development shouldn't translate into development as seen by the elite. It must be development as seen by those whose lives are to be transformed.

A development strategy that has been successful in one village may not necessarily give the same results in a neighbouring village. Hence the renewed emphasis of planners on area specific plans. Transplanting cultures has been a favourite idea of armchair development experts, but time has shown that nothing could be as damaging as the imposition of alien culture. Each society, howsoever nascent, has a social and cultural apparatus that regulates and balances the divergent traits and traditions. I have always been guided by Paul Devitt's famous words: "The poor are often inconspicuous, inarticulate and unorganised. Their voices may not be heard at public meetings, in communities where it is customary for only the big men to put in their views. It is rare to find a body or institution that adequately represents the poor in a certain community or area."

The reforms in the areas of land, water, forests and environment will be ineffective if they don't give space to the voice of those affected by the reforms. These communities comprise eighty-five percent of the country's population, yet none find even half a percent's space in these seminars and conferences, in particular when we are deliberating programmes targeted towards women.

Participatory development attempts to move away from externally led interventions. It aims to facilitate action and social change that is led and shaped by the so-called 'beneficiaries' themselves. It emerged as an alternative to the top-down development approaches of the 1950s and '60s.But as participatory development gained importance so did the critiques from other scholars. At the turn of this century, *Participation: the New Tyranny?* challenged the assumption that participatory development represents a shift in power relations from development experts to the local communities. The main critique is that development practitioners and organisations are not passive facilitators. They own the tools, choose the topics and ultimately shape and direct the processes. So rather than a shift in power relations, participatory development was seen as a mask perpetuating the dominance of Western actors over the recipients of Indian aid.

Participatory development has now adopted a more pragmatic approach, which results in a wide spectrum of methods used, most of which are less idealistic than their original Freirean roots. Participatory projects can also differ from one another in their nature and objectives; there is no easy single answer to how to implement them, but looking at what pitfalls to avoid can be a place to start.

The early nineties of the last century saw the introduction of a sound participatory paradigm initiated by Robert Chambers, known as Participatory Rural Appraisal (PRA). It was designed to involve all the stakeholders of a development programme in the entire decision making process. It caught on when microfinance gained vogue and was meant to involve the villagers themselves in identifying prospective borrowers, loan activities and loan amounts. Participatory Rural Appraisal is an approach to the analysis of local problems and the formulation of tentative solutions with local stakeholders. It makes use of a wide range of visualisation methods for group-based analysis to deal with spatial and temporal aspects of social and environmental problems. It mainly deals with a community-level scale of analysis but is increasingly being used to help deal with higher-level systemic problems.

The techniques are typically used in the field to gather qualitative data, often to complement quantitative data derived from traffic counts and origin and destination data. We have to begin with the people who know most about their own livelihood systems. This approach must value and develop the recipients' knowledge and skills, and put into their hands the means to achieve self-development. This will require a reshaping of current practices and thinking associated with development assistance. In short, it will require the adoption of a new paradigm. This emerging participatory development paradigm suggests two perspectives: involving local people in the selection, design, planning and implementation of programmes and projects that will affect them, thus ensuring that local perception, attitudes, values and knowledge are taken into account as fully as possible; and to make more continuous and comprehensive feedback an integral part of all development activities.

More an eclectic situational style (the humble, learning outsider) than a method, the Participatory Rural Appraisal is distinguished at its best by the use of local graphic representations created by the community that legitimize local knowledge and promote empowerment.

The important concepts of PRA are:

- **Empowerment**. Knowledge is power. Knowledge arises from the process and results of the research that, through participation, come to be shared with and owned by local people. Thus the professional monopoly of information, used for planning and management decisions, is broken. New local confidence is generated, or reinforced, regarding the validity of their knowledge. "External" knowledge can be locally assimilated.
- **Respect**. The PRA process transforms the researchers into learners and listeners, respecting local intellectual and analytical capabilities. Researchers have to learn a new "style". Researchers must avoid at all costs an attitude of patronizing surprise that local people are so clever they can make their own bar charts etc. The "ooh-aah" school of PRA works against its own principles of empowerment and indicates shallow naivete on the part of the researcher. A good rule of thumb is that when you can really understand the local jokes, poetry and songs, then you may feel you are starting to understand the people's culture.
- **Localization**. The extensive and creative use of local materials and representations encourages visual sharing and avoids imposing external representational conventions.
- **Enjoyment**. PRA, well done, is, and should be, fun. The emphasis is no longer on "rapid" but on the process.
- **Inclusiveness**. Enhanced sensitivity, through attention to process; include marginal and vulnerable groups, women, children, aged, and destitute.

Despite its limitations, the concentrated power of formalization of community knowledge through participatory techniques can generate an impressive amount of information in a relatively short space of time, leaving time for more selective structured formal surveys where they are necessary and of value. However if PRA becomes part of the global development agenda, there are risks of:

- **"Hijacking"**. When this occurs, the PRA agenda is externally driven, and used to create legitimacy for projects, agencies and NGOs.

- **Formalism**. The "PRA hit team" arrives in a local community to "do a PRA". This abrupt and exploitative approach is all too common in project-based PRAs where there is a deadline to meet, or in scheduled training courses.
- **Disappointment**. Local expectations can easily be raised. If nothing tangible emerges, local communities may come to see the process as a transient external development phenomenon. Threats. The empowerment implications of PRA, and the power of its social analysis, can create threats

Poverty cannot be measured by income alone, hence the need to identify categories of wealth relevant to the specific village or locality, e.g. animal ownership, type of house, size of family, farm size and other criteria. Wealth ranking enables villagers to rank households in the community according to economic and other 'well-being' categories. This helps identify target group members for projects, specifically the poorest sections of a society. It also subdivides larger groups for further PRA discussions. Differences in wealth and well-being affect people's perceptions and coping strategies. It is important to understand this prior to further appraisal or planning. This type of ranking not only discusses relative positions of households in a community, but also points to local indicators of wealth and well-being.

Another very important technique, complementary to PRA, is resource mapping. The women can be made aware of rudimentary planning skills that can help in mapping the resources in their settlements, and initiating a discussion on how to increase their access to resources. It is for the first time they use *rangoli* (powdered chalk of diverse colours) powder, chalks and pens to draw maps of the village on the temple platform, wall of the gram panchayat building or under a tree. They sketch a map of their settlement, featuring houses, infrastructure, roads, boundaries, and survey specific services—drinking water sources, assessment of schools and health centres. Once the map is drawn, the community identifies the features they want eliminated or added in five years' time. They then draw a map of the future settlement comprising elements they want to see in the community and spell out steps they must take to achieve this. They estimate the time and resources needed and identify the people who will be responsible for each of the steps. Whether they are attending a dialogue with the block officials or in training, they are able to articulate the village problems and assess what needs to be done. They then use this as a record to monitor and track whether these activities have been carried out and whether their development objectives have been achieved.

It is possible to distinguish three distinct objectives of self-education: development, local governance, and empowerment. The first enables women to identify their survival needs, map available resources to address those needs, decide upon an appropriate strategy through participatory planning, acquire requisite skills (be it masonry or keeping accounts), mobilize community resources and act in a collective manner. The second concerns skills required for local governance, the possession of which allows for greater and more fruitful interaction with the local political structures and ultimately a more inclusive vision of social development. The third is about the strength that women derive from being members of collectives, which allows them to be more assertive in dealing with issues and also have an expanded coverage (geographical as well as issue-wise).

A decade ago, many in the development community acted with the best of intentions, but without the best of evidence. If households lack clean water—help build wells; if people suffer ill health—health services; if the poor lack capital to start businesses, give them credit. But reality is complicated. Well water can be contaminated, people don't always use their local clinic, and savings or insurance may be better than credit. In theory, the poor themselves are in the best position to know what their communities need and to demand accountability from their governments. In reality, however, community-driven development is one of the least understood areas of poverty work.

The problem with the villages in Central India where I spent a major part of my career in rural banking was that the people were known for following their instincts; they followed each other. There was not one leader in the bunch; there were scores of them. They followed each other into oblivion. The womenfolk would huddle behind curtains, giggling shyly at us, content to fade into the background, letting their husbands speak for them or they would blink a coded language to fellow women with their eyelids.

I saw my role as that of the initiator. I was a catalyst for change and the one who 'intervened for change'. In other words, the perception was that of myself as the leader, insomuch as the group action traced back to a set of actions for which I was responsible. It may have been an idea or a set of ideas. Gradually, I began to understand that the perceptions and ideas exist in different forms in people's minds already. What is really needed is the time and space and opportunity for putting them into action.

All around me, I saw development programmes failing because they did not take the politics of the ground reality into account. An effort for deep-rooted social change needed to derive its strength from the people it intended to benefit. I worked in rural projects for close to three decades, and throughout this time was disappointed by the way government, banks and development agencies approached rural development. Their traditional approach failed to build the capacity of the people. They undertook projects that kept funds flowing, but failed to consult the affected villages. The projects weren't collaborations with the people and the result was a lack of sustainability. Most importantly, the people were not empowered or valued enough to learn and think for themselves in finding solutions. Instead, they were simply instructed and subsequently followed direction like servants.

Tackling poverty requires a fundamentally different approach: one that starts with people themselves and encourages the initiative, creativity and drive from below that must be at the core of any transformation of their lives if it is to be lasting. If people can be given the support they need to make important decisions in their own communities, to build their own democracies in their own ways, they can do the rest themselves. In doing so, they will not only move their own communities out of poverty, they will take the world with them. Change must come from within: communities must make their own decisions regarding their future. We have to promote participatory approaches that address the specific needs of each community, as well as increased education.

The bit-push thinking brushes over one of the underlying problems of aid, that it is fungible—that monies set aside for one purpose are easily diverted towards another; they can be set towards agendas that can be worthless, if not detrimental, to growth. Proponents of aid themselves have acknowledged that unconstrained aid risks being consumed rather than invested, of going into private pockets, instead of the public purse. When this happens, as it so often does, no real punishments or sanctions are ever imposed. So more grants can and usually do mean more graft.

Economic development and social change cannot be imposed from without. They must be sought by the individual pursuing opportunities for self-realization. People considering giving aid should have the open mindedness to listen to those who work in the field and live the day-to-day challenges. That respect opens many doors. Lasting change comes about so slowly that you may not notice it until people resist being taken care of—they need to be given a chance to fulfil their own potential. If we can inspire people around the world to reconsider what it means to be poor, then we will have made a real impact. When we design solutions that recognize the poor as clients or customers and not as passive recipients of charity, we have a real chance to end poverty. And I believe we can do that in our generation. I learnt very early a lesson in the importance of empathy—not one that comes from a place of superiority, but one born from a profound humility and sympathy.

If the primary focus is ending poverty, we must establish partnerships between communities so that they learn practical knowledge and skills from one another. Importing unworkable ideas, equipment and consultants destroys the capacity of communities to help themselves. That model encourages colossal falsification of figures, excessive hiring of private consultants and contractors, conflicts of interest and a massive patronage system. The development community seems constantly and restlessly in search of a singular approach that will 'solve' poverty. The fundamental flaw with this system is that each new approach fails to break out of the underlying technocratic and specialized paradigm in development work. I have found armchair and ivory-towered development experts apt to unveil new buzzwords every few years, only to toss them aside. I have also found how creative risks and an innovative spirit can revive development work.

In his reflections on fieldwork, the doyen of Indian anthropologists, Professor M.N. Shrinivas, described successful ethnography as passing through several stages. An anthropologist is 'once-born' when he goes initially to the fields, thrust from familiar surroundings into a world he has very little clue about. He is 'twice-born' when, on living for some time among his tribe, he is able to see things from their viewpoint. To those anthropologists, fortunate enough to experience it, this second birth is akin to a Buddhist urge of consciousness, for which years of study or mere linguistic facility do not prepare one. All of a sudden, one sees everything from the native's point of view, be it festivals, fertility rites or the fear of death. A banker or a development expert is no less an anthropologist than a sociologist: he is a financial or a development anthropologist.

There was a need to find a research method that would give power to the powerless and make people the subject, not the object of research. The methodologies employed by the anthropologists marked a radical departure from the research methodologies of the social sciences and the mathematical objective systems of the physical sciences. These methodologies provided 'windows' that took people's own words and ideas at face value. As participant-observers, the anthropologist, the social activist and the development worker lived together with communities and chronicled their felt needs, priorities, art and worldviews. This marked the beginning of the practice of a participatory alternative to conventional research. There was also an intellectual ferment that permeated academe during the 1960s that questioned the ivory tower stance of development research and how the results were being used.

Take a lesson from this field experience. Laxman was an extremely poor landless agricultural labourer who lived in a village in Chandrapur. A well-meaning official decreed that Laxman should be given a subsidised loan to buy a rope-making machine. Laxman, afraid that he might not be able to repay the loan, tried to resist this offer, but by that time the loan had already been sanctioned and he was firmly told to take it. The rope-making machine turned out to be defective, and while the bank officials kept promising that they would send someone to repair it, this never happened. Unable to get the machine repaired himself, Laxman sold it for a relatively small sum and bought seven goats with the proceeds. One year later, six of the goats had died. Laxman was left with one small goat and a debt larger than his entire annual income. It is extremely necessary that we ensure that development programmes have relevance to the beneficiary and can be profitably sustained by the local economy.

When programmes viewed their clients as beneficiaries, they tended to see them as relatively passive people and to picture microenterprise finance as a transfer of money from rich to poor. In such a context, decisions about what type of help to provide were made on the basis of what programme designers thought would be good for the beneficiaries. At the same time, such programmes spent a great deal of effort deciding which beneficiary groups were the most deserving of assistance and how to target them. The new microenterprise finance programmes look at clients as customers they wish to serve. Policies need to be understood in their proper context. We need to try them, fail, redesign, and succeed.

Think of policy as a live object, a domain to engage all stakeholders in. Talk to customers, because they have a sense of what they want, the life they want. Every time we make policies we forget that the customers have ambitions, aspirations. They are not zombies.

When foreign dollar investors make millions off the backs of the poor, the poor are liable to display a decided lack of gratitude. This is a global issue, which should be addressed by scaling back, going local, giving borrowers ownership of the loan process, and generally being much less ambitious when it comes to growth rates. Much better that full-service banks grow organically out of local communities than monoline microlenders parachute in, flush with venture-capital funds, make a huge splash, and then implode.

The idea is to use local wisdom before we involve expertise from outside. Encourage private initiative without commercializing education. Give private initiative more responsibility, more space, more freedom. As things stand now, the formal system alone cannot answer the challenge of rural education. It destroys initiative and creativity. Tackling poverty requires a fundamentally different approach: one that encourages the initiative, creativity and drive from below that must be at the core of any transformation of their lives that is to be lasting.

The failure of so many development interventions over the past half century can be partly attributed to their lack of rootedness in the society they were designed to change. For development interventions to catalyse fundamental change, they must engage with people's identity and values, whether they be individuals, communities, organizations or indeed nations. Capacity-building needs to be grafted onto pre-existing foundational values, rather than importing another's value base. Experience suggests that a participatory process helps ensure more active engagement by local people, a greater degree of local ownership, and increased reliability and quality assurance. It also helps overcome some of the ethical issues around such processes, including agreeing on its scale and scope, who is involved, and who has access to the data.

The key to strengthening the sustainability of livelihood strategies lies with the empowerment of the primary stakeholders or users. Additionally, it is necessary to provide them with the ability to link with state, market or civil society participants. These linkages provide access to assets which are a critical factor in strengthening poor people's livelihoods. Access to assets through participatory management does not simply mean access to use of resources: it also means the capacity to act, to negotiate, to debate and to make decisions. Participatory methods, creatively evolved and carefully facilitated, have opened up aspects of life which have been thought too private, sensitive or dangerous to make public or to analyse.

An early example was wealth or well-being ranking, in which members of a community first draw a social map showing all households, then list these on cards, and then sort them into piles according to degrees of wealth or, more usually, some concept of well-being. Middle-class urban professionals often regard this as either impossible, or unethical, supposing it will be demeaning for those who are worse off. These fears have proved unfounded.

Although the data is skimpy, many of the anti-poverty schemes don't appear to have a beneficiary orientation. The beneficiary perspective, that is, the scheme seen from the point of view of the beneficiary, the rural poor, is missing. Targets, commands, exhortations and threats come from above. From the periphery and bottom comes a weaker flow of filtered information which placates and misleads. In meetings, subordinates are upbraided, cajoled and given orders and plaudits from visitors. A few prominent villagers are cultivated, and to them are parroted sentences that can sound musical to the ears of visitors.

Inundated by the demands of high profile visitors, the managers set up public relations units. When visitors come, a fluent guide follows a standard route and a standard routine. The same people are met; the same buildings entered, the same books signed, the same polite praise inscribed in the book against the visitors' names. Questions are drowned in statistics; doubts inhibited by hand-outs. Inquisitive visitors depart, loaded with research papers, technical evaluations, and annual reports which they will probably never read, with a sense of guilt at the unworthy scepticism which promoted their probing questions, and impressed by the charisma of the exceptional leader or manager who created it. They write their journey reports, evaluations and articles on the basis of these impressions.

The first participatory camp for mapping rural resources I conducted was in a village called Saori Bidkar in Chandrapur; we had a day-long camp in which residents of neighbouring villages and the staff of banks, government departments, NABARD, NGOs, and representatives of IFAD participated. Under a canvas in kaleidoscopic colours, strung on poles for shade, festooned with buntings and colourful helium balloons, with pennants in bright colours flying exuberantly, we sat in groups each of which had a heterogeneous composition.

Participatory development stands for partnership which is built upon the basis of dialogue among the various actors, during which the agenda is jointly set, and local views and indigenous knowledge are deliberately sought and respected. This implies negotiation rather than the dominance of an externally set project agenda. Thus people become actors instead of beneficiaries. Participation is concerned with the organized efforts to increase control over resources and regulative institutions in given social situations on the part of groups and movements of those hitherto excluded from such control. The importance of participation can be particularly seen in decision-making and evaluation, rather than stressing control and, by implication, issues of power. Participation can be seen as a process of empowerment of the deprived and the excluded. This view is based on the recognition of differences in political and economic power among different social groups and classes. Participation in this sense necessitates the creation of organizations of the poor which are democratic, independent and self-reliant.

For rural communities, participation is a way to identify and implement priority rural development activities through better use of existing resources. To do this, communities analyse constraints as well as resources available, identify and agree upon priority problems, develop action plans to address the priority problems, take charge of implementing the action plans, and pressure the service providers and development organizations to provide the necessary assistance. Communities also identify what incremental resources are needed and organize themselves to try to mobilize these resources. Moreover, villagers themselves influence how the development organizations and service providers organize their work with the village. Through their strengthened organizations, villages can more strongly voice their satisfaction or dissatisfaction with the services received, and indicate how service delivery can be improved.

The process is:

- *Diagnosis.* Through village mapping exercises, semi-structured interviews, transects, daily and seasonal schedules, and social structure diagrams, villagers analyse their situation and identify problems, challenges and possible solutions. To ensure the active participation of all members, the villagers are asked to divide themselves into groups based on age, gender, ethnic group or other affiliation. Different tools used in the diagnostic exercises allows for the villagers to complement and cross-check the information obtained through one tool with information from another.

- *Identifying priority problems.* The diagnostic exercises can result in a long list of village problems. Each group is asked to select four to five priority problems.
- *Problem and solution analysis.* The priority problems are analysed in mixed groups, using a method called the problem tree. For each problem, the group analyses the underlying causes and identifies the effects of the problems. This raises villagers' awareness that many problems are due to their own actions (for example, cutting of trees leading to erosion and soil degradation). Finally, villagers name possible solutions. Here again, villagers become aware of their capacity to influence priority problems using their existing resources.
- *Action plans.* Village groups, together with the team of facilitators, identify the actions most likely to produce the desired results and develop detailed action plans specifying responsibilities, labour and resource needs, implementation timetable, and monitoring indicators.
- *Village organizations.* Once the villagers adopt their action plans, they decide whether their existing organizations are adequate to oversee the plans' implementation or whether they need to create a new organization to handle this responsibility. In addition, villagers also identify committees that will be in charge of implementing specific activities.

General principles of the participatory approach

Although there is no singular and uniform participatory approach, all conform to certain general principles:

Encourage participants to take responsibility

Participatory approaches encourage the community to take responsibility for its own development agenda. Rather than wait for outside assistance, the community can undertake activities that they themselves regard as the highest priorities.

Respect village diversity

Although the village is a discrete geographic and administrative unit, it is not homogenous. People or groups have conflicting interests or perceptions. Development practitioners should be careful to give all socioeconomic groups equal weight in decision-making.

Promote participation for all

For socio-cultural reasons, it may be a challenge for women, youth, the poor and others to speak out in village meetings. Facilitators should make sure that people from disadvantaged groups are able to express their opinions and participate actively in decision-making.

Reconcile different interests

Many problems require group decisions. Actions which solve the problems of some groups can harm other groups. The participatory approach recognizes that different groups within villages have different interests, and that the decision-making process must take all groups into account.

Listen to the community

Service agency staff arrive in villages with expertise but not with ready-made solutions. Rather, they are expected to focus on problems that they consider most pressing and that should be addressed immediately. The compilation of the list of individual groups' priorities becomes the list of village priority problems.

Listen to the villagers

They also encourage villagers to think through their own problems. Each person has knowledge and ideas which can contribute to finding solutions to village problems. There is a proverb from Benin, "Knowledge, like fire, can be found at the home of one's neighbour."

Involve multidisciplinary teams

There is another proverb, "Two know better than one." Involving people from different service agencies, with different training and backgrounds allows the group to benefit from different knowledge and perspectives.

Collaboration among service agencies is essential to integrate the activities of all those working in the village.

Examine the situation from different points of view

Approaching a problem with only one point of view, based on one tool or technique, can lead to wrong solutions. It is better to use a triangular approach, looking at a problem from at least three different perspectives, to ensure that the information collected will be more reliable.

Adapt to local situations

Although the participatory methods and tools are large and diversified, it is up to the team of facilitators to decide which to use and then adapt them to local conditions.

The actors and their roles

Each actor involved in village participation—community members, service and development agency staff, political and administrative authorities—has a unique role to play and task to perform. As facilitators, development agency staff must encourage villagers to reflect on their situation, analyse their problems and identify possible solutions. As specialists with expertise, they are responsible for informing the villagers of technical solutions to the problems. They can also facilitate contact between the village and service and development agencies. The challenge for administrative authorities at regional and national levels is to take the concerns of local people into consideration when allocating resources for development activities. Quality village-level planning can serve as the basis for regional development planning and programming of service agencies' activities. The participatory approach thus implies that the attitudes and behaviour of each actor in local development must change. Participation leads away from a relationship based on dependence and hierarchical position to one based on partnership and collaboration.

In one case story, the village organization found resources to buy seeds by reallocating funds meant for a tarpaulin to protect funeral-goers against rain. The organization also influences villagers to manage their natural resources more effectively, such as encouraging villagers to use organic matter as fertilizer rather than as fuel, construct terraces to protect soils against erosion and use more efficient stoves to conserve fuel and therefore trees.

Villages are confronted with so many problems that it is impossible for the villagers to handle all of them with their meagre existing resources. How can the team of facilitators avoid creating unrealistic expectations when asking villages to identify their priority problems? It is important to highlight the difference between consultations of villagers on the use of external resources on the one hand, and discussions on the better use of existing resources on the other.

Many years ago, Pandit Jawaharlal Nehru made a speech that is often quoted by our co-operators. It was the speech in which he spoke of "convulsing India in cooperation". Less noted, but far more important, were other words he spoke that day, words that were highly relevant in 1993:

I do not accept the statement often made that the Indian peasant is so frightfully conservative that you cannot make him come out of [his] rut. He is a very intelligent person—given the chance—only a little cautious, only wanting some proof, some evidence of what he is asked to do...and not taking too much for granted. Now that makes cooperation in India for the rural people absolutely essential.

That is why we do not want, as in the past, the district official, or any other official, to throw his weight around too much. Again, he is the adviser and friend, but not the boss.

...we wanted to draw the mind of the people out of the old conception of some big officials sitting on top and ordering people about to do things...

Nehru expressed his faith in our rural people and remarked:

...theirs will be the decisions and if they make mistakes, they will suffer for them, and learn from them.

Nehru must have had village menfolk in mind when he dreamt of a participatory financial democracy in rural India. Nehru was right in his assumption but he was wrong on the constituency from which he expected this change. He would never have imagined that the revolution would be ignited by an almost mute constituency—the leadership of the women of rural India.

6

Odyssey With Dairy Farmers

The friendly cow, all red and white,
I love with all my heart:
She gives me cream with all her might,
To eat with apple-tart.

Robert Louis Stevenson

The cow is of the bovine ilk; one end is moo, the other milk.

Ogden Nash, Free Wheeling

To country people cows are mild,
And flee from any stick they throw;
But I'm a timid town bred child,
And all the cattle seem to know.

T.S. Eliot

In the early morning hour when the sun is still a brown moon, a lovely landscape stretches along both sides of the highway from Nagpur to Chandrapur, two important towns in India's major province, Maharashtra. The overcast sky softens the landscape and flimsy wisps of cloud drape the shoulders of hills like gauze scarves. Much before this blurred silhouette of the morning starts its lazy climb, the broken leaves start billowing like the wings of exotic butterflies. Outside the thatched huts, men sleep sprawled on the ground, their faces covered with torn sheets in an attempt to shut out the sun. The dawn coming out of the cusp of hills pinkens the eastern sky and makes the Wardha River as lustrous as silk. Even as the men snore, the women are up, the bronze pots on their heads glinting in the sun as they trudge across the barren fields. The tinkling of their anklets is soon joined by the harshly rhythmic song of a nearby hand pump. At the edge of a muddy path, a woman squats by a fire, preparing breakfast. A haze of smoke drifts somnolently over the countryside, as the morning meal is prepared. We are in Ashi, a village in the Chandrapur district of Maharashtra, which I intended to serve as an epicentre for dairy programmes for marginal farmers in the area. It was in this village that I would have my first brush with dairy farming in India.

The morning bus to Ashi will take you past dry fields of jowar and wheat and other seasonal crops. A two-kilometre stretch of freshly-laid glittering asphalt separates the fields from the main road. This tarred road stands out like a fresh scar on the red soil. The road is eminently motorable, giving no tell-tale signs of the backwardness of the village. The road makers seemed to have been in a hurry, however, as the road ends, incomplete, a mile from the village. A rickety wooden shack stands at the entrance to the village. On my first visit to the village, I had tea there that was so cold, so stewed, and so thin that you had to be a tea addict to get through it all; the cafe shop had an owner so absent-minded that he poured salt into the tea instead of sugar.

When we left the narrow strip of asphalt, we began bumping alarmingly over a cart track, with bamboos and tree branches scraping the sides of our vehicle, until we suddenly saw green fields of thick, lush millet, with a row of simple huts down one side of the cultivated area; beyond was thick jungle. My colleagues gazed at the crops with visible emotion. This was the first time that this land had been sown, the first time ever that it yielded productively. The cycle of sowing and reaping has always been like a creed to me. The mystery of life is all around us—right here, for anyone who has eyes to see or heart to feel.

The main laneway was lined on each side by thick mud walls spotted with hundreds of dung patties, a mix of manure and straw, slapped on to dry in the warm winter sun. Once the dung cakes were dry, the village women stored them in mounds, which they sealed with more mud, giving them the appearance of anthills, to serve as family woodpiles. We followed a narrow cobbled path beyond one of the big new water pumps, around the water hyacinth-covered swamp and past two women bickering about a broken wall between their huts.

One of the oldest traditional occupations of humankind is herding and grazing of cattle. Providing cows to the poor was one of the most common programmes I pursued, to equip villagers with a business they could manage while at the same time meeting the nutritional needs of the family. When I travelled for my first assignment to a village as a bank manager, I kept this learning in mind. I believed the best way I could help the poor villagers was by helping them with loans for purchasing livestock. I dreamt of beginning my career on the idealistic note of providing goats or poultry so the poor could swiftly pull themselves out of destitution. I believed a goattery or dairy was a much easier source of income than training a poor family to set up a small business, as it could be conveniently managed by the female of the family also.

Goats and cows are sturdier than paper money. Friends and relatives can't ask for small pieces of them. If you own a cow, it yields milk, it can plough the fields, and it produces dung that can be used as fuel or fertilizer. Goats also have economic value, as they cost little to maintain and breed fast. In a pinch, they can be slaughtered and turned into saleable meat or simply eaten. The same is true of ducks and chickens, which are valuable for their eggs and their meat. If the business profited, the borrower could graduate to a buffalo. Dairy animals' end product is the same whether you own an expensive imported breed or an inexpensive native: all manner of cheese, yogurt and butter. Cows are the main draught animals of India, their manure is the fuel which cooks Indian food and their milk is an important part of Indian diet.

Financing cattle is a routine business strategy in rural banking, as it benefits the local economy in terms of generating income and providing employment. Rural poor, who have no agricultural land, or only small landholdings, can manage both a goattery and a small-scale dairy. The simplest way of assisting the poor in this regard would be to lend them Rs 4000 to buy a cow that will yield four litres of milk during the lactating period and then dry up. We can work out a nearly uninterrupted flow of income for the dairy farmer if we provide a second cow to provide milk till the first cow calves again. The recipient of the loan will have an income sufficient to only slightly improve the quality of his daily meal, but not enough to permit saving.

Although goat-herding is one of the world's oldest economic professions, it turns out that goat-herding is a little more complicated than it appears. First, the normal life expectancy of a goat is around ten years. This means you will lose about ten percent of a herd to old age annually. Secondly, although goats typically give birth twice a year to one or two kids with each gestation, the viability rate is around seventy-five percent such that each goat will only net an average of 2 kids per year. The kids are worth about fifty percent of the mother goat's price. So conservatively by the end of the year, you have a hundred percent return: the doe, worth Rs 2000, and two kids, worth Rs 1000 each.

Even if you took out the cost of capital at twelve percent of the loan, you're making in the range of seventy percent return on invested capital.

Goats had intrigued me for years–their intelligence, their seeming disdain of human dominion. I once trailed a herd of goats in India through the sandy dunes of Rajasthan. The goats marched single file, hoofs clicking cobbles, while scooters and trucks squeezed past. At each narrow curve, another goat broke from the parade and turned into a home where a member of the household–a child or a woman–held open a wooden door and greeted the returning goat with a palmful of salt. The goats had returned from the desert to be milked and bedded with their family at night. In the morning they'd gather again with the herder. I'd never seen such a wonderful arrangement before–goats and humans living side by side–but it was one of the most ancient of the relationships between mammals.

Back home I was pained by the tragic fate these poor goats suffered at the hands of other marauding animals. I happened to be present one day at the veterinary clinic close to my office when a client of ours, an old man, a wrinkled farmer, walked into the dispensary. He held a bleeding goat in his arms. The goat had been bitten on the neck by a dog. The farmer pleaded with the doctor for help. The doctor administered an injection, but he said the goat would die. I heard the old man tell someone that the goat was all he had–no land, no children, and no other livestock.

Goats were to be my priority, followed by cows. This was a popular and easy way for villagers to make money: you could buy a goat and take it along with you to the agricultural fields, where it would graze while you worked, as a goat will eat just about anything. You could then breed the goat and sell its kids when you needed money. To me, it appeared a simple but magical formula. I even wondered why banks and government and development agencies needed highly qualified bankers and veterinary staff to handle such a simple task. Perhaps even a villager with some basic level of literacy would do a more efficient job than we bankers who couldn't distinguish between a Jersey and a Holstein or the average milk yield of a local breed. It was only later I found that the wily villagers had turned goat financing into a notorious farce. It took lot of time for bankers to get rid of the aversion they had developed for goat financing thanks to this.

Goat-rearing was the top priority in the programmes meant for combating poverty. Those who were eligible for finance would buy a flock and tend it; the surplus goats would be sold off during festival time. All the bank's village units distributed many such loans. Past loan ledgers showed that the number of goats financed often exceeded the population of the village, but signs could only rarely be found of either the goats or the cash from their sale being ploughed into the economy. It was much later that I solved the mystery of both goat economics and the vanishing goats.

My first exclusive loan camp for goats provided the first clue. The government had already issued a notification for purchasing goats from cattle auction markets located out of the district area. The purpose was to promote interbreeding that could improve the strains. However we suggested that we continue the practice of purchasing animals locally for some time. The local administration accepted our request and a camp was organised in our village with great fanfare and success.

Two days after the camp opened, an old woman walked into my office. She was sobbing inconsolably, her eyes red, tears streaming down her cheeks. I asked my lady peon to offer her a chair and fetch a glass of water. As the woman settled down and the sobs grew weaker, I asked what tragedy had befallen her. "Aajibai, (old mother) why are you in such great grief? Has any tragedy befallen you or your family? We are here to stand by you." She seemed to be unrelenting. "Sir, thank you for your good words. My problem is that I have lost two of my healthiest goats in just one day." I asked her to properly explain the entire issue.

She calmed down and assumed a stern expression and started speaking. "I think the entire system of financing and insuring cattle is wrong, you should have properly verified the goats and ascertained their true owners," she said.

"But what is wrong in the present system?" I asked.

"Wrong?" she burped as she raised her decibels. "This has been happening for years. We have been complaining for such a long time but nobody wants to believe us."

A veteran borrower who was watching the whole drama suddenly interjected as he found both me and the woman beating about the bush instead of grasping the problem by the horn. He explained that some of the notorious borrowers of the village would borrow goats from the villagers for a day. In return they would promise Rs. 10 per goat and return the goat by the evening. These borrowers bring these goats to the camps and get their earlobes tagged on the strength of which the money is released. If the owners resist, they convince them that these tags are necessary for warding off evil influences. I now understood the entire operation but was still not clear how the lady was affected.

The daughter of the women who accompanied her stepped into the conversation. "Sir, the tags used for the goats were rusted and the rust poisoned them to death. We want the bank to pay us the cost of those animals to compensate for the loss." It was my first encounter with the netherworld of goat finance. I later came to know that it was an old and routine practice which had imparted notoriety to the government's goattery programme.

In another case we financed a borrower to purchase a flock. In this case, we knew the borrower already had one goat, but she wanted to increase her business. The week after we gave the woman her loan, we came back to check on whether she'd actually bought a new goat. This is one of the cardinal principles of lending: it is good to check on borrowers to make sure they are using loans for their stated purpose. Otherwise, the money too often ends up going for household expenses or other non-income-generating purchases. We call the process by the technical phrase, verification of assets. Suresh and I drove to the village, and we met the woman at her house. "I bought the goat!" she said brightly. "Here it is!" With a flourish, she gestured to a skinny brown goat standing nearby.

"Great," I said, and smiled at the woman. It was the beginning of a goat revolution which we had so passionately planned. I didn't quite realise that this embryonic revolution had within it the seeds of one of the most rampant malpractices that plagued the goat economy.

"Wait!" said Suresh. "This is not a new goat. This is the one we saw last week. It's the same colour, with the same markings." I looked at Suresh, amazed. How many goats had we seen, in how many villages? And he remembered that this goat was the same one he'd seen a week ago? How could he tell? I felt Suresh was unnecessarily trying to micromanage things in order to impress me.

"No, it's not the old goat!" the women protested. "I just bought it! The one you saw last week was black."

But Suresh stood firm. "We're not stupid," he told the woman. "This is the same goat we saw last week."

I felt abused, standing in a dusty village in the middle of nowhere, arguing with a woman over the colour of a goat. Was this what I'd spent all these years preparing to do? But we knew we had to make it absolutely clear, from the very beginning, that we wouldn't bend the rules for anyone. If we were going to establish a culture of accountability, we had to be firm.

Suresh wouldn't back down, and the woman finally confessed. Yes, she admitted, this was the old goat. She intended to use the loan to buy a silk sari. "You can't use it for that," Suresh told her. "Buying a sari doesn't generate any income, so you'll be no closer to getting out of poverty that way. Either buy a new goat, or give us back the loan money."

My experience has shown that most loans fail because bankers do not ensure that the borrowers purchase the asset for which finance has been extended. For instance, if a loan is given for a grinding machine and the borrowers purchase a television, there will be no return on the asset and the borrowers will not be able to properly repay the loan. Thus making sure proper end use of funds is an important canon of banking

During my association with dairy programmes as part of my assignment as manager of a village branch of a bank I found that the extension departments of the government have an innate obsession with exotic breeds of cattle as against the native or local variety. My disillusionment with most state-driven dairy programmes was mainly on account of the inadequacy of skills and knowledge of the poor in handling exotic varieties; mortality can rip a huge hole in the precious savings of the farmers. The climate may not suit the cattle and the farmers can ill afford the luxuries and amenities that need to be provided to the vulnerable exotic breeds. These breeds must be promoted for prosperous farmers who can provide luxurious parlours to house them and have a sufficient buffer of assets to cope with contingencies. In poverty alleviation programmes, most of the beneficiaries are the poor who do not have adequate savings to meet the expenses of proper veterinary care. Moreover, the entire cost of travel, stay and local transport of the officials accompanying the farmers for purchase of cattle is recovered from these farmers. The final count turns out to be a sizeable sum.

It may be a coincidence that the development programmes have a greater fascination for cows, when several other alternatives could work better. For instance, goattery doesn't require any complex veterinary care. In case of a crisis or financial emergency, a single goat can be sold off with the business remaining intact.

My initial exuberance and enthusiasm suffered early jolts and I soon realized that financing cattle was not a simple apprentice's job. My notions of dairy finance being the simplest of all types of finance was based on my naivety and lack of exposure to rural realities. I later realized it was the diciest finance in which nature's hand had a greater role than our financial and agricultural skills. As long as the cows keep gushing out gallons of milk, yoghurt and cream and keep padding their wallets with wads of cash, and the gravy train keeps chugging on; it is a happy romance for the dairy farmers. The problem starts when the cattle start falling ill. An ailment, if left unattended, may lead to mortality resulting in a heavy loss for the poor household.

My plans soon vaporized as illnesses wiped out the livestock like a baboon plague. I slowly started moderating my enthusiasm. In one of my assignments I found that several of these decimating waves were man-induced and had nothing to do with nature. My knowledge of cows was restricted to what we had learnt in schools. We knew that the cow was a highly revered animal for Indians and several healing properties were associated with it. The dung was of great utility to villagers who used it for making fuel briquettes.

In a city, cow's milk was a rare commodity and much more expensive than buffalo milk, which was a preferable choice. It was only when my grandma had to prepare medicines or somebody was recuperating from a long illness that cow's milk would be needed. We had to cajole the local milkman to help us with half a litre each day. Grandma would tell us how to distinguish cow's milk from buffalo's. Cow's milk was thinner and slightly yellowish, that of buffalos was thick and viscous. However, since cow's milk was so scarce and yet much in demand, milkmen would often try to dilute buffalo milk with water and dye it with an edible yellow colorant to pass it off as cow's milk. The only way of being sure that it was genuine cow milk that we had was the reputation and credibility of the milkman and possibly getting the cow milked in our presence. I learned to keep a keen eye on the milkman to make sure he didn't, via a well-concealed tube, water down the milk.

A cow (or any animal, for that matter, but let us stick to the cow) has many relationships. It is related to the farmer who has bought it, it is related to the farmer's wife who feeds it and milks it, it is related to the farmer's child who takes it out to graze, it is related to the local doctor who cares for it in sickness, it is related to the market, it is related to the shed in which it lives, the land on which it grazes and the pond from which it drinks. The productivity of this cow depends upon the quality of all these relationships. Therefore, a cow cannot be seen in isolation, but in the context of its environment. A healthy cow in an unhealthy environment is of no use to anyone.

I found the best of intentions could produce negative results if they are based on faulty assumptions. This is true as much for animal husbandry programmes as for any other programme. Somebody (let us say the veterinarians, or the bankers, or farmers from high-rainfall, well-developed areas) tells us giving good, crossbred cows to farmers in our area will improve their economic status. But will it really?

I found that veterinary services in villages are very poor and veterinary doctors behave like sharks, trying to fleece the poor even for treating common ailments. The much-touted insurance of livestock is quite cumbersome. Techniques for increasing the quantity of milk are but one part of a vast repertoire of practices in which dairy farmers must be thoroughly grounded. They must also have thorough exposure to traditional veterinary practices.

I worked out a strategy to outsmart the despotic local veterinarians' guild. With the help of a few veterinary friends from college, I developed a small veterinary kit for common ailments, and we designed a simple chart indicating the ailment and the medicine for fixing it. The village woman who was a peon in my office served as barefoot veterinary doctor. We included medication capsules and tablets of the lowest dose. A single tablet was enough for a cock or hen; a goat required two, a cow three, a bullock four and a buffalo five. The strategy worked very well and the mortality rate came down drastically. My bosses agreed to absorb the cost of medicines in the monthly overhead costs. Drug companies supplied the medicines at concessional rates and also generously provided us charts and other product material which we disseminated to cattle owners. It was a novel initiative which was highly appreciated by visiting dignitaries from development agencies who would enthusiastically share it with other organizations. Several newspapers gave positive coverage for the innovation.

My initiative drew a lather of protests from veterinarians who were slowly uprooted from their business. They banded together to start a smear campaign against me, alleging that I had become an agent of multinational drug companies, whose medicines I was promoting in exchange for fat commissions. They also started advising people that the medicines were harmful for animals, attributing some of the regular ailments of the cattle to the effects of these medicines. "Will you ever accept medicines without consulting a doctor? How do you know whether the drug is benefiting or harming the body?" they would ask the superstitious villagers. I knew they represented an institutional lobby which could block my innovative efforts, but my dogged persistence thwarted their attempts to sabotage this initiative. The local block development officer tried to unnerve me by saying that anonymous complaints against me were pouring into his office and he could not postpone action on them any longer. I knew these were all tactics meant to discourage me from disturbing the status quo in development programmes. I had to straighten these fellows out, although by now they had got a fair idea of what we were up to. Critics scoffed at my notion of getting much traction from the initiative, but I persevered. To my good fortune, most of the borrowers were quite happy and came out openly in support of mc.

This unique idea won me a lot of goodwill and popular support even though we had to face an avalanche of protests in the beginning. The veterinarian guild was incensed. I had pitched the doctors back into their lairs. They couldn't swallow such bravado from a puny manager pretending to have the gall to confront the giants. They tried every sort of trick and stratagem to entrap me. Despite the smear campaign though, there were sensible people who lauded my initiative and debunked the veterinarians' charges, labelling them as greedy merchants. It was gratifying to see that the main stakeholders–the borrowers–vehemently protesting the veterinarians' stance. Rural programme managers must remember that innovation and creativity have always met with obstinate resistance from those who gutlessly follow a path someone else blazed for them. Rhetoric is cheap, action is always demanding.

The cattle suppliers have a powerful cartel fully blessed by the veterinary doctors and development staff of the government. Unlike medical professionals, veterinarians' filial feelings for each other are strong, but when it comes to treating animals, they are hard-hearted and careless because the mortality of an animal doesn't suck them into the legal hydra of consumer protection.

The Animal Husbandry Department was following a faulty mechanism for releasing payments to suppliers: it was to remit the loan sanctioned by the bank to the veterinary department at the district headquarters. The department then released the total amount (bank finance + capital subsidy) to the supplier after the delivery of animals. Since the government officials promised full cooperation and the villagers also appeared enthusiastic, I decided to implement the project on a larger scale. The veterinary lobby of the district had overhyped the benefits available to dairy farmers under the scheme and there was a scramble for including names. The most attractive feature of the scheme was a subsidy component of fifty percent, irrespective of the families' income level.

As a manager of a bank branch dealing with peasants, I accompanied the farmers to negotiate the purchase of dairy animals. I could have delegated the task to my junior officer, but I felt that I should make personal efforts to negotiate a fair deal for them. The farmers too were apprehensive, as this was the first time any of them had purchased exotic varieties, and they were keen that I should join them. The government's Animal Husbandry Officer fixed up transactions with a cattle supplier from Bihar who had settled in Wardha. We travelled together by jeep. I would have normally checked into a hotel but the farmers were insistent that I should be present through the entire dealings. I was habituated to night halts in villages and it was not a big challenge to accede to their request.

We visited Wardha where the famous cow supplier, Musa Sheth, had his barn. Inside the stables, three hundred cows were jammed flank to flank, and behind the stables, fringed by manure, was the pool where dairyman washed themselves, their cows, and the milk containers. As we sat down to find our places for the night, we found a small closet adjacent to the pens.

The dairy cows smelled. All farm animals do, of course, but these particularly pungent Jerseys had just come in from the rain. They were huddled in open stalls, swishing their tails, chewing on bales of hay, and remarking on the terrible weather with a series of disappointed moos. Musa Sheth chatted with the farmhands, inspected the milk storage tank, and laughed when a curious cow followed him around the barn. The cows mooed *ooaaw, ooaaw*.

The Jersey cow is small, amiable and very pretty, with fine, deer-like limbs, enviably long-lashed eyes and caramel colouring, sometimes embellished with cream or dusky markings. Farmers and breeders laud the Jersey's capacious udder, her impressive conversion of fodder into milk, her ability to calve early and easily. The rest of us marvel at the special richness of Jersey milk, like liquid silk to drink, and cream that churns to deep golden butter. The exceptional composition of her milk, her tolerance of poor pastures and hot climates proved unbeatable in world markets.

The cows were first cleaned, and the teat cups put on. A pulsating vacuum drew the milk into a receiver through piping into the farm milk tank. Musa Sheth ordered his servant to boil the milk and serve us with a glass each as we sat discussing common issues pertaining to milk dairies. Musa Sheth was rueful about the government's apathy: the shrinking of the grazing land and frequent droughts had compelled farmers to rely more on market fodder which had spurred milk prices higher. "It is our life and we invest a lot of emotion and energy and money into developing a cow herd that is genetically what we want," he said. "When we are forced to liquidate, it is not an easy thing to do. It is heart-wrenching sometimes, but is part of the business. Cattle have been streaming into auction yards across the country in recent weeks as grazing land burns up in the sun, ponds and streams evaporate and prices for feed corn rise. With land these days commanding heady prices, as financial investors snap it up to plant high-value crops like corn and owners put more into conservation easements, finding land cheap enough to raise forage for cattle is hard."

Most ranchers, like Musa Sheth, focus on their animals' lineage and weight. "The glitz and glamour is in the genetics," he said. "The value we see in what we sell is in the calf. Ranchers breed calves, raising them on pasture and hay for six to nine months, until they separate from their mothers and are sold to stockers. Stockers pasture the cows and fatten them before selling to feedlots. There the cows are penned in corrals on protein and starch-rich diets."

Our cattle supplier's house was a small one and we decided to sleep close to the spacious courtyard, redolent with the fragrance of jasmine. We shared the cowshed with the bawling calves and the wafts of cow dung that kept producing an acrid tang and doused the sonorous effect of jasmine. To freshen the air, our host opened the windows, and in rushed flies from the stable. Shooing them away, we stretched out. It was a mildly chilly night and I kept myself swaddled in a thick blanket. I was given a cot and the farmers slept on the floor where a huge, coarse carpet was laid out for them. They had had an enormous meal and farted painfully through the night.

Although the cloudless sky was spangled with a million twinkling stars that glistened like sequins, I couldn't enjoy the beauty of the moment. My mind was clouded with all sorts of worries. All the borrowers were illiterate and very poor decision-makers, and had entrusted the responsibility of the entire transactions to my judgment. While we were there, a fistfight broke out among the farmers and I had to intervene to restore order.

We were planning to buy at least a dozen cows. If the planning went well, the scheme was going to improve the life of the dairy farmers of Ashi. If the planning failed, it would mean an uncertain and painful job controlling the primary and collateral damage. There was already bickering among the farmers; from tongue-lashing to abusive outbursts, as each one tried to project himself as a dairy wizard. I had to pull away the blanket and get out of bed to restore order. I raised my voice and asked the farmers to concentrate on sleep so that everyone could rise early for the morning ritual of milking the cows.

A flood of questions kept tossing around in my head. The average milk yield of two days–at least two times in a day–is used as the metric to calculate the milk output of a cow. For every one litre of milk, the cost of a cow was fixed at Rs. 1000. Thus a cow having a yield of eight litres was priced at Rs. 8000. After jerking awake several times, I dozed off into a fitful sleep around midnight but the bustle of activity aroused me early.

My hosts didn't want to wake me up at that odd hour. They knew I was very tired and a lot of work lay ahead of me for the coming day including finalization of transactions and then working out logistics for transport of animals. I was jousted out of sleep by the sort of violent effort with which one wrenches one's head away from the pillow in a nightmare. After a bath, I decided to have a stroll to purge my mind of confusion about negotiations for the purchase of the cattle. A haze of smoke drifted somnolently over the countryside as the morning meal was prepared. Then the sounds of the rural dawn came like a jarring note to the ear—coughing and wheezing, raucous clearing of throats and nostrils, spilling water and brushing of teeth, the clang of utensils, the sputtering of taps, the slurping of hot tea. For the older village men, there is nothing like a deep chestful of bidi smoke to quell a morning cough.

Stepping into the gentle sunshine of a spring morning, I heard the lowing of snowy white cows impatient for milking to ease their udders. Musa Sheth had already organized the buckets and was gently caressing the cows. I could see how dearly he loved them. I was sure that after the cows reached the villages, the yield would straight away dip by a litre because none of the borrowers would extend such fond care to the animals. Musa Sheth's palms were greased with vegetable oil which the cows licked with relish.

The first thing Musa Sheth would do after getting up was to quaff a goblet of cow's urine. He believed it was a great rejuvenator. One of the aides brought a tray of steel tumblers with steaming tea made out of milk from the cow tethered in front of us. It was the best way to start the day. With the occasional massages, careful milking twice a day, and the spacious living quarters, to the cow community the farm was the bovine equivalent of a five-star hotel.

Musa Sheth and his aides sang a lovely pastoral tune as they went about the task of milking:

Oh, the maid who
Minds the dairy
Is a barnyard dignitary
And her rule is arbitrary
Where the brown eyed bossies browse
Everyday she has to putter
And at twilight out
She'll flutter with her pail
To milk the cows!

The calves were separated from their mothers, and he and his aides began milking the cows. He was wrapped tightly in a brightly washed loincloth raised up to the knee as he squatted in a hunch positioning the pail to collect the milk. Musa Seth and his friends milked the cows so enthusiastically that I was afraid little would be left for the calves. Musa Seth put my mind at ease. "We milk only three teats and leave the fourth for the calves. They never complain." He dipped his forefinger in a small pool of milk and lifted it up in the air. The white blob clung to his fingertip; not a drop rolled down. It spoke of the quality of the milk.

I asked some of our borrowers to participate in the milking ritual so that they could assess the quality of the animals. I was disillusioned with the poor pace at which they milked the cows. It appeared they were the best candidates for animal welfare awards, too gentle and kind to squeeze out even the surplus milk. Musa Sheth placed three buckets full on the table when our farmers were still halfway through the first cow. Peeved at the superlative performance of Musa Sheth, they started making unnecessary complaints about the cows, blaming them for being uncooperative with strangers. They asked me to reject these cows as they were sickly.

Musa Sheth pushed the farmer aside, took the bucket from his hand and sat below the udder with the bucket firm between his two legs and jets of milk started streaming into the bucket. It looked as if milk was almost on the point of bursting through the udders as Musa Sheth's lubricating hands hastened the flow. I was left with ample proof that milkmen who practice dairy as a hereditary vocation turn milk into gold.

Anthropologists tell us that indigenous people who are practicing their traditional vocation inherit practices handed down through generations and apply them successfully in their vocations. Modern dairy farmers who have large mechanised farms with professional support are a different case but small farmers cannot afford any of these facilities. The milk was thick and creamy and I had never seen such dense cream. When I asked Musa Sheth why such good quality milk was not available in cities, he picked up a wicker basket and showed me the fodder he was feeding these cows. He told me that he always ensured high quality nutrition for the animals; this was the secret of the quality of his cows' milk. Musa Sheth said that he was really pained that villagers were grazing these exotic cows on country grass and heaping so much cruelty on them. "They don't deserve to be given these cows," he railed.

His comment provoked an angry response from the villagers who contended that a luxurious gruel was out of question for the cattle when they themselves were unable to properly feed their families. I tried to reason with the dairy farmers that if the quality of milk was good, they would get better rates and this could help them purchase superior quality fodder.

We spent two days and two nights identifying the animals, measuring the milk output and then negotiating the price depending on the milk yield. We purchased animals worth Rs. 4.5 lacs. On the evening of the third day, the veterinary officer latched the insurance tags onto the earlobes of the cattle. The cattle were loaded and we saw them off. The borrowers and my junior colleague accompanied the animals while I proceeded to Warora, the block headquarters for Ashi village, by jeep.

Back home, I was caught in a bout of malaria and was in great pain. When I resumed my office, I found myself deluged with files which had been awaiting my clearance during my agonizing odyssey with cows and their old and new masters. I decided that I would visit these borrowers at their villages on a Sunday, but the farmers appeared to have messed up everything. By evening, our cup of woes was brimming over.

Rekha Teltumbde, who had purchased a pair of cows, walked to my cabin with moistened eyes. "Both my cows disappeared during the night. I had no experience of handling this strange breed; you should have given me the local variety," she started wailing. She was accompanied by the local councilman who launched on a long condescending discourse, "Poor people have to unnecessarily suffer because the banks do not understand their needs correctly." I told the councilman that the scheme was designed by government experts and there were different schemes for different borrowers. I tried to calm Rekha, assuring her that I would try my best to seek a solution and requested her to meet me after two days. Rekha tossed a polythene pouch on my table, asking me to relieve her of the loan. "I would prefer to put up a grocery shop; at least I would not have this headache of keeping a watch on the buffaloes".

Before departing, the councilman insisted that I give a written guarantee absolving Rekha of the debt. I bluntly told them that it was public money and I had no power to forgive the debt, and if they needed any further clarifications, they should meet the Animal Husbandry Officer whose office was just across the road, opposite the bank. Fifteen minutes after they had left, my telephone buzzed; it was the Animal Husbandry Officer. To my shock, he sang the borrowers' tune: "When the animal has been stolen, wherefrom will the borrower repay the loan?"

"The next time your department talks of targets for financing livestock, I will lodge a written protest," I railed, as my high-pitched voice trailed off into the main hall. I demanded a written communication about his views so that it could be deliberated at the monthly meeting of bankers, NGOs, insurance companies, development officers and the state government and slammed the phone down.

We held a meeting of the staff at which everyone suggested that we must adopt a tough stance. "Too much compassion is bad. It can boomerang on us," chimed in my farm credit assistant. "If the government staff was so casual as to misguide borrowers, we may have to spend most of our time fending off accusations from local leaders who are always keen to tap the discontented voices." interjected another colleague, a senior and wizened man.

We were yet to come to grips with the problem when Mangla walked in with a photograph of the buffalo which died during transportation. "Sir, you had advised me that whenever an animal dies, a photograph should be taken showing the tag latched to the earlobe. I think too many animals were stuffed in the mini-truck; it must have died on account of suffocation." She tossed a polythene pouch containing the detached ear lobes of the cattle on my table. Each buffalo cost Rs 10,000. I telephoned Musa Seth and narrated the incident to him, sharing with him the tight situation into which I had been pushed. A gentle and understanding human being, he discerned my plight from my plaintive tone. "Please don't worry. We will help you in every possible way. I have handled this sort of customers for years. I will send you two buffaloes to make up for the borrowers' loss." I assured him I would compensate the loss in the next round of purchases, but he suggested that I wait for two days saying the buffaloes would either be found or return on their own.

Two days later, I received a call from Musa Seth informing me that both the buffalos had reached his farm. To this day I still believe that Musa Seth must have gifted me the buffalos to redeem and strengthen my trust in him. Although the event astonished me, Musa Seth was not the least surprised. He said it was a routine affair and he knew of cattle which could nose their way back over distances of almost three hundred kilometres. The buffalos were transported back to Warora and transferred to a new borrower in Ashi. Rekha signed the transfer deed and settled for an auto trolley in exchange for the buffalos.

I dashed off an excoriating letter to the District Collector, vehemently pleading for a thorough inquiry into the way dairy programmes were being implemented and the problems in which I had got trapped on account of both the defects in the programme formulation and also their inept handling by the development staff of the government. The same week I received a telephone call from my boss in Nagpur asking me why I was creating unnecessary problems for the bank. He advised me that entering into altercation with the government could be detrimental to the bank's business. I resisted the provocation and gently replied that there appeared no immediate threat to the rising graph of business at the branch. He was a little uneasy with my answer and advised me that as long as I was representing my bank, I should keep my personal emotions in check and focus on the interests of the organization. The message was clear: even if I had a healthy ego I should not regard others' egos as unhealthy. If I ruffled the feathers of my peers in government, the government bosses would settle scores with us. I knew the only solution lay in brokering a peace deal.

The solution to Rekha's problem was not to be the end of my woes. Vandana Dhawas, a farmer from Mohbala who had purchased Jersey cows, confronted me the very next day in my office. She had not yet found sufficient customers for her milk, and the milk had soured in the summer heat, putting her to heavy losses. She had come with a small canister containing the foul-smelling milk. "Sir, you should have given me a refrigerator before you gave me these cows. How can I repay your loan now? I want to return these cows." We sought the help of one of our customers, the leading sweet mart of Warora, and they agreed to buy bulk quantities from Vandana every day.

These experiences opened my eyes to the vast issues involved with helping the poor, particularly when you don't have the support of various linkages to make the business deliver. On paper, the dairy programme appeared wonderful, but in practice I found myself sinking deeper and deeper into problems.

The most unnerving part of cattle finance is the handling of cattle insurance. If a manager doesn't handle it shrewdly he can get trapped in a cesspool of shady practices. The problem becomes complex if the cattle die before the insurance is done. Theoretically, such a situation should not arise at all because the financing and insurance of the animal are supposed to be simultaneous. But the field worker knows that there are umpteen times when, during the purchase, the loan is released earlier and the cattle remain uninsured for days, even weeks.

The date, time and venue of purchase of the transaction have to be fixed in advance by the Animal Husbandry Officer, and there are occasions when he fails to turn up at the market. Since the borrower and the bank's field officer have already agreed on the purchase price and the loan amount released, the deal must be finalised before the market closes. If the cattle die before being insured, it may mean a long and unending ordeal for the banker as the borrower may disown the liability for repayment of the loan and the manager must then undergo the excruciating rigmarole of enquiries, explanations and reprimands. The insurance company has a safe haven under its ubiquitous template: "no tag, no claim".

The owner has the impression that the animal is insured and the animal's death relieves him of the responsibility of repayment of the loan. I have personally come across cases where the borrowers have avoided treating the animals during sickness hoping the ailment would hasten the animals' death and relieve them of the burden of the repayment of the loan.

I would like to recount a case where a particular insurance company had run out of stocks of tags and which led to my horrifying ordeal of searching for genuine help for the poor beneficiaries. Since the animals had to be purchased under the government's Integrated Rural Development Programme, everything needed to be completed by the end of the financial year, March, or the government funds earmarked for any development programmes would lapse. With time already running out and chances of the consignment of tags being received looking dim, the bankers and block development administration decided to complete the process of financing and purchase leaving the tagging to be done after the tags were received. To my good fortune, no animal died during the intervening period; otherwise it would have meant a few more sleepless nights and another journey through a dangerous blind alley. Outsiders would be amazed to know that bad debts resulting from failure of realisation of insurance claims form the major portion of overdue loans under animal husbandry programmes.

The formalities for lodging a claim with the insurance company are cumbersome, time-consuming and entail costs which a small borrower may not be able to meet: a photograph of the dead animal positioned such that the ear with the insurance tag is visible, a *panchanama* (statement attested by five witnesses), a post-mortem report from the government's Animal Husbandry Officer, and so on. Often the owner simply knifes the ear and dumps the foul-smelling decaying morsel at the bank branch. Even if the manager has the necessary forms required for claiming the insured sum and is willing to provide assistance for comleting the insurance formalities, the borrower often has the gall to say he has nothing to do with the paperwork as he has already been discharged of liability. If a cooperative and sympathetic manager decides to take care of the formality (in most cases he is compelled to, despite his aversion, because recovery of the bank loan is at stake) he would be able to handle only a few cases. The insurance companies are no saints, there to do charity. They can't keep paying claims and losing profits. They too have understood the clever tricks of villagers the hard way. They have devised methods to filter claims to the minimum.

One such method may have been the issuance of plastic tags in place of brass tags, ostensibly as a cost-cutting measure but nevertheless something that worked in favour of the insurance company but was detrimental to the poor farmers. When the cattle grazed in the thick underbrush, the plastic tags often snapped off when the animal scraped through bushes. The procedure for getting a new tag latched was as tricky as getting a new insurance cover done. The nearest insurance company branch to villages financed by our bank was at Chandrapur, almost sixty kilometres away. The borrower would, therefore, submit the application at the bank branch known to him. The bank forwarded the claim to the insurance company, whose representative came according to his own sweet convenience, as retagging was not fresh business and hence he was not entitled to any commission. This whole process would take ten to fifteen days.Meanwhile, if the animal died before the insurance was done or the tag had fallen off, the insurance company had no liability. All insurance policies carried a terse fine-print message: "No tag — No claim". And then you have the arcane asterisk in an obscure corner of the insurance policy indicating the ghastly omnibus phrase "Conditions apply". I personally feel this clause is a licence to the company to treat each complaint the way it likes. Moreover, for a post-mortem to be carried out on the animal, the borrower has to spend days chasing the veterinarian, who will often insist on an unofficial fee for which the banker has to give a temporary overdraft to the borrower.

There was a bewildering array of forms to be filled when making an insurance claim or filling in subsidy claims. Rural bankers and veterinarians must know technical Marathi vernacular, especially the jargon and phraseology used in government notification. I remember my visit to the local *panchayat* office; I was utterly confused with the maze of unruly papers. One of the men, his face softening with an embarrassed grin, matched my linguistic attempt in Marathi with a few trial words of English. The grin spread around the table. Finally identifying the right form, we were filling it in when the section chief appeared. We told him what had happened, and he offered his profuse apologies in quite adequate English. Escorting us to our car, he said, "I hope, please, that you will try to be understanding."

Insurance is one of the biggest markets in rural India, but depending on the region, cattle insurance poses high risks to the insurer. Arranging an agent to underwrite the cattle's life and also to prove the death of the cattle at the time of making a claim, entail extraordinary cost and efforts. There are master policies issued by insurance companies in efforts to reduce the cost of underwriting, and such policies are normally taken by banks, cooperative societies and also by the departments of state governments. However, the insurance companies have not been happy with the ease with which villagers manipulated proof and certification offered for the death of animals.After the first lot of policyholders universally claimed to have lost their cattle, the insurance companies decreed that in order to place a claim, the owner would need to show the ear of the dead cow. The result was a robust market in cows' ears: any cow that died, insured or not, would have its ear cut off and sold to those who had insured a cow, so the farmer could claim the insurance and keep the cow.

The issues to checking frauds in cattle insurance are being slowly resolved. A recent breakthrough is insurance against drought: pay-outs are triggered when satellite images show grazing lands in the region have deteriorated to the point where herders are expected to lose more than fifteen percent of their herd, with the fifteen percent threshold acting as a sort of deductible. Tracking forage cover–rather than the number of dead animals–circumvents claims being made for animals that have died of disease or neglect rather than drought. Previously, insuring livestock for pastoralists has proved near impossible due to the difficulty of verifying the death of animals over a wide and remote area.

Ashi had acquired the reputation of a model village and I decided to try the programme here. The Veterinary Officer at the local block headquarters insisted that the cattle must be purchased from outside the district so as to prevent the practice of dummy purchases, but this entailed higher costs. Moreover, we must deal with suppliers with whom we were not familiar, whereas not only did the local markets offer an abundant variety of local breeds, but the suppliers were known to us, and we were conversant with the local trade practices. The specified supplier was Kishor Thakur, a tautly-muscled macho man who resembled a Mughal warrior with a splendid manly moustache and menacing glare. The bank manager normally does not interfere with the veterinary doctor's choice, but I was hesitant to deal with this particular supplier. Even the villagers endorsed my opinion and felt uncomfortable in dealing with him.

I tried to convince the Animal Husbandry Officer of the need for negotiating with other suppliers to safeguard the interests of the farmers. This nettled him: I had encroached on his turf, chipped at his authority. I recalled how possessive his tribe could be, and here it could only be explained by the bloated unofficial fees built into the transactions involving purchase of animals and thereafter on settlement of insurance claims in case of the death of the animal. I had to cave in to their pressures. However, I kept the campaign going by writing letters to their bosses informing them of these abusive practices. I did not have the faintest suspicion that this decision would later trigger off a chain of problems and finally snowball into a serious personal and professional crisis for me.

I was alone in my office one evening when I heard a patter of cowboy boots and a western belt clanking with every step. I could see the silhouette against the wall. Kishor, radiating a pure animal anger, was at the entry gate negotiating with the security guard. He had shaved badly that morning and the tiny patches of stubble lay under his throat just above where the polo-neck collar touched his skin. The ends of his moustache twisted to a rapier's tip, standing clean away from the cheeks. Every few minutes he reached for them and gave them a slow, hard twist. Spittle flecked his betel–reddened lips as if they were bleeding. He wore a tight black shirt, hair spiky with gel. On his fingers he wore several rings, each set with a different stone. He was a man of pancake makeup, hair dye, and aviator sunglasses.

He swept into my office. After a bit of confusion over where everyone would sit, Kishor selected a chair on the far side of the room, with his back to the wall. With a sweep of his large hand, he instructed his underling to take the chair to his right. I retained enough composure to offer him tea and ask him what had brought him here at this weird hour. He downed the tea in a single swallow and swirled the dregs around in the glass. He let his aide open the conversation, but when he found his aide fumbling, he took over the conversation. He said that the Animal Husbandry Department of the government had still not released the payment and he was passing through a financial crisis. He wanted the payment or the animals would be returned. I told him that I had already remitted it to the government, and politely told him that he should follow it up with the government department. I explained my difficulties and pleaded with Kishor to understand that I was an employee bound by certain rules, but he insisted that the staff at the branch had told him that I could sanction a temporary overdraft that could be liquidated on release of payment by the government. "You can't give excuses. Your staff has fully briefed me. They have even told me that you have released an amount in a similar case to a cattle supplier." I reiterated my stance but he left my room in a huff. I felt relieved, not knowing that I would be confronted by him again.

The drama of the previous evening was still brewing in my mind when I arrived at the office the next morning, only to find Kishor reappeared there. He said that the Animal Husbandry department had not received the necessary grant and there was no possibility of any payment materialising in the near future. He wanted me to help him with a temporary loan. At first he was calm, but then, on impulse, he became hoarse with anger. The words hit me as if someone had punched my heart. I snivelled and actually flinched backwards in my seat. I asked Kishor to meet me during office hours and I promised to do something in the matter. After he left, I rested my head against a stack of files.

He returned that afternoon accompanied by the government's veterinary officer. I decided to sanction an overdraft hoping that when the payment was released by the department the bank account would be liquidated. I was sucked into the passion of the moment and didn't read the undercurrents of the racket which operated in the veterinary transactions.

My action in helping Kishor proved to be my undoing and set me on a long and painful journey of vigilance enquiries by my employers leading to mental suffering for my family. Kishor's money was released by the veterinary department without our knowledge and the only remedy we had of recovering the overdraft amount was lost on account of the connivance of the veterinary department.

I remember our visit to Mumbai's Aarey Milk Colony, accompanied by two village elders (including the local village headman, or *sarpanch*), the government veterinary doctor and our field officer. The Colony is one of India's prominent emblems, on a par with Anand of India's White Revolution. We stayed at the New Zealand hostel, constructed out of funds from donors from New Zealand. I was tired after a long journey and preferred to rest, so I skipped the dinner and had a slice of toasted bread with buttermilk. The next day was Sunday and we were told to stay indoors as there was some trouble outside and the area was under police patrol. We came out of our rooms only for lunch and dinner.

At the lunch table we met officials from other centres. The initial pleasantries over, all of us got involved in an animated discussion. Some of the veterans who were regular visitors spoke bitterly of their past experience but admitted that there was little they could do with the system. I sought their advice on my responsibility as a banker in the whole transaction. They said since we sanctioned the loan amount, the accountability would naturally rest with us, but suggested a few simple tests to independently verify the quality of the animal. Examine the animals' eyeballs, make it stand or sit three or four times to determine its agility and gait. The appetite and the rate of belching give an idea of the intestinal health which is the most critical aspect of cattle's well-being. During negotiation we should keep reminding the suppliers that we were disappointed with the quality of animals and we could have bought much superior quality anywhere else. We should still think twice. The sting in the message straightaway knocks twenty percent off the price and puts the seller on the defence.

The next day we visited the *tabelas* (cattle camps). I had expected something cheerful, maybe with dancing and music, but I saw quickly that there were no festivities. The atmosphere was serious, even tense; it reminded me less of a fair than the floor of a stock market. It appeared as if the country's buffaloes had converged for an annual convention. Men, carrying or counting bundles of pink thousand-rupee notes, shouted and shoved their way into deals, occasionally getting into heated arguments that hovered at the edge of violence. Cattle brokers, called *dalals*, go from farm to farm buying buffaloes just before they calve, and send them by train to the market where they are bought by city dairymen. The *dalals* and the dairymen consider the new-born calves to be expendable, and it is a common sight to see dead calves piled high outside the stables.

The entire fair stank. I was surprised at the insensitivity of my new friends' olfactory organs. All of them moved around without the least trace of revulsion. Their noses didn't seem to register even the slightest whiff of the stench that wafted through the sky. Soon the sky was hailing mosquitoes. The eagles were also working a frightful racket around us. My nose kept on registering so many different odours that I felt I would have to be driven straight to a hospital to pump out poisonous gases from my lungs. The scene from the Bhopal tragedy started crossing my mind.

By evening, I emerged from the scrum, dishevelled, glassy-eyed and soaked in sweat, and wearing mismatched sandals packed with grime and cow pee. The moist heat was intense enough to steam up my glasses. I was so exhausted that I could not negotiate even a single transaction My villagers were equally overawed by the mad cattle bog. My shirt was sodden and beads of sweat trickled down my face and neck. I later discovered that somebody had picked my watch, which had adorned my wrist ever since I joined my bank. During the afternoon, they had fetched me a few greasy snacks daubed with lots of chilli powder, wrapped in a torn newspaper. I immediately signalled an emphatic no as my mind would always hallucinate explosive gunpowder when I saw the flaming red ochre powder resembling the diffused particles of an angry sun.

The veterinary doctor was waiting impatiently, accompanied by a ferocious-looking man with an outrageous moustache and whiskery cauliflower ears. I could see wrinkles of suppressed rage on his face. He couldn't express his displeasure to me, but he told the farmers to give up the village slack as long as we were in Mumbai. He then asked them to settle the transactions with the *dalal* (broker), the man standing beside him, whom he introduced as a renowned authority from Haryana on buffalos.

He could apparently tell by looking at a buffalo how much milk it would yield. The farmers looked at me, expecting me to lead the negotiations. I made it clear that if the entire procedure turned out to be faulty, I would not spare anybody. I told the doctor bluntly that I wouldn't hesitate to complain to the government. The frowning faces of the doctor and the buffalo master relaxed, the creases on the faces dissolved and their tone became conciliatory.

The buffalo master took the initiative to break the stalemate and said that he was open to further discount as he was keen to get a foothold in Chandrapur, the district from which our farmers hailed. "Rs 8000 for each buffalo, transportation cost to be borne by the borrowers." The farmers shook their heads and raised their eyes upwards to show how puzzled they were.

Finally after a discussion with the Dairy Commissioner at Chandrapur on the telephone, we finalised the deal. It was agreed that the vendor would also provide one month's fodder free along with the buffalo. Two huge wagons were hired, each of them almost double the length of a truck. The doctor and the farmers accompanied the cattle. I boarded the night train. There were no mobile phones then and there were no means through which I could remain in touch with the buffalos and their new owners or the doctor. The buffaloes arrived forty-eight hours later, to much excitement in Ashi. In Warora, the people were seeing these huge vehicles for the first time. The two well-built Sardars who drove them were quite upbeat and still fit enough to commence their return journey immediately.

At this juncture, I realized that every dairy loan must have a component for veterinary care and the government can chip in with a fodder allowance to be paid to the farmers till the cattle calve. Before taking this risky step, I sent urgent messages to the veterinary staff but no help appeared to be forthcoming. The only way out of the predicament was to sanction overdrafts. It was a minor liberty I was taking with the rules, but my auditors could very well label it as a major transgression because it was a scheme designed by the government.

A few days later while going through the minutes of the monthly review meeting, I was astonished to find an obscure remark mentioning that the District Collector had lauded the veterinary officers for their zeal and commitment in achieving the target for supply of dry buffaloes. There was no reference to the travails and agony the bank staff had undergone. I felt deeply hurt that the government had such a myopic view of rural development programmes, feeling that the government staff must be under the impression that we were naïve. When we coolly analysed the processes involved in the programme, we found that the programme had been foisted on us. I wrote a very strong letter to the Dairy Commissioner, pointing out that the poor tribals had been cheated under the guise of a programme ostensibly designed for their welfare.

This term "rehabilitation and relief" has in truth become a much-abused term in relief manuals and has been used as a smokescreen to camouflage corrupt practices. I cannot but marvel at the title which P. Sainath, the well-known rural affairs editor, gave to his wonderful book *Everybody Loves a Good Drought.* Natural calamities like drought and floods lead to inundation of relief material and provide excellent opportunities for self-aggrandizement of the relief staff.

My complaints evoked a snigger from the lower veterinary bureaucracy, and my letters did create a flutter in the veterinary department and an inquiry was set in motion. I later came to know that the dairy officials visited Ashi and got a signed undertaking from the borrowers to the effect that the dairy department had extended its full cooperation and the scheme had failed owing to the negligence of the borrowers themselves. I don't know whether the borrowers or the local *sarpanch* were bribed for obtaining the declaration.

There is a great risk involved in financing livestock, particularly where the veterinary infrastructure is weak. Large numbers of milch animals are often bought for beneficiaries at the same time in cattle fairs, pushing up their price. The difference in the price and quality of financed assets over their market price, along with the costs of time, out-of-pocket expenses and payments to middlemen is estimated to raise the transactions costs to the borrower by an estimated twenty percent. It takes a discerning eye to know when to sell a cow, such as in the early stages of an outbreak of bovine disease.

The real villains who sabotaged the development agenda of the banks were the staff of the local development administration. The veterinary doctors made life miserable for banks, insurance companies and the poor. At the time of purchase, these doctors would charge exorbitant fees for certifying the health of the animal and then again charge the cattle owner an equally hefty fee for endorsing the insurance claim when the cattle died. The veterinary doctors' certification about the quality of animal and the suitability of the price is ten percent of the loan value and when the animal dies, you have to shell out another ten to fifteen percent for the so-called post-mortem, which is actually a written recording of the cause of death as reported by the borrower. I used to envy these doctors, whose fee was higher than that of even the best cardiac surgeons in the country. The insurance procedures are very complicated and the veterinary doctors create further problems by insisting on conditions which are difficult to meet. The veterinary doctors have their own cartel which is in league with the cartel of suppliers. A bank manager is not in a position to break this cycle to explore better markets and wider choices for the borrowers.

I became aware of the messy procedure much too late. I found that whenever a poor farmer thought of availing himself of any assistance from the government, he had to brace himself for the usual struggle with a venal and slothful bureaucracy. The so-called purchase committee for purchase of livestock under the government's development programmes is a big sham and it is the veterinary doctor who indulges in outright manipulation. If the borrower or manager doesn't accede to his diktat – there is no other way to describe his dictatorial role–he has to face severe outright non-cooperation from the veterinary staff. In case of death of the animal, the borrower cannot think of even a faint possibility of claiming his insurance.

I remember a young, hard-working boy whom I financed for the purchase of two buffaloes so that he could have his own independent business. The extra income gave the boy the luxury of visiting the nearby township and befriending youth from elite families. In the process, he got involved with a girl with whom he eloped. The panicked family, which used to earlier sing my praises, suddenly started charging me of having spoilt the boy with the loan. The boy's mother would wail that the family had lost their peace after their son got the loan. After the boy left, there was no one to look after the buffaloes and the mother flatly told me that she and her husband were not in a position to take care of them and they would not be able to pay the loan instalments any longer. I spent an almost sleepless night wrestling with this typical problem.

My colleague who had until now only watched the situation, found it necessary to intervene. He made short shrift of the *sarpanch* and, sensing our mood, the *sarpanch* softened his stance. I then pleaded with the woman to engage a labourer and manage the dairy by herself for the time being. I promised to lend her any support she needed, like arranging for veterinary care and stocks of fodder to help her in the calamity that had befallen her. This allayed her trauma. I also asked my clerk to explain the financial transactions to her and also how she could manage her loan account without any hassles. The shy housewife turned out to be a very efficient manager and by the time I was transferred, she had repaid almost the entire loan. Later I came to know that the boy had also returned to the village with the girl whom he had married. The boy and his wife had been gracefully accepted by the family. The loan was finally paid, but in the process, I underwent a protracted period of agony.

Fast forward 2010.

The boy's hard-working parents have both expired. The boy is settled with his wife in a bigger town. His younger brother is the lone inhabitant in the big house. He looks after the family's grocery shop, the biggest grocery in the village. He retains his loyalty to the bank and having seen my plight, he is always forthcoming to advise villagers properly in case of any banking dispute.

Even in this bleak world, I could see silver linings. Gulab Kshirsagar was a landless agricultural labourer belonging to a family whose income was below the official poverty line. He had been working as a labourer almost since his childhood. Owing to illness and old age, he had lost the physical stamina for undertaking any strenuous work. He was financed by the bank under the IRDP for setting up a goattery unit and purchased seven does and one buck. He was able to repay the entire bank loan at the end of three years, by selling goats during festival seasons, particularly Holi and Id when goats are in heavy demand for sacrificial slaughter. He used his profits to enable his daughter to marry. One significant factor that enabled Kshirsagar to succeed was that he devoted abundant time in tending the goats. He grazed them personally, bathed them daily with soap and disinfectant. But he could not afford any supplementary food or veterinary tonics for stimulating their growth.

He fell in love with goats when he was a teenager. Now when people ask, "How come you got into the business of goats?" he answers, "I didn't get into goats; they got into me." He now has 150 goats of varying ages on his small dairy farm, and he knows them all by name. Kshirsagar's flock of goats was much healthier than those of other villagers who had more money and could afford a servant for grazing the animals and professional veterinary care. Kshirsagar is an example of what distinguishes successful goattery units from those that fail: the commitment of the owner to his flock herd.

Basic veterinary knowledge must be imparted to individuals who are engaged in goattery and they may be provided with emergency veterinary kits. In the present case, the bank branch maintained this kit and periodically medicine was supplied to unit owners. It was found that goats have to be given a periodic dose of wormicide to disinfect their intestines and prevent occurrence of intestinal infections. Worm infection is the most common problem with cattle; but wormicides can be administered on the basis of symptoms. In the case of successful units, it was observed the owners were very diligent and careful in sticking to proper medicinal schedule.

In the case of cattle loans, a majority of cattle owners reported that they had either sold off the animals bought with the loan or that these animals were dead. Cattle loans were financed without adequate attention to other details, such as fodder availability, marketing of milk etc. Buffaloes, whose milk has higher butterfat content than cows, are the mainstay of the commercial dairy industry. Today's dairy farm is mechanized, computerized and, above all, big. The end product, however, is the same as it was a century or five centuries ago: all manner of cheese, yogurt, butter and, in perhaps its purest form, the stuff you put on dry cereal or use to wash down a piece of chocolate cake—milk.

As these stories show that development programmes, particularly dairy programmes for small farmers, can be counterproductive unless we provide fodder and veterinary allowances. Take the example of the much-discussed IRDP buffalo. For a farmer who already owns land and animals, it is easy to make good use of an additional buffalo. For an asset-less household, the same animal can be a Damocles' sword. If the buffalo falls ill and cash is not available to take special care of it, or if it grows weak during non-lactation periods when fodder also has to be bought, the household can easily be ruined. I think it is time we stopped asking the BDO what villagers want. Perhaps it is time we ask the people what they want. Or, better still, leave it to the people to ask each other what they want and then decide themselves how they want to spend their resources.

In Yavatmal, for example, many poor individuals signed up to receive microfinance to purchase a cow in order to generate a little additional income from the sale of raw milk. While this was widely seen as a very sensible and compassionate intervention by the international donor and NGO community, the development outcome was extremely problematic. The local over-supply of raw milk in many communities led to a general price decline. This undermined all incumbent producers, of course, but especially other non-client 'one-cow farms' who quickly saw reduced margins and incomes, and were thus more likely to fall into poverty than before. It also had a negative longer run effect by undercutting the day-to-day operations of potentially sustainable larger dairy farms

The onset of internet and mobile phones has revolutionized dairy, like all other businesses. Veterinary assistance is readily available. The story of the cow and the computer is a local parable showing that sometimes the simplest information is the most valuable.

Some months back Sangita Kitey, a round-faced woman who cannot read or write, sat in the courtyard of her small home in Wanoja in Chandrapur, with the family's only milch cow. For five days and nights, the cow moaned while in labour. Sangita grew ever more fearful that the cow would die. "This is the only good income we have," she said, explaining that the four gallons of milk the cow produced each day paid the bills. Word of Sangita's woebegone cow soon spread to Ashok, a public-spirited farmer who uses one name. The village's computer is in the anteroom of his home. The computer is operated full time by Ashok, who used it to call up a list of area veterinarians. A doctor arrived that night and, by the light of a bare electric bulb, stuck his arm into Sangita's cow, extracted the calf's spindly leg and tied a rope to it, then dragged the calf into the world.

One thing that I admire in my cattle owners is the priority they attach to their animals' health. If his milch cow or his prized bull is ill, the owner will rush the animal to a veterinarian even though he may not take his child who may be a victim of chronic diarrhoea. "A man can breed children. But if his bull dies, he loses his livelihood. What gives man bread should be cared for and worshipped," says Ledange, another farmer.

In villages, a day is set aside to honour the bull. In the festival of *pola*, the bulls are massaged and bathed, fed on eggs, and made to participate in a race. "He is my child," says Ledange, as his hand rests tenderly on the head of a sturdy white animal. He feeds his bull on wheat and himself eats *ragi*, a coarse grain. And when his bull becomes a father, he celebrates the occasion in a manner that befits the birth of his own son. "Do you know how to judge a bull?" he asks, as his eyes glow. "You first look at its horns, then its hump and watch closely how it crouches down. When mine does, it deserves an *arti*(sacred ritual)." The bull is Ledange's companion. He brings him home in the dead of night. The bull is more than a wife, who he only sees at certain hours. His wife to him is a mere tool, necessary to keep a unit complete and further a generation. He has no room for her. She finds room for herself in her motherhood.

After my bitter experiences with dairy financing, I vowed never to get into the nightmarish ordeal again. As I moved up the ladder of senior positions in the bank hierarchy, I came in contact with promoters of giant dairy plants, particularly in Western Maharashtra, who had modern salons and parlours for housing animals, state-of-the-art chilling plants and the required infrastructure in terms of veterinary care. These dairy plants were real wealth creators and sources of pride and revenue for the banks. This model, I realized, was the only viable route for dairy businesses: small dairy farmers need to be aggregated and linked up through a value chain to these sophisticated projects.

But I found that the penchant of development agencies for high-yielding cows has never abated. Long after I had lost direct contact with dairy farmers and the dairy circuit, no less a person than the Prime Minister announced a package of wagonloads of these Holstein and Jersey cows that were to be handed over to farmers in the suicide-affected agrarian belt of Yavatmal and Wardha. The farmers were themselves in great distress and were now supposed to feed these royal guests. Newspapers columns bled with morose headlines: 'Princely cows for measly families.' The results were on the expected lines. The farmers, unable to feed these cows, sold them off at paltry prices and were back to their original plight.

The stories of proxy purchases of animals and fleecing of clients for insurance claims continue, but the processes have become transparent and scrutiny tough and rigorous. It is good for honest borrowers. Private veterinary doctors have proliferated but the poor are now more empowered and aware of their rights. Their innocence has gone.

Incidentally small dairy farmers continue to flourish in India primarily on account of the white revolution pioneered by Verghese Kurien. He has left a legacy that will continue to nurture and suckle dairy farmers. They say great men are not normal. If one is normal, one tends to act within the limits set by his surroundings. What makes the great men great is their ability to transcend obvious limitations. Their vision and supreme self-belief drives them constantly until they achieve what they wanted to.

Kurien was one such man. Otherwise, he would not have – almost singlehandedly – cranked up the co-operative sector in India and that too in milk production. It was unimaginable in the middle of the twentieth century that small farmers and cooperatives could take up dairying. Western experts saw dairying as the exclusive preserve of big dairy companies conducted over expansive ranches. Dairying has become a common farmers ally, thanks to the vision of Kurien,

Kurien's words in his biography remain a guiding credo for rural development managers handling dairy programmes for farmers:

I opted to remain an employee of farmers all my life ....I did it because I realized I had a job which gave me the greatest pleasure, the greatest satisfaction. The idea of working for a large number of farmers translated itself into the concept of working for social good. I soon realized that money is not the only satisfaction that one can seek, that there are several other forms of satisfaction and all of these were available to me at Anand

7

Vignettes From Villages

If the villages perish, India will perish too. It will be no more India. Her own mission in the world will get lost.

M.K.Gandhi

Our rural people could never become really free until they were liberated from the exploitation of money lenders, from the social ills and burdens of caste and class

Verghese Kurien

The inertia of a jungle village is a dangerous thing. Before you know it your whole life has slipped by and you are still waiting there

Tahir Shah, House of the Tiger Kin

The hoary stories of legendary banks and their lords are now part of public lore. The history of banking is itself akin to that of wars or of kings and queens. Of late, rural banking has emerged as one of the top priorities of developing nations. After Mohammad Yunus was awarded the Nobel Prize in 2006, rural finance remains on the top of the agenda for even the World Bank.

At a time when rural banking is emerging as a strong sibling of other banking segments, I think it fit to share my experience in rural finance, which has been my abiding passion for well over three decades. The experiences have been varied: some chilling, some amusing, some exciting but they nevertheless serve as a prism which provides a view of every facet of rural society. The scenario has undoubtedly undergone a radical transformation in the last decade. Rural banking has lost its sheen because development bankers now feel that commitment has no relevance, especially when you are pitted against a rural society that is becoming more politicised with time.

On the institutional front, the greed for profits has diluted the original mission of Muhammad Yunus, the man who revolutionized the financial model for the poor; the mission has shifted from serving the poor to skimming profit off the poor. To ensure that the small loans would be profitable for their shareholders, the banks needed to raise interest rates and engage in aggressive marketing and loan collection. In some cases, especially in the area of commercial microfinance, several excesses were committed. The kind of empathy that had once been shown to borrowers when the lenders were nonprofits have faded away.

Here are some of the most amusing high points in my career that took me to the remote hinterland of India. It spanned several cultures and states.

While I was a bank manager in Bina, the government introduced an insurance programme for men and women below the age of sixty. As a local bank manager, I was also associated with this important exercise. A huge crowd collected, beginning in the early morning at the *gram panchayat* (village council) office where the government officials were holding the camp. My curiosity piqued as I found the camp crowd growing out of proportion to the population of the entire village. The formation of the camp had been announced far enough in advance that even villagers who had migrated from the village to their cousins in cities had also turned up, with some of them so old and infirm that they had to be carried on the heads and shoulders of their relatives. It appeared as if some temporary migrants were also being enrolled, albeit for a commission charged by local agents.

The officials at the camp tried to convince the youth leaders and the headman of the village of the serious implications of the wrong declaration of age. The officials finally decided to accept the applicants' own declaration of age, as they felt that any attempt at trying to investigate their proper ages could touch raw emotional nerves and trigger the ire of the villagers. The insurance formalities were finally completed and a few weeks later, the insurance policies were handed over to the beneficiaries.

Coincidentally, *Sanjay Gandhi Niradhar Yojana*, the government's pension scheme, was introduced in the village for people above sixty years of age not too long thereafter and similarly evoked a huge response from villagers. We started an elaborate process of sorting the documents of those who apparently qualified from those who fell below the Plimsoll line. I had retained a copy of the earlier insurance statement. There were at least two dozen women on my rolls alone already covered in the earlier insurance schemes who wanted to get the benefit of the pension scheme also. We categorically told them that, apart from being covered under the previous insurance, they were by their own declarations for that application not eligible for this pension scheme. These garrulous women did not buy our logic, feigning ignorance of the fact that an individual would not be allowed to figure in both the lists because it would amount to gross contradiction in the declaration of age. The naïve villagers were unaware of the serious consequences of these false declarations. Their only goal was to get benefits from as many government schemes as possible.

The village headman protested that the villagers could not be penalized for the error. He insisted that the insurance officials had not correctly conveyed the eligibility criteria and most people had declared their age without seriously getting them verified. He also agreed to certify the declared ages of these individuals irrespective of what the consequences would be for him. We told the headman that he held a political position and any certification from him had no validity for official processes. Some of the sensible officials in our group preferred not to disturb the fragile political eco-system of the village and finally decided to incorporate the ages as reported by the applicants and attached a note explaining the aberrations in our compilations and the anomalous situation that had arisen out of the discrepancy in ages declared on the pension application and the insurance application.

By the time the final scrutiny was done, and the list finalized by the block authorities, I was transferred. Years later, I came to know that a large number of villagers continued to figure in both lists.

Before the new international financing norms based on stringent evaluation of banks financial assets were introduced, Indian banks performed in a traditional manner that could never throw up a realistic picture of the quality of financial health of their loans. The lending banks and borrowers were both parties to what was once known as evergreening of loans. The annual profit of the bank would be calculated at the end of the financial year on the basis of the notional interest income that would accrue to the bank, not the interest actually realized.

For example, when a borrower defaulted on his loan, the bank sanctioned a new loan to close the old loan. Thus, in the account books, the borrowers' dealings and transactions with the bank appeared regular. Some borrowers required perennial evergreening. Finally, a loan would balloon to, say, five to six times the original loan. Thus whatever interest income was being booked on the loan was illusory. When the loan finally failed, it sank a big hole in the bank's balance sheet and the health of the loan would have deteriorated so badly that there would be no scope for salvaging it. Most farm loans, especially those which were given for the purchase of farm inputs and had to be repaid on harvest after the half-yearly or annual crop cycle, turned into financial graveyards on account of this faulty practice of evergreening. Thus, instead of checking the baleful tendencies of the borrowers whose repayments ethics were being slowly weakened, the evergreening strategy boomeranged. In turn, the implications of these events foreshadowed the growth of the Indian farmer's aversion to loan repayment.

The survey for identifying BPL (below poverty line) families in villages has always been a contentious affair. Both the international poverty line and the Indian poverty line are based on the income of and calorific value of food consumed by the village residents. The BPL surveyors have always found that working on this matrix in certain village conditions is not only complicated but results in false data. The current procedure for surveying the present BPL families is still very crude and did not appear a convincing matrix, doing proper justice to its avowed objective, Moreover, it does not promise being even remotely close to the position at ground level.

The present system, designed locally by the village administration, works by elimination. A decade back, it was a very simple affair, with families having a concrete house, moped or TV being automatically disqualified. Very few people had concrete houses at that time, and those who owned mopeds and televisions hid them at the time of survey. In effect, almost 80 percent of the population would get a smooth entry into the BPL domain. It was only when the state governments decided to allot an aggregate number of BPL families to be identified for each state that the local administration started winnowing out at least those families who could hardly be considered BPL even by the wildest standard established by the states. To muddy matters, the criteria for each state is also different. Thus an applicant who is eligible in one state may not qualify in a different state on the basis of consumption of same calorific value of food or annual income.

The international poverty line is based on the basic needs approach. 'Basic needs' are factored into 'food-related' needs and 'non-food-related' needs. In the first, the expenditure required to meet food-related needs is estimated; this 'food poverty line' is employed, in the second stage, to estimate an aggregate poverty line intended to comprehend non-food needs. The first-stage problem is addressed in terms of the cost of a food basket that will meet some pre-specified nutritional standard (such as a calorific norm of, say, 2,400 kilocalories per person per day), while also satisfying some constraints imposed by 'palatability' considerations. One difficulty with this procedure is that there are likely to be differences in the food preferences ('palatability constraints') between the rich and the poor. Howsoever scientific and accurate this procedure may be, the village level assessor can hardly comprehend this concept well enough to correctly measure the income levels.

The Indian government has now declared that it will take into account multiple factors of deprivation for arriving at specific entitlements that rural households will receive, and that the current poverty estimates based on these declared numbers will not be used to impose any ceilings on the number of households to be included in different government programmes and schemes. We still have to see how this will play out, but here is a first step in the right direction:

The yardstick for determining the eligibility for most government subsidised programmes is measured with the help of a Below Poverty Line Census (also known as 'Socio-Economic and Caste Census"). The criteria for determining BPL status continue to be puzzling, however, and often exclude those who deserve it. If you have a pucca house, a two-wheeler, a fan...you are ineligible. The pucca house could have been in your family for generations and is not necessarily a reflection of your present situation, to name just one ambiguity. There was a government scheme once in which girls were given cycles to ensure they went to school. Because the girls had a cycle, they were not counted as BPL.

There was a time in the early 1980s when populist politics was at its zenith in India. Freebies, hand-outs, subsidies and soft loans were the call of the day. Loans were being extracted from banks under pressure of threats and intimidation. For the first time, bankers were exposed not just to politicians but to ruffians masquerading as political workers and youth leaders. The government designed these products as loans without guarantee or security, cutting off bankers' access to their recovery. Moreover, these loans were distributed by politicians at public melas, giving the impression that they were largesse from the government rather than loans from the banks. These practices were the first in a series of events that contaminated the rural credit culture and the consequences continue to batter rural bankers.

During my first assignment at Aurangabad, my boss, R. P. Mehta, was a little bemused at the amicable way I treated my clients, given banks' notoriety for poor customer service. Mehta was given the impression by my colleagues that I was liberal in my approach with borrowers and hypersensitive to customer complaints. Mehta could be ruthless with errant staff and recalcitrant borrowers, but there was also a soft side to him. Whenever any staff member got into trouble on account of a bonafide lapse, he would always take whatever risks were necessary to rescue him. His mantra was simple: be good with good customers; be casual with routine customers; be wary of new loan seekers.

He did not appreciate my gentle approach of lavishing cordiality and hospitality on every customer. He conveyed his displeasure to me through other colleagues. Mehta was a great master in man management and he would always drop subtle hints to ensure that his instructions do not demotivate the officer. When he found it necessary to counsel me, he called me to his residence, which was just above our banking hall. When I visited him, he was dressed in an impressive full-length coat and was probably enjoying a drink. An exquisite cigar would always be between his teeth. Mehta was a warm-hearted person but always wore a stern glare that evoked a feeling of awe. I was slightly nervous when Mehta ushered me into his drawing room; he was frowning slightly, which did not augur well for me. He gave me, if not indeed a barbed hello, a sort of reproaching welcome.

As was his usual style of conversation, Mehta cleared his throat, raised his legs to the table and asked me what drink I would prefer. I knew he was not referring to a soft drink, but rather the premium wines that adorned his small cellar. When I suggested lemon water, he burst into peals of laughter, but this laughter was not sardonic. He took pity at my innocence, "Do you know bankers are hard boozers?" I sulked for a moment but then got the better of my emotions and feigned not to have heard him. He gestured his servant to fetch me lemon water with ice.

He then proceeded to enquire about my personal experiences in the town and my interactions with the staff and customers. He complimented me for my sincerity and commitment at work and spoke about the positive feedbacks he had received, then recounted how he too had been flush with idealism and revolutionary zeal in his college days. He vowed to his teachers and friends that he would not marry till he cleansed the system of its veniality. But all his idealism vaporized after he experienced the tyranny of employers. Idealism had receded and finally faded as family matters started claiming him.

He recounted a fable of a millionaire who had to undergo a heart transplant. The doctors asked him to choose which heart he wanted to receive. The millionaire's fortunes were so vast that he could afford to buy anybody's heart: the heart of a film star, beauty queen, politician, sportsman, politician, scholar, astronaut, doctor and, if required, even that of a ruling king or queen. The millionaire wanted a heart that would be both sturdy and tough, one that could remain unruffled by emotions. He mulled over the suggestions of his surgeons and said, "I should be fine with a banker's heart. Bankers don't use their hearts; a banker's heart will be impervious to external emotions. I don't think that there could be a sturdier heart."

It was a very clear message for me. Mehta perked me up, saying there is always a way in which compassion could be blended with prudent financial judgments. He conveyed through his nuanced suggestions that, as a banker, I should have the head of a hawk and the soul of a dove. The hawk worries about the safety of the bank's money; the dove wants the maximum number of individuals to get access to banking and in turn assistance by way of loans at soft terms of interest.

With the repayment culture contaminated and delinquent tendencies of borrowers so firmly entrenched, bankers became wary of extending rural credit. They started practicing credit apartheid. Our planners responded to this situation with a totally myopic idea: target loans to women, the most important and stable constituency for vote-hungry politicians.

Nobody wondered what use a loan could be for village women who played the triple role of mother, home-keeper and wage earner, not to mention lacking business skills. Their only qualifications were reliability, honesty and trustworthiness, qualities which a bank's conventional appraisal methods cannot quantify.

This resulted in men using women as fronts for loans for a wide range of technical equipment: tractors, harvesters, grain mills and pump sets. The worst was to come when, on account of defaults, women started receiving court notices, became parties to lawsuits and were subjected to harassment at the hands of recovery officers.

This was happening at a time when the neighbouring countries of Asia were undertaking a sensible experiment in rural finance. Poor women were being trained in book-keeping, business skills and leadership qualities. When they became qualified, they were provided small loans for goat-keeping, cycle rickshaws, and hair salons, basket-making and other businesses. The women themselves serviced the loans and ensured that all conditions were fulfilled. It took almost two decades for us to realise our folly and take lesson from experiments elsewhere. It was in the early nineties that we conceived of our indigenous Self Help Group model of rural finance.

Most people believe that social control of banks was necessary to make banking accessible to the huge rural population that remained unserved by the conventional banks. The branches of public banks were so thinly dispersed that even those villagers who had access to banking were vastly underserved. In 1984, these banks were nationalized because of the perception of politicians, particularly the socialist lobby, who believed that the poor and marginalised were being bypassed by the banks and big businessmen were monopolizing banking services. The politicians felt it was necessary to impose social control over banking to give it a developmental thrust and laid a special emphasis on extending banking in rural areas. Bank branches mushroomed at places of politicians' choices with scant regard to the viability of the bank branch and availability of necessary infrastructure. Establishment of a new type of structure was needed, one specifically for the needs of the rural population. These banks needed to be staffed with low-cost employees familiar with the local culture. This could increase both the efficiency and viability of the branches.

The Regional Rural Banks and District Cooperative Banks emerged in response to this thinking and were initially driven by a philosophy of dedicated service to that segment of the population which could not be covered by the formal financial system. But these institutions got so brutally politicised that they became tools in the hands of politicians. Instead of fixing the problem or learning lessons, our politicians decided to use the mainstream public banks to achieve their socialist and populist agenda.

The problem with all new development practices is the excessive haste with which the policy makers and practitioners peddle half-baked ideas without first piloting them to assess their suitability for scaling up across diverse geographies. One field study, which by itself cannot be conclusive evidence of the efficacy and sustainability of a new innovation, is picked up by market leaders who are keen on pushing the new idea which is bundled as a dream route to prosperity. We have professionalized and glamorized the strategic communication departments which are manned by experts who have mastered the art of selling ideas. The most gullible groups are normally the marginalized communities whose meagre incomes keep their raw minds groping for ways of getting rich the quick way. There is a scramble among the development scientists to score points on the board of new innovations. Development journalists are always sniffing for stories that please their editors and earn them by-lines.

The disastrous end to the National Biogas Programme of India serves as a stark example of the monumental failure of the alternative energy model. Initially termed a revolutionary project which was expected to transform the economy of India's hinterland, the administrators allocated huge targets for the installation of biogas plants and doled out loans on a massive scale. These loans were honeyed with dollops of subsidies. They did not, however, make any effort to train masons or create a pool of service agents to ensure proper construction and maintenance of these plants. The entire programme proved to be a financial tsunami for poor villagers, who were left with a legacy of unpaid loans. The loans were written off later, but in accordance with the banking norms, the borrowers were no longer entitled to new loans as they fell in the category of defaulters. It was a typical case of a credit-worthy borrower became bracketed as an untrustworthy borrower on account of the over-enthusiasm of the staff of the development machinery whose careers were linked with the juiciness sweetness of targets achieved.

This programme is the most glaring example of how a top-down approach can play havoc with the life of the very people whose lot it proposes to improve. All households in Visakha, a village in Gadchiroli, within an eponymous *gram panchayat*, were covered under the programme. A recommendation that the concerned development officer should be publicly felicitated was pending at our zonal headquarter in Nagpur when a senior officer who had vast experience in grassroots programmes insisted that all such recognitions must wait for two years to allow evaluation of the results. After two years, the ghost of the National Biogas Plan haunted the villages even as the spectre of drought sucked hundreds of farmers into its vortex of mass suicides.

Rural bank branches became the shrines of a failed rural revolution. In my own bank branch in Chandrapur, I wrote off hundreds of loans as if ploughing a mountain of rotten potatoes just to rid the balance sheet of the toxic assets. Every quarter, the concerned clerk would brand the yellowing dog-eared ledger sheets with a remark, *nonperforming asset* so that interest income on these accounts would not be erroneously booked as profit. The deadweight was a drain on our manpower because, during the quarterly financial tally, these dead accounts had to be jotted down and the figures entered at various places in the bank account books. They also contaminated the balance sheets.

The original banking concept, based on security-oriented lending, was broadened to a social banking concept based on purpose-oriented credit for development. This called for a shift from urban- to rural-oriented lending. Social banking was conceptualised as "better the village, better the nation". However, opening new branches in rural areas without proper expansion, planning and supervision of end use of credit or creation of basic infrastructure facilities meant that branches remained mere flag posts. it was a make-believe revolution that was to lead to a serious financial crisis in the years to come.

The Integrated Rural Development Programme (IRDP) is a grim reminder of how mechanically trying to meet targets can undermine the integrity of a social revolution to such an extent that a counter-revolution can be set into motion. Arguably India's worst-ever development programme, the IRDP intended providing income-generating assets to the rural poor through the provision of cheap bank credit. Little support was provided for skill-formation, access to inputs, markets and necessary infrastructure. In the case of cattle loans, for example, a majority of cattle owners reported that either they had sold off the animals bought with the loan or that these animals were dead. Cattle loans were financed without adequate attention to other details involved in cattle care: fodder availability, veterinary infrastructure, marketing linkages for milk, etc.

Working for the poor does not mean indiscriminately thrusting money down their throats. Unfortunately, IRDP did precisely that. The programme did not attempt to ascertain whether the loan provided would lead to the creation of a viable long-term asset nor attempt to create the necessary forward and backward linkages to supply raw material or establish marketing linkages for the produce. Little information was collected on the intended beneficiary. The IRDP was principally an instrument for powerful local bosses to opportunistically distribute political largesse. The abiding legacy of the programme for India's poor has been that millions have become bank defaulters through no fault of their own. Today, the people so marked find it impossible to rejoin the formal credit stream.

The IRDP alone accounted for 40 percent of the losses incurred by commercial banks in rural lending in India. By the end of the 1980s, great concern began to be expressed about the low capital base, low profitability, and high percentage of non-performing assets of public sector banks, whose earnings were invariably lower than their loan losses and transaction costs. They required continual refinancing and recapitalisation by apex institutions. The final nail in the coffin was the official loan waiver of 1989, which destroyed whatever semblance of credit discipline remained.

There are two basic pre-requisites of a poverty eradication programmes. Firstly, reorientation of the agricultural relations so that the ownership of land is shared by a larger section of the people. Secondly, no programme of removal of poverty can succeed in an economy plagued by inflation and spiralling rise of prices.

A poverty eradication programme, therefore, must mop up the surplus with the elite classes. These two pre-requisites a strong political will in the national leadership to implement the much needed structural reforms. Besides, the government must aim at a strategy for the development of the social sector of which the key component should be population control, universal primary education, family welfare and job creation especially in rural areas. These and the other aspects of poverty alleviation have not given any importance so far in our planning, though we have always thought that poverty can be removed through economic development.

I feel that all rural finance programmes should have substantial inputs in rural sociology as a part of the training kit for rural managers. Rural banking requires a greater insight into rural sociology than on banking practices and as far as finance is concerned, even a basic knowledge is adequate to handle these simple transactions. A fair exposure to primary sources, like the works of Shrinivas, Beteille, Ghurye, Mandelbaum and Jodhka can provide strong academic tools for rural managers. I would recommend Robert Chamber's *Putting the Last First* as the best introduction to the grammar of rural development, particularly its exposition of participatory approaches now being espoused by the World Bank.

Policy wonks have always projected the banking correspondent model of the commercial banks as a revolutionary transformation of the landscape of financial inclusion. It made a poor beginning, because initially the correspondents or BCs were inadequately trained and banks found most of the business they sourced unworthy of processing. The expectations were that they would be able to take up credit functions. Now it is clear that only larger entities with competent manpower and proper logistical support can handle the credit functions required for modern banks.

The intentions of the business correspondent may be genuinely good, but it is a fact that he is not properly remunerated for his efforts and upfront investment. Most of these BCs are financially stable and are setting up financial franchises for enlarging their local clout, as it can give them a platform for much larger agenda, be it politics or business. If we can encourage agricultural graduates to become BCs, the credit functions will be strengthened. Dairy and agriculture are specialised activities and generalised bankers have been averse to taking decisions on high value projects for that reason. Fortunately now almost all banks are recruiting in large numbers agricultural and veterinary graduates.

During the massive banking expansion phase in the 1980s, opening a bank branch was made to look as casual as punching a flag post. This lacked the soul of a genuine economic revolution because it was not conceived by the grassroots agents but assembled by starry eyed mandarins who had picked up bits and pieces about financial inclusion from pompous new fangled and half baked ideas generated at seminars and conferences. The district coordinators of the public banks who handled the process for individual districts were astounded by the strange-looking names of villages where banks had to be opened. As a district coordinator, in charge of overseeing this expansion programme for my district, I saw how an unenlightened politician can play havoc with financial systems.

I was handling Wardha district, identified by the Planning Commission for overall development purely on Gandhian lines, with an emphasis on Gandhian values and economics. It was impossible to locate a proper structure to house the bank. The possibility of a toilet or a medical centre or a police post or a primary school in a village as a precondition for a bank branch was simply overlooked. In several cases where the expiry of RBI licence for the opening of the bank branch approached without proper premises for the bank being identified, banks had to be opened in a local temple or a community centre, marked by a small banner, and a photograph screened as evidence of the launch of the bank's operations.

Juicy numbers give musical resonance to the ears of all bosses. Numbers have been a great obsession with Indian planners in particular. Number of men & women sterilized, contraceptives circulated, wells dug, toilets constructed, villages screened for polio, TB, or malaria, children enrolled in schools, saplings planted. There is no accountability for fudged figures. In fact, the majority of the rewards are given to officers most adept at massaging figures. The game of numbers without a concurrent focus on social performance and evaluation of quality of assets created has been the bane of most credit programmes for poverty reduction and self-employment.

Rural branch expansion during that period may have accounted for substantial rural poverty reduction during the period, largely through an increase in non-agriculrural activities, which experienced higher returns than in agriculture, and especially through an increase in unregistered or informal manufacturing activities. But there was a significant downside; commercial banks incurred large losses attributable to subsidized interest rates and high loan losses - suggesting potential longer term damage to the credit culture.

There was a village called Pimpri, close enough to Pandharkwada block in Yavatmal district. The villagers were both smart and shrewd and most of the men were salary earners with full-time employment in a local ginning factory. I discovered the women's tenacious ability to hold on to each other's intimate information. One of the women perpetuated a fraud and no amount of cajoling or threats could elicit even a remotest clue from those who knew of the crime. The affected members preferred to remain tainted as defaulters rather than exposing Jyoti, the suspected culprit.

Jyoti was the *sarpanch* of this village and she had cleverly persuaded a few women members of her Self Help Group to protect her. Far from being a threat to the village, Jyoti was an affable person, but emotionally so tough that her expressions didn't give the faintest hint of her role in the fraud. My staff and I had to finally waive the loan amount because recourse to legal channels would have been both costly and time-consuming. It was not worth harassing borrowers who were themselves living on subsistent wages.

The real issue for the bank was not the loss of Rs. 85,000 but the damage it caused to the local credit culture and the casual approach with which the borrowers started viewing bank loans. If one defaulter could go scot free, what was the sin of others that they had to pay the defaulted loan amount? Was it not a penalty for being honest and meek? One of the lessons I have learnt the hard way is that like a pest when an individual borrower starts getting delinquent, the others can catch infection and the malady can grow into an epidemic. In the same village, we had a defaulter of just Rs.500; we used police help and spent about Rs. 2000 (four times the value of the loan due) to seize his goat and sell it in the market to realize our amount. Our action was meant to be a message; we will not spare a recalcitrant borrower, howsoever small may be the default and howsoever difficult it may be for us to rein a recalcitrant borrower.

I remember the case of Manik Meshram, a progressive farmer from Charurkhati in Chandrapur, whose father had been financed long previously for a bore well and an electric pump. The general complaint was that the bank-assigned contractors did poor work. The villagers could not benefit from the well, yet the loan continued to grow even after the final notice from the bank. I extended an olive branch and agreed to substantially reduce the repayment on account of interest but Manik's father refused to pay the loan as a protest against the callousness of both the bank and the contractor. Our relations became highly strained. I decided to wind up the matter at that stage.

One day I heard Manik's father was ailing and was virtually in the throes of death. I decided to visit him because I considered Manik the most decent farmer in his village. I found the venerable old man propped up in his hospital bed, monitors beeping and flashing graphs measuring his vital signs. His frail arms had been punctured with endless needles and a tube ran through his mouth into his lungs. The room was illuminated only by the psychedelic images on the television screen, blackout curtains having been drawn to block out the sunlight. Manik briefed me on the health of his father, saying that his father's chance of surviving appeared quite dim and he was clearly marking time. As I sat with Manik, I casually mentioned the outstanding loan of the failed well and requested that he pay at least some portion to demonstrate his credibility. I also advised him that his refusal to do so would demean him in the eyes of the bank and taint his father's high reputation..

It seemed the very mention of the loan aroused the olfactory organs of Manik's father and triggered the raw nerves. He jolted back to life, and started accusing me me of unnecessarily insisting on recovery of a loan that yielded no benefit. I was terrified that his very ghost would chase me after his death, so wild was his rage. He let loose a barrage of invectives against the bank.. We mollified him and put him back to bed with generous dollops of assurances.. Such was the sharpness of the senses of Manik's father that my casual remark wrought a wonder that intensive medication could not achieve for almost two days.

I remember we had a tough, rocky soil in Wanoja's fields where most previous efforts at digging wells had turned out to be failures.. The region was rain-fed, and agriculture was dependent on the vagaries of the monsoon. I received an application from a farmer for a loan of Rs. 1 lac for digging a well, installing a pump and energizing it with an electric connection. The farmer was highly enterprising and wanted to make a serious attempt. He planned to dig it much deeper than what was attempted by farmers earlier. He tried to justify the higher amount on the ground that it involved excavation to a depth of almost seventy-five feet and entailed deployment of heavy-duty pulverisers and dynamite. People in the village had cautioned me about the farmer's notorious past record and the tragic trail of failed wells. However the farmer's zealous enthusiasm led me to believe it would be worthwhile; if the farmer could achieve a breakthrough it could open new vistas for irrigation in an arid region. I always had an open mind and was a great admirer of innovative and progressive farmers..

Since it was my first assignment, I didn't realize I had to inspect the site at every stage of construction and release the amount in tranches depending on the progress of the work. The farmer had informed me that the entire stock of cement and steel had to be purchased at wholesale rates from original suppliers so that he could enjoy a decent discount. He assured me he would give me periodical feedback reports about the progress of excavation and construction of the well.

In one of his feedbacks, the farmer stated that water had been struck at 120 feet and concentric concrete rings were being built along the circumference to reinforce the outer support for the well. Finally the only formality left was installation of electric poles to connect the transformer and the pump by wires. Meanwhile I had also sanctioned a temporary overdraft to meet the expenses on account of the increased depth of the excavation. I had been insisting with the farmer all through to plan my visit to the site as I had to compile a report for headquarters.

The farmer agreed for an inspection after it had rained heavily for almost three days, saying that the project had been completed and was an astounding success. The water level was so high that I smelled mischief. The village headman who had accompanied me saw my disbelief and brought a long bamboo and asked me to lower it into the well to get a rough idea of the water level. The bamboo hit an obstruction just eight feet below. I cornered the farmer and threatened to book him with the local police for fraud unless he coughed up the entire amount together with the interest that had accrued on the amount. With the help of local farmers and assistance from the local police, we were able to recover the entire loss. However the incident severely eroded my faith in the innate goodness of villagers. This is not to detract from the character of most poor and marginal farmers whose reputation for honesty should not be allowed to be sullied by the crooked actins of such evil minded elements. The common peasant is still a paragon of great virtues.

A farmer and his family once visited my branch with two satchels of currency notes. The farmer emptied the bundles and placed them neatly on my table. The cash was probably about Rs. 2 lac. Since they were low denomination notes, the cash had built up into a small molehill. The family sat in awe, flush with pride at their 'wealth'. It was clear from their faces that they had achieved a remarkable feat. I called my cashiers who brought their counting machines. In a matter of minutes, they'd counted the money and a prompt acknowledgment was given to the farmer. But the farmer and his family looked a little disappointed and seemed to be in no hurry to leave. When I assured them that their work was complete and that they could go, they walked out with sullen faces. Later, I met their village headman who mentioned the family's disappointment. They had built their savings over two years and had expected that the bank staff would take at least four-five hours to count the notes while they sat back taking pride in their great efforts. They were disappointed that their two years of toil was worth just ten minutes of the bank's time. After that, I instructed cashiers to count the notes slowly whenever poor villagers came with bulk saving so that the client could savour the efforts required to count their cash. It would also help in inflating their ego. It is since then that I realised how important is the understanding of behavioural patterns for managing customers.

One of the key businesses at rural branches was loans using gold ornaments as security. If anybody opened the bank vault, he would find tiny cloth sachets containing gold ornaments. In some parts of South Asia, there is a long-standing tradition of gold as a preferred form of saving. Small amounts can be accumulated at different intervals; it is not easily lost or destroyed; it is compact and lightweight compared to its value; and it is easily divisible into small units which can be sold off as needed. Indian households typically have an emotional attachment to the gold they own, which is usually in the form of jewellery, coins or bars. Thus gold owned by Indian families is rarely liquidated unless in extreme financial distress. But pledging gold ornaments and other gold assets to local pawnbrokers and moneylenders to avail loans has been prevalent in the Indian society for many decades particularly in rural areas. Jewellery shops and pawnbrokers do brisk business in buying or pawning gold. The bankers have taken cue and are also pitching in aggressively. I remember that during peak season we had to sanction at least twenty to thirty loans each day.

The financial institution's main responsibility is for the safekeeping of the gold jewellery. This requires well-developed logistics to prevent fraud or tampering. Each jewellery item is kept in a tamper-proof sealed sachet that is carefully labelled and tracked by meticulous inventory systems. During our days, vaults were imported from England and the suppliers were so meticulous about quality and security that vaults took months to be designed, assembled and delivered.

Loans against gold were popular at village banks because they required very simple paperwork. Customers just had to walk in, wait for an hour or so and come out with the loan amount. Since most borrowers at villages were agriculturists, they could get the loan at the concessional rate. They just needed to produce proof that they owned agricultural land.

This was not without its hiccups, however. At our village, there was no goldsmith who could certify the quality of gold. Just imagine the plight of a bank manager who must assess the gold without any technology for assaying its purity. Secondly most jewellery was studded with expensive coloured stones. The bank's instructions were to discount these external hedges and give loans against the net weight of the actual gold content. Weighing the gold, assessing its quality and the extent of purity was the exclusive responsibility of the branch manager. In fact when I started my career as a bank manger, I had not purchased even a finger ring and here suddenly I was an authority on gold. We were provided with a bottle of nitric acid and some bleach chemical paper to help us in assessing gold.

My mantra was simple. First ascertain the integrity and character of the borrower and then accordingly use our judgment based on his feedback of the percentage of non-gold accessories and the composition of the gold. Our coordinator was a wonderful man with practical common sense, ideas and solutions. The first question he asked at a meeting of officials drew a lot of angry complaints. The core issue was how to distinguish whether it was genuine gold or spurious when one had little familiarity with gold jewellery and there was no assistance available to evaluate it. The coordinator came out with a simple solution: the moment a gold loan customer shows you his ornament, you should immediately put him on the defensive, challenging that it is not gold but copper. This haggling continues but the tone, confidence level and body language give an idea whether the borrower is honest in his claim or not. He said this simple rule of thumb held and he had handled thousands of gold loans. Surprisingly, his simple advice appealed to the entire audience. I have never used this technique out of the fear that some sensitive customer may retaliate, but lot of people tell me that in those old days it did work.

There was a time when villagers perceived the 'Village Adoption Scheme' of public sector banks as a holistic programme for catering to all needs of the entire local population — credit, health, education, livelihood, housing, food security and sanitation. The scheme became a rod for politicians to whip the banks and absolve themselves of the fundamental responsibility of delivering the entire gamut of services needed to develop for a village to enable its inhabitants to live with a basic modicum of dignity. It was in fact a holistic credit programme which envisaged one bank to be a provider for all the credit needs of their adopted villages.

A unique feature I found among the villages was a highly institutionalized practice of communal defecation which provided both time and privacy from homes for the gossip and rumours mill. The most popular topic among women would be gossip spiced with burlesque sexual revelations. Most illicit liaisons took place during the day in the thick hedges of the farms where women and men worked together. In many cases, farmers used the female labour for satisfying their lust.

Managing a farmer's credit requirements is a very tricky business for a bank manager. It is really a gut-wrenching exercise handling the farmers who have become seasoned in handling the bankers, particularly after being mentored by the new breed of canny politicians who have come up with ingenious methods to flummox banks.

When the sowing operations begin, the farmers will start grumbling about the growing cost of farm inputs, and try to get inflated sums sanctioned. When the crops reach the mid stage and need fertilizer support, the farmers will be in an exuberant mood telling the bankers of the possibility of a booming harvest provided proper, timely and adequate quantity of fertilizers is supplied. But when the harvest season approaches and bankers start courting them for recoveries, the farmers put up grim and sullen faces saying the crops suffered damage during harvest and it would be difficult to meet the repayment obligations. They would ask for relaxation in interest rates or rescheduling of their loans or waiver of the interest portion, adding their masterly histrionics and lamentations bemoaning the government's apathy towards them. They would then unleash a litany of complaints against farm input suppliers accusing them of selling spurious products and cheating them on prices.

At first I would get emotional and spend endless hours trying to work out relief packages. But later I began to realize that I was burning myself out for these undeserving farmers who were hoodwinking me just because they could.

I remember a colleague who was doing his first rural assignment, when he was immediately confronted with a government programme for financial assistance for digging wells. This manager had spent his entire career in a metro region and carried the impression that villagers were saints. He worked very hard to ensure that all proposals for dug wells were processed speedily and the amount disbursed to farmers. He handed over the money to farmers directly as he felt that if he released the amount directly to contractors/vendors, they would exploit the farmers by inflating the costs.

A fortnight after the loans were disbursed, the manager decided to inspect the sites in order to submit a progress report to his head office. He was shocked to find no indication of work having commenced at any of the sites. He met the representative of these farmers to question him about what he perceived a big fraud. The smart and highly suave farmer feigned total innocence. He asserted that all the farmers had dug their wells but a mischievous contractor, who was jealous of the new found prosperity of the farmers, had dumped waste material from construction sites in their wells.

The compassionate manager was so moved by the farmer's histrionics that he immediately decided to work out a relief plan. He consulted his bosses and decided to give an ad hoc bridge loan to help the farmers cope with the crisis. It is experiences like these which have most committed bankers turning their hearts against the villagers they have come to assist.

It was much later that the manager came to know he was beguiled by the canny farmers. An enquiry was ordered and an exhaustive training module on irrigation projects was introduced for the managers. The manager was a highly demoralised and sought a transfer. The event tore the credibility of the villagers in the area and severely crimped the implementation of the development programmes already underway.

I vividly remember the sweeper at our branch who would turn up religiously at dawn, from his house, small but self-owned, near the bank building. I admired the way the family presented themselves; a portrait of resistance, tenacity and sincerity. I greeted him when I passed on my morning jog. I would give the family gifts on every festive occasion. Uikey had a son, his only child, and they were keen that he should not suffer the ignominy and humiliation they suffered to make a living. The boy was not a matriculate and could not qualify even for a menial job in the market. The only option was to set up a small business. This required capital which Uikey could hardly afford. The only option was a loan from a bank. This appeared a fair and workable alternative to Uikey as he knew the staff of our branch quite well. I sympathized with Uikey's sentiments and his intentions for his son but could not assure him a definite solution because his son didn't qualify for any of the government's subsidies under loan schemes administered through our bank.

I was contemplating extending a loan to Uikey's son but couldn't work out how. A very good opportunity came my way when I came across a government circular that I had skimmed over earlier and filed and forgotten, calling for applications. My curiosity now piqued. I retrieved it from my slush pile of discarded correspondence. The circular gave the details for a non-refundable loan of Rs. 25,000 to scavenger families. That was in 1996. Today the amount would be the equivalent of Rs. 2 lacs after factoring in inflation.

I called Uikey, filled the application form and got signatures of Uikey's son and other supporting personal documents organised and sent the application to the District Collector, putting in my strong recommendation for the loan to be sanctioned immediately. Uikey purchased a wagon-load of stock and his son's shop was overflowing with a diverse variety of commodities. No customer could turn back for the non-availability of any item. The shop became popular and the Uikey couple also helped manage the shop. With the son well settled, the Uikeys started looking a good bride for their son. With their reputation for honesty, they were able to get a good bride from a well-settled middle class family from nearby Nagpur. The girl was a matriculate and was deft in handling household chores. She started helping the family in managing the shop and introduced some professional business practices, like maintaining the inventory of stocks, recording sales of every item and monitoring the cash flow so that idle cash and stocks could be properly reconciled.

Things went well for the family and I was happy that I was part of his success story, but the glory was short-lived. One day I heard that Uikey had sold his merchandise. When my colleagues confirmed the information, I was broken. I visited Uikey, who trembled as I confronted him.

"Sir, my only daughter-in-law was ill and the local doctor advised me to get her treated at a multi-specialty hospital to avoid risks. I decided to sell the stocks to another shopkeeper and moved her to a high tech hospital in the neighbouring city; all of us had to stay for more than a month. I am broke and I have run up debts. It is the will of God."

I was unmoved, even though Uikey's tears kept rolling, as he sobbed and mumbled in his plaintive voice. "What if you didn't have all this money?" I thundered.

"Sir, I would have taken a risk and treated her at the government hospital. But I thought that since I had the resources, I should not chance my daughter-in-law's parents taking me to task." I was held shocked by Uikey's reasoning and logic and I was wracked with guilt that I had become a tool for a wasteful drain of public money.

Events like this have been a routine experience in my career in rural India and have made me rethink the myths of innocence and simplicity surrounding the rural population. At the same time, I would not care to generalize these experiences. They are aberrations in an otherwise placid and value-driven rural society. When a development manager has undergone only a short stint in a rural area and most of his experiences are flooded with such events as I mention above, he is bound to become pussy-footed and pusillanimous in his approach.

The banking system stipulates a filing of a police FIR for the misuse of assets but the police system is so slow to respond that a failed case can do much greater harm to the banker's efficiency than simply leaving the case alone. It is better not to file an FIR at all. Threats, legal notices, lawsuits have lost their bite after people have seen their inefficiency.

A bank manager's entry into the village sets in motion the ferociously swift word-of-mouth communication machinery. The defaulters get alerted and most of them take shelter in the fields. The family members are experienced in handling the broad array of lenders and have parroted a well-rehearsed procedure for shooing away the visiting recovery staff. As soon as you knock the door, which has normally been locked by the inmates after sensing your impending visit, it will be opened after a great deal of persuasive tapping.

The lady of the house will emerge with a frown at this act of intrusion, knowing full well the purpose of the visit. She will put up a deadpan expression, pleading total ignorance of the matter. When you ask her about her husband's whereabouts and the fate of the loan, she will narrate the usual script with the same manipulated emotions of her face. "I don't know anything about it. He alone manages it. He may have gone to the market, possibly to organize money. He is under severe stress as the crop has failed. We have not been able to pay our schoolchildren's fees for two months. Please show mercy to us"

If you are fortunate enough to meet the borrower, he will reel out a list of assurances: "I have already sold the stocks and I am awaiting the payment. The first thing I plan to-do is to square the loan." The confident and assuring tone of the borrower with make-believe sincerity on his face may beguile a neophyte into believing the credibility of the bogus theories spun so effortlessly by the peasants. The farmer will go further. "Why do you unnecessarily waste your time coming all the way to the village? I am more concerned than you. I have to safeguard the reputation of my father for timely repayment of debts. His record is impeccable. He would rather pledge his wife's gold than be bracketed as a defaulter…I really don't understand why God has been so cruel with farmers this season."

The Personnel Department at our bank was gifted with a rare talent of ensuring that an official was put to the greatest possible discomfort. I think they had a suave intelligence network that located centres where their target officer would suffer mental hardship. Once the department unwittingly transferred an officer to his preferred posting. Elated, the officer thanked the Personnel Manager and distributed sweets in his department. When the Personnel Manager realized what had happened, he cancelled the transfer and instead got him posted to a place which he greatly abhorred.

I was also a victim of this cruel strategy. Normally, a rural posting is seen as a punishment. I opted for it because I had a passion for working in rural areas particularly with the poor women. My performance was appreciated by the government and my work was often covered by the media. As a reward for my contribution to rural development, UNDP deputed me to University of Manchester, Malaysia's Ministry of Rural Development and later Grameen Bank, Bangladesh. Sensing that my wings were spreading fast, and that I was enjoying my assignment, the Personnel Department transferred me to Kolkata at the bank's Foreign Department. I was assigned a dull job of handling mirror accounts of original transactions in overseas branches.

My posting had no relevance to my expertise and it was going to be a dislocation for me and my family. In fact for the bank, this posting entailed a loss because it drained the experience I had gleaned in rural finance particularly when there were few officers willing to work in rural areas. Since I had voluntarily opted for the informal rural cadre, I had admitted my children in schools where the entire teaching was in a regional language. The officers in the Personnel Department defended their move and said that I was being rewarded for my work with this post at the Foreign Department. The truth was the Foreign Department was a backwater in the bank's foreign business firmament; the lucrative postings were located at the bank's overseas centres. Everyone in the bank was convinced that the department to which I was posted was full of frauds and irregularities requiring a sledgehammer to fix the problems there. I put up a bitter fight with the management and bounced back into my natural territory, which is development finance, after the bank realized that the rural finance portfolio which I had so assiduously built had begun to rot. It was this bitter experience that warned me to be very careful with the Personnel Department lest I stepped on their toes and invited their wrath. I also realized that the Personnel Manager was an unanointed deity. We would refer to him as the jailor or the hangman whose noose was keenly waiting for anew prey each day.

I remember a woman client, Chandrabhaga Bhajne, in Bina in Nagpur, whose alcoholic husband had made life miserable for the whole family. He finally died on account of a failing liver. I appointed Chandrabhaga as a canteen worker in my office. Since she was staying in a rental house, she found her savings inadequate for meeting the family expenses. I was able to come across a government scheme for a concessional loan for acquiring a house. I personally negotiated the dealing with the house owner and finalized it. I felt immensely satisfied that I could extend some concrete assistance to this widow. Unfortunately my sense of fulfilment was short-lived. Chandrabhaga's two sons died within a span of two months after the family shifted to the new house, both claiming their lives by consuming pesticide. The whole village believed that the house was inhabited by evil spirits and Chandrabhaga made a mistake buying it. It was then that Chandrabhaga started cursing me and continues to curse me even till this day, accusing me of trapping her in the deal involving the haunted house. A Good Samaritan is painted a devil. That is the tale of a poor rural manager.

Banks have attempted to rein in recalcitrant borrowers who misuse funds but considering borrowers' ingenuity (what has now come to be termed as local innovation or 'jugaad') bankers keep testing new ideas, and discarding the old.

The system of making payments directly to vendors had also not worked. The vendor deducted twenty percent of the payment and released only eighty percent to the borrower with the result that the asset for which finance had been provided was not acquired. There were vendors who were not traders but agents for assisting the clients to encash the fungible assets and earn huge profits. Ghost loans have been another bane of the development finance arena. Most ghost loans have been products of ingenious crooks in the financial system. Most development programmes of the government have been contaminated by ghost clients, which are conduits for siphoning off institutional funds.

In 2011, the farmers in northern Maharashtra suffered badly on account of low yields of cotton; additionally, the government procurement prices for cotton were pegged low. As a result, our loan recoveries plummeted. I conducted a detailed assessment of the farmers and realized that their plight was genuine and a rehabilitation package had to be worked out.

I informed my bosses in my report that on account of the twin effect of low yield and low prices, the farmers didn't have enough money to service our loans and would have to be provided some concessions. No one from my head office came down to meet the farmers and verify the situation themselves. Our boardroom pundits, whose method of monitoring the portfolio was confined to meticulous reading of business newspapers, came across a news item which stated the state government had worked out a new paradigm to address the woes of the farmers: instead of raising the prices paid, the government had decided to compensate the farmers by paying subsidies based on landholdings. Our senior officers must have felt terribly excited at having got a fix and believed they had scored victory.

But I was not the one to get trumped by these armchair know-all toadies. I was familiar with this tribe and was convinced that the poor reading of the problems and unrealistic solutions were the root cause of anti-farmer policies being churned out in regal boardrooms. Moreover, most senior executives were out of touch with ground realities, their only source of information being the newspaper where experts' opinions could be grounded in a particular ideology. Also, these opinions take a macro view and do not account for the wide diversity of regional problems. I shot back a tart letter informing them that the government move was in fact a conspiracy against small farmers and smacked of outright feudalism; since eighty percent of my farmers were either tenant farmers or share-croppers, they would not stand to gain anything. Instead, the rich landowners would get this subsidy without having cultivated their land or suffered any loss.

I had seen for myself how the anti-poor-farmer lobby operated and how its policies impoverished the farmers rather than offering succour. Had I not been aware of the pernicious implication of this policy at the ground level, I would have kept building pressure on the farmers. Such serious ethical dilemmas keep buffeting the conscientious manager's mind on account of blatantly political exercises like this. I don't want to talk of how loan waivers have penalized and demotivated good borrowers and vitiated the credit culture in rural India.

Apart from routine occupational hazards, a serious security threat for rural managers looms when they have to ferry cash by motorcycle without armed guards. Smaller village branches are prescribed a cash-holding limit and if the cash exceeded this limit, after a larger number of receipts from customers, excess cash had to be immediately deposited in the parent branch. If there was heavy demand for cash from customers, it had to be withdrawn from the parent branch and then carried to the paying branch. Cash has to be transported in a concealed van, manned by an armed guard. The logistical planning for this arrangement can take two-three days; an armed guard cannot be arranged when cash has to be transported at an hour's notice. Any delay in handling cash can hamper the banking services and put customers to great hardship.

The only solution is to transport the cash on the bank's battered motorcycle through tough, desolate terrains with no hope for any respite from bosses in case a tragedy struck. The bank's stringent punch line would be that the officer had violated the bank's instruction. If you were robbed or waylaid, you would have to reimburse the loss amount and face a volley of office memos seeking explanation.

The bank's instructions in case of an attempted dacoity were quite strange and naïve. The circular said that when dacoits seize the currency vault, the staff should encourage them to fill the gunny sacks with small denomination currency notes so that the loss to the bank would be minimized. Similarly, the attention of the dacoits was to be diplomatically focused on cash, and access to gold jewellery was to be carefully avoided. I always wondered whether Indian dacoits were such dimwits that they could be led into such foolish traps. How did the management expect its unarmed staff to stand up to these professional thugs? I am sure the instruction was written by someone who had himself not encountered any dacoits.

In my early banking days, the commonest of all loans was the lock and key limits. The godowns in which the stocks of the traders were stored had two sets of locks, one of the traders and the second of his banker. The goods in the warehouse were pledged to the banker and the money was released after the inspection of stocks and computation of its monetary value by the bank's representative. Whenever the money had to be released against the security of stocks, the godowns were opened in the joint presence of the trader and banker and an inventory of the stocks was undertaken. The banker always preferred to take a gross estimate of the stocks by counting the containers. It was much later that banks found several of these containers empty, usually ones stacked in the rear so they might not catch the bank representative's attention. Then banks started the practice of shaking a few containers to verify whether they were empty or filled. Much later it was found that the witty traders were filling these boxes with waste paper so that they didn't appear empty when they were shaken. These sorts of loans have been done away with, but retired bankers keep bandying about these stories when recounting their nostalgic memories.

An even greater fraud was traders taking out credit from two banks against the same stock. On one occasion, one of the two bankers was taken in through the route which displayed the second banker's name and bore his lock. Thus it was discovered that the same stocks were pledged to two banks.

The Reserve Bank of India took a tough stand around 2002 to rid the banks of dirty smudged currency notes and replace the entire currency stock of the country with crisp notes. Bank cashiers had had a tough time convincing customers to accept old notes. Customers would sometimes throw the packet on the cashiers' faces, muttering foul language. We had a senior cashier, Babulal Sondhiya, who was on the verge of retirement. He had spent his career at several places and was highly adept at handling customers. He designed a unique strategy. Whenever a customer threw the packet at him, he would raise a hue and cry, shouting, 'This person has insulted Laxmi (goddess of wealth) and people should condemn him!" The customers would then meekly apologize, hurriedly pick the cash up and make a quick escape before suffering somebody's wrath.

My friend from World Bank, Gautam Ivatury, who was then a microfinance specialist, would regularly visit our village to study first-hand the impact of new models and policies at the ground level. When he arrived at the hall where colourfully garbed and decorated women waited to welcome him, Chanda the leader stepped up to welcome him. Gautam raised his hands in a 'Namaste'. He was stumped when Chanda beamed a loud hello and stoutly offered her right hand for a warm handshake.

I translated Gautam's words for the audience. My friend was so overwhelmed by the enthusiasm and energy of the women that he answered he would learn Marathi, the local language, and would speak to them in it the next time he visited them. It evoked a spontaneous comment from Chanda who assured Gautam that if he would speak in Marathi next time, she would speak in English.

One of the most agonizing roles in a bank manager's career is coping with frivolous and baseless complaints, particularly from political elements holding out threats when loan applications are rejected. It is laudable that the banks' customer grievances disposal machinery is sensitive to their complaints, but the whole process is quite demoralizing for the bank manager. The job of the complaint cell at the bank's regional head office is to affix a pre-printed letter asking the manager to redress the complaint and obtain a letter from the complainant stating that his complaint has been resolved to his full satisfaction. This letter is followed by a stereotypical reminder at periodical intervals. In most of the cases, the complaint will be baseless or it may be couched in aggressive phraseology trying to portray the manager as a villain. The new semi-literate breed of leaders of villages and small towns have a lot of time and the fervent desire to project themselves as saviours. They are the real complaint factories, using the complaints as a weapon of blackmail.

Seeking a letter from the complainant even if the complaint is resolved puts the manager in a highly vulnerable position. There will always be a residual problem animus in the complainant and the fact that most will try to exploit the opportunity in order to extract concessions put the manager in the dock. The banks must design a system whereby false complainants are booked by lodgement of *First Information Report* (FIR.), the first formal complaint to the police. They must learn a lesson from the judiciary which has started litigants filing frivolous lawsuits.

Most complaints are doctored or sponsored by disgruntled insiders who provide the precise names, job titles and addresses of the bosses, and often even the various codes under which the complaint attracts judicial or police attention are parlayed so the complaint is, in effect, a well-crafted legal petition. The insider may also go to the extent of drafting the entire complaint without writing in their own hand to avoid suspicion. These insiders also follow up the complaints by peeking into the correspondence between the local branch and head office. On several occasions, the internal remarks on confidential notes relating to loans are known in entirety to the concerned clients. The clients would also come to know the name of the specific official instrumental in the rejection of their loan cases.

The issue becomes thorny if the information source is a union leader. The industrial laws in our time provided union leaders such a solid protection that, despite stark evidence of their wrongdoings, management would quail to take them head on.

Another weapon akin to complaints is a hunger strike or threat of immolation. At the height of the agrarian crises which led to mass suicide in Yavatmal district in Maharashtra, loan defaulters would sit in front of the bank manager's residence with kerosene cans in their hands, threatening to set themselves afire if they were not given new loans. Many a time, bankers gave in to unreasonable demands to escape the vicious and endless cycle of police enquiries. Several young bank managers in Yavatmal put in their papers, cutting short their bright careers, in order to survive the orgy of arson and violence. Political leaders who prefer to use populist tactics keep sharing the fire by virulent rhetoric. Much can be resolved if they are even-handed in such crises.

One of the greatest weaknesses of public banks is their inaccessibility to the media. As one who handled this for my organization for almost a decade, my primary task was to diplomatically keep the media away from bosses. That is why most media leaks are attributed to sources that prefer anonymity. No one who reads it can be sure whether it is authoritative or authentic. Bosses always fear they would be quoted out of context. Middle level and even senior level officials do not have the authority to speak, even if they are fully informed on the subject. It was a funny situation from which I could not escape. I used to take the press delegation to remote rural places to build awareness among journalists about the revolutionary work being done in the hinterland by bankers. However, whenever they were curious about certain policies and wanted clarifications, I was allowed to share only the innocent facts. If I allowed myself to be drawn into discussion, I would be overstepping my brief and inviting disciplinary proceedings.

On their part, the bosses always shied away from the media and would prefer to barricade themselves through a variety of strategies. Controversies would rage, confusion over policies would run riot, causing immeasurable damage to the organization's image and brand, but the doubts in the media would be allowed to linger and fester. On several occasions, even when I had made it strictly clear that I was not the official spokesman for my organization, the media would refer to me in good faith. But this innocuous act of theirs would lead to nightmares for me, with bosses angrily questioning my priority. During my extensive travels in rural India in connection with our rural finance programmes, I had to be cautious not to encounter the media. Whenever I conversed with them, I would always clarify that it was more of an informal feedback from someone working in the sector than part of an official briefing.

One of my most audacious acts as a rural banker was one which almost cost my job, in a situation which resulted from the infamous Telgi scam, in which fake judicial stamp papers flooded the government treasury. The Government was left with no choice but to impound the papers. Judicial stamp papers constitute a security document like a currency note and are used for executing all legal contracts. All loan agreements have to be executed on these papers. In lieu of a stamp paper, agreements can be executed on regular paper against the necessary fees paid in the government treasury which attests them and embosses them with revenue stamps. The Telgi scam was basically a flourishing racket of circulating fake stamp papers. With the dubious stamp papers withdrawn, all loan processes had to be suspended till the new papers were printed and released by the government.

There were almost two hundred marginal and tenant farmers in the village attached to my bank branch, who were totally dependent on us for credit for farm inputs. The season had approached and there was no possibility of stamp papers being issued. The bigger farmers elsewhere had several other sources of income, particularly dairy, and were able to meet the contingency. The farmers at my village had a very good track record and their credit history demonstrated good credit culture and repayment ethics.

When I was convinced that I wouldn't be able to help them through official channels, I decided to disburse loans on printed documents instead of the government embossed security paper. I took a joint undertaking from the village headman, village officer, two prominent agriculturalists, one of whom was from the Dalit community and one from the Kunbi community, which happened to be the majority constituent of the village council. I got them to pass a resolution in the *Gram Sabha* (village assembly) taking full responsibility for the loans in case my action in releasing the loans on the strength of agreements on non-government security paper came under the scan of auditors.

The outcome of my action was along expected lines. The auditors were in a rage, and my bosses were exasperated and the gossip channels among my colleagues were abuzz with news of my mad action. I got telephone calls asking me whether it was really true that I had been divested of all authority on account of my flagrant violation of rules and was merely an official sans authority. My only weapons against my adversaries were my clients. I have never compromised on even the slightest injustice to my clients, particularly because most of my clients have been poor, unsettled and underpowered. My sincerity is demonstrated through the warmth of the gratitude that my clients have evoked in their communication. Added to this has been my strong focus on proper documentation of facts and communication of my actions to all functionaries who are part of the loop.

I prepared a small dossier in which I filed the resolution of the village council, village assembly and representation of the important local citizens. I scanned these documents and sent a properly drafted letter to the revenue department of the state government, explaining the circumstances of my action, my intention and the hypothetical consequences of my non-action. I still carry a firm conviction that all bonafide actions, if supported by proper documentary evidence and attestations by influential individuals, will sail through troubles. That doesn't mean you don't have to answer explanations or face enquiries. People misunderstand a call for explanations or holding of enquiries as vendetta. I think facing all these and coming out clean enhances one's credibility and strengthens the confidence required for decision-making.

Most managers relied on the conventional wisdom of city dwellers, which projected villagers as meek, innocent and ignorant. They are not to be blamed; all anthropologists and public administrators from Metcalf to Shrinivas have hailed villages as self-contained republics. Their writings also bristled with noble characters who exemplified the basic human values of compassion, honesty and hospitality. These managers got tripped like lame ducks when a new generation of villagers who had extensive exposure to television caught them off guard.

When the managers visited the farms for inspecting wells for the excavation and construction of which a loan had been released, the borrower wore a sullen expression, and meekly admitted with moist eyes, "Sir, my well has been stolen. It was nearing completion when my jealous neighbours dumped stones and mud down the diggings. I am now planning to engage labour for removing the rubble." The manager usually did not have the heart to do anything but commiserate with the borrower. I was told by the villagers that the borrowers used similar tricks in cattle finance. They would take the manager to the field and show him a herd of cattle from a distance, indicating some of the beasts as being those financed by the bank. These events became commonplace in banking lore.

The Integrated Rural Development Programme suffered a cruel end on account of the ingenious but foul-minded villagers. During farming season, when the initial tranches of the loan have to be released, the farmers are usually in an upbeat mood: "Rain may not have been up to our expectations but we are sure the crops would be better this year. We will be able to clear all bank arrears this year." Or, "I don't want to remain a defaulter any more, I have decided to settle all my overdues and become debt free." Buoyed by the encouraging sentiments of the farmers, the bankers also get into a bullish gear and start releasing funds without serious inspection and assessment.

Come harvesting time and the smile turns into a frown. "We were expecting this year to be better, but it seems it may turn out to be worse. The government should come out with a relief package now that the harvest isn't going to be good, markets should behave well; good rates alone can save us".

In most villages, the mountain of bad loans had turned larger than that of good loans. With the downturn in the rural economy, banks were looking far less inclined to add bad loans to their asset portfolio — unless they could snag them at a serious discount and have a guarantee of great return. At the same time, farmers were passing through such a critical phase that if the pain from taking action was great, the pain from not acting was even greater. The literature of the late twentieth century, which for the most part consisted of polemic and counter-polemic rather than of empirical investigation, did not answer these questions, and so all we could do was to pass on the flavour of the debate to our practitioner colleagues. Most poverty-alleviation schemes wrote off loans. The lending officers of banks seemed more concerned with balancing their accounts than seeing poverty and injustice disappear from the countryside.

I learnt that the government has been subsidizing toilet installation, but that the money either didn't get into the plumbing, or, worse, it went down the drain: the toilets were built, and then used for grain storage. Subsidies are useless if the people are not educated about why plumbing matters. My new friend's husband had a fantastic strategy which worked with telling effect. He toured poor villages, giving a lecture about sewage, during which he would place a pile of human excrement on the ground, and a few feet away, a plate of food. Soon a cloud of flies buzz about, landing on first one plate, then the other. After the lecture, the man turned their attention to the plates. He showed the villagers how the flies contaminated their food; how the villagers were therefore eating their own shit. And they begin to understand.

During our early days in rural banking, wheat chapattis were still a luxury in cities. While some had to make do with substandard quality wheat, many ate the fodder-like milo, which was imported under the PL 480 food programme. We ate this with dal and tamarind water. In villages, the jowar bread, popularly known as *bhakri*(jowar), was the universal bread; a thick, earth-coloured, flattened circular bread which would crumble into pieces at any effort to slice it.

Once we were accompanied to a village by visitors from a foreign donor. At the villagers' request, I had got an assurance from the visitors that they would have meals with the village headman's family. The headman's wife was always a gentle and hospitable host for our visitors and herself locally acclaimed for her country cuisine. She served luscious dollops of spinach flecked with sprinklings of raw cucumber and carrot in her nicely baked *bhakri* (flat rounded bread made of jowar). All the visitors, without cxccption, licked the entire serving of the vegetable from the bread and placed the *bhakri* in a corner mistaking it for something akin to plantain leaf or half-baked clay.

During the period when the government subsidy programmes for poverty alleviation were at their zenith, there was a spate of corruption charges against all local officials associated with them: the government officials, bank managers and local bodies handling these programmes. The officials were charged with extracting hefty commissions on these loans on the pretext that they had to bribe their bosses for getting subsidies released. The subsidies ranged from twenty-five to fifty percent of the loan amount. The Anti-Corruption Bureau of the Police Department also had a field time laying successful traps, and in the process helping its staff burnish its credentials in my district. The department surpassed its yearly target in just one quarter.

Since I had agreed to the bureau's suggestion to be a part of the team whenever it involved corruption on the part of the bank staff, I got an insider's view of the entire operational exercises. The first case involved a junior manager of a very small bank unit who had demanded Rs. 500

for sanctioning a loan for the purchase of a flock of ten goats. The bribe was to be delivered at a tea stall on the road traversing the village. The farmer had visited the bureau office in the morning, where the currency notes he was to deliver were sprinkled with chemical powder which was later used as primary evidential exhibit for nailing the criminal. The acts of bribery of public servants are covered under a law called Prevention of Corruption Act which stipulated a maximum sentence of seven years in jail. It covers bribes taken by the staff of government departments and government-supported institutions.

Our team stationed itself at the residence of a villager close to the tea stall. At the appointed time, the manager arrived at the tea stall and the farmer handed over the amount, which the manager immediately inserted in the side pocket of his pants. The Sub-Inspector leading our team immediately pounced on him like a crouching cat upon its prey and waited for us to join him in relishing the kill. The manager insisted that the farmer had forcibly inserted the amount in his pocket, but the veteran police officer asked the manager to take his pants off as they were to be seized and sent for chemical examination of the powder that had stained his pocket. It looked a hilarious scene and life's severest embarrassment for the poor manager but the tea stall owner came to the manager's rescue. He organized a lungi and then located a man whose pants somehow fitted him so that he could accompany the police in at least tolerable dress. A *panchnama* (recorded statement by five witnesses) was penned on a coarse paper typical of government stationery but the 'writer', as he was officially designated by the police, wrote it in highly technical Marathi in a lovely handwriting with every sentence in a perfect straight line. With the *pahchnama* completed and signed by us, I was relieved.

I once decided to drop in at the bank branch whose manager's trousers we had seized. I introduced myself to the new manager and I could sense the fear on his face that I was perhaps on a hunt for new prey. I told him I had nothing to do with the unfortunate incident and I was part of the drama only as a witness. He then narrated to me the long ordeal he had to suffer while handling the whole affair. The routine enquiries following the incident were done at the branch level but most of the disciplinary procedures were handled by the bank's administrative office. The real problems arose when the police returned the pants to the bank after completing their enquiries and finally closing the case.

The manager asked his peon to get the file which could give me an idea of the drama that unfurled in the aftermath of the return of the pants. The file was appropriately titled 'Correspondence relating to the seized full pants of the suspended manager'. There was a large stack of papers in the file pertaining to the correspondence shared between the branch and the various departments of the bank. I could make out that it was probably the first such case to be handled by the regional headquarters of the bank and it took a few months for the bank to formally decide which department should handle this matter.

It seems that for several days, this became a high priority matter at the office and the gossipmongers had used their own creativity to embellish the story into a film script. The bank's manual of procedures was of no help and a creative exercise had to be undertaken to decide the procedure for handling the matter. After the necessary journey of the trousers through several departments, they finally arrived at the branch where they were consigned to flames in the presence of the branch manager and the staff. A document confirming it and signed by those present at the funeral of this unique customer of the branch was sent to the administrative office. The matter was closed but I could well understand from the file the amount of manpower consumed for closing an aborted bribery of Rs. 500. And yet, the ghost of those pants continued to haunt the new manager and his colleagues!

Superstitions appear to have become an integral part of rural life, even if these have singularly done the greatest damage to rural society. Superstitions enjoy a long and rich history in India. Although some of these practices may seem poetic to outsiders they can have deadly consequences. Superstitions are based on faith, not fact. They have a placebo effect-if we believe them, they benefit. But they can paralyze the society–take away people's faith in themselves. Changing entrenched traditional beliefs is not simple. Information must come from a trusted source, not from a foreign expert who takes little or no time to understand local culture and customs. When one deity fails a devotee he approaches another in much the same way as when one patron failed him, a client approached another. To put it crudely, devotees expect to benefit from propitiating deities, and the benefits sought are health, wealth, children, good crops, victory over rivals, and a sense of security.

While the theologian conceives of god as immanent, ineffable etc., the villager deals with him as he deals with his powerful patron or his trader, smith, barber washerman or potter. He wants benefits and favours from the deities he propitiated. While the villagers cite supernatural events and happenings as evidence of the handiwork of god, they were not a credulous lot. They are shrewd, commonsensical and hard headed, and this trait of theirs was seen repeatedly and in a wide variety of contexts.

Naturally, such an attitude tolerates a great deal of superstition and ritualism. There is no rationality in what may please a personal deity, or invoke a dormant benediction. The offering of a lock or hair, a donation, a pilgrimage, a penance, a vow, a fast, an amulet, the feeding of monkeys or cows- anything may work to alter the apparently unalterable framework of our lives. This irrepressible faith gives to Hindus a buoyancy that refuses to fully deflate.

There is a popular superstition in some villages in India. As soon as the sun sets, the villagers fear that ghosts and demons will come to their homes. So in order to save themselves, they have a sign painted in red at the door that reads "Naale Baa," meaning "Come Tomorrow." The idea is that, on seeing the message, the ghosts and demons will know that they are supposed to visit this house the next day. But as tomorrow never comes, neither do the demons! Isn't that wonderful? Similarly rumours are an equally big bane of rural society. They prey on the weak eared and the vacuous mind ingests everything that is offered to it. It doesn't have a sieve or filter. In villages rumours spread like bushfire. Then there is the flourishing chat mill in the village that is hyperactive. It doesn't have a holiday. Rumours swirl the villages. They suffice to feed indignant theories. People indulge in wild speculations. By virtue of frequent repetition, rumours acquire an air of unassailable truth. The villages are traditionally part of a vibrant universe of fast hatching savants and supermen who have dominated grandma's childhood lullaby stories. There was a considerable amount of gossip in our village about extra marital sex relations and some of the reported liaisons across the lines of caste. But the only thing, I could conclude from all this was that rumors about extra marital relations were widespread and widely believed in. This was only what wad to be expected in village society where every bit of gossip moved along well established networks and the networks of different individuals at many points.

I remember one farming season the relentlessly scorching sun had cracked the earth and deep fissures opened up their sagging mouths desperately crying for water. For weeks the sparse clouds cast only shadows. For days I had been watching the clouds -- first gray and flaky, and then black and heavy -- as they descended ever lower; but there was no rain. The sage would tell me that God was punishing people for their sins. Just before the monsoon, farmers in tribal villages arrange frog weddings to welcome the rain god. Villagers make one male and one female frog pose in separate earthen pots for their 'baraat' (wedding procession). The procession finds its way to the local temple, where the frogs are "married". After the wedding, the couple is given a send-off to a local water source and set free. If they croak, it means that they have been told that the monsoon is near. (Local people believe that frogs are harbingers of rain). "Our lives are wrapped up in the rain," explained a woman named Laxmi Kelwade, using a countrywoman's version of Marathi, the regional language. "When it comes, we have everything. When it doesn't, we have nothing."In the meantime, everyone kept scanning the empty sky. If the people of Bina once believed the gods controlled the rain, they were starting to move beyond that. Even as they carried betel nuts and cones of incense up to the goddess's temple, even as one by one the village women knelt down in front of the stone idol that represented her, they seemed merely to be hedging their bets. Krishna Bhadang, a sober-minded, mustachioed farmer in his 30s, sat on one of the low walls of the temple, watching impassively as his female relatives prayed. "Especially the younger people here understand now that it's environmental," he said.

All day, villagers had been speculating about those distant clouds. It was gambling time for rain-dependent farmers across India. In the weeks leading up to the monsoon, many would invest a significant amount of money, often borrowed, to buy fertilizer and millet seeds, which needed to be planted ahead of the rains. "Like fools," said Krishna Bhadang, sweating beneath his white Nehru cap, "we just sit here waiting." He kept running a continuous wager. There were many ways to lose this wager. A delayed monsoon likely would cause the seeds to bake and die in the ground. Or if the rain fell too hard before the seedlings took root, it might wash them all away.

I cannot forget a late-night meeting in the village of Walni, in the district of Chandrapur in Maharashtra during which rain poured down in a pitiless torrent. My colleague, Vinod Yeramwar, a senior UNDP representative and I were climbing through the jungle on a very steep ascent up a deep gorge. A bolt of lightning, luminous like Indra's weapon, tore open the dark sky, and thunder roared in the gorge like a famished beast carrying the echoes of its clamour to neighbouring villages. The entire village had turned into a swamp.

We had to cross a small drain across the road that ran to Walni. It was in full spate when we reached the low bridge. The driver was afraid of driving the vehicle through the puddles, and we decided to wade through it. I found myself in waist-deep, muddy, swirling water. I grabbed a thorny bush only to find clustered round it snakes, scorpions, frogs and field mice. In common peril they did no harm to each other. A few villagers were also planning to cross the bridge on foot. As families waded through the water, sometimes slipping in the marsh, small children and babies wailed in the darkness. I listened to one approaching, crying, snuffing in his mother's arm as she passed and then listened again as they scrambled by me. The distance was not as forbidding as the condition of the pathway in bad weather was. One slip and you would fall three feet in one direction or twenty in the other. The downpour soaked me. The sun finally came out, so we just lay down on a small outcropping of rock to soak up a little heat. Soon it dried out our wet clothes and put us back to life.

As far as the devilish side of rural character is concerned the most scathing attack came from Ambedkar. Ambedkar spoke about it bluntly and unsentimentally. He articulated a kind of experience that neither Tagore nor Gandhi could have possibly had in their formative years. He told the Constituent Assembly:

I hold that these village republics have been the ruination of India. I am therefore surprised that those who condemn Provincialism and communalism should come forward as champions of the village. What is the village but a sink of localism, a den of ignorance, narrow-mindedness and communalism? I am glad that the Draft Constitution has discarded the village and adopted the individual as its unit.

While Gandhi and Tagore had a sober view of Indian village, Marx had condemned it as closed, stagnant, and a victim of nature. In a vitriolic passage he said, "these idyllic village communities... had always been the solid foundation of oriental despotism… they restrained the human mind within the smallest possible compass, making it the unresisting tool of superstition, enslaving it beneath traditional rules, depriving it of all grandeur and historical energies."

Gandhi was the most ardent supporter of the Indian village *:*

I have believed and repeated times without number that India is to be found not in its few cities but in its 7,00,000 villages. But we who have gathered here are not villagers. We are town-dwellers. We town-dwellers have believed that India is to be found in its towns and that the villages were created to minister to our needs. We have hardly ever paused to inquire if those poor folks get sufficient to eat and clothe themselves with and whether they have a roof to shelter themselves from sun and rain. Now I do not think any Congress worker has travelled through the length and breadth of India as much as I have done during the past twenty years. That in itself is hardly a thing to be proud of. I, however, humbly claim, as a result of those peregrinations, to know the Indian villages more than any other Congress worker or leader. I have found that the town-dweller has generally exploited the villager; in fact he has lived on the poor villager's substance. Many a British official has written about the conditions of the people of India. No one has, to my knowledge, said that the Indian villager has enough to keep body and soul together. On the contrary they have admitted that the bulk of the population live on the verge of starvation and ten percent are semi-starved, and that millions have to rest content with a pinch of dirty salt and chillies and polished rice or parched grain. You may be sure that if any of us were to be asked to live on that diet, we should not expect to survive it longer than a month or should be afraid of losing our mental faculties. And yet our villagers go through that state from day to day. (Harijan, 4-4-1936)

The great sociologist Charles Metcalfe was an equally ardent admirer of Indian villages which he considered as republics:

....I admire the structure of the village communities, and am apprehensive that direct engagements for revenue with each separate landholder or cultivator in a village, might tend to destroy its constitution.

The village communities are little republics, having nearly everything they want within themselves, and almost independent of any foreign relations. They seem to last where nothing else does. Dynasty after dynasty tumbles down. Revolution succeeds to revolution. Hindoo, Patan, Mogul, Mahratta, Sikh, English, are all masters in turn, but the village communities remain the same.

In times of trouble they arm and fortify themselves. An hostile army passes through the country. The village communities collect their cattle within their walls, and let the enemy pass unprovoked. If plunder and devastation be directed against themselves, and the force employed be irresistible, they flee to friendly villages at a distance, but when the storm has passed over they return and resume their occupations. If a country remains for a series of years the scene of continued pillage and massacre, so that the villages cannot be inhabited, the scattered villagers nevertheless return whenever the power of peacable possession revives. A generation may pass away, but the succeeding generation will return. The sons will take the places of their fathers—the same site for the village, the same positions for the houses, the same lands will be re-occupied by the descendants of those who were driven out when the village was depopulated; and it is not a trifling matter that will drive them out, for they will often maintain their post through times of disturbance and convulsion, and acquire their strength sufficient to resist pillage and oppression with success.

This union of the village communities, each one forming a separate little state in itself, has, I conceive, contributed more than any other cause to the preservation of the people of India, through all the revolutions and changes which they have suffered and is in a high degree conducive to their happiness and to the enjoyment of a great portion of freedom and independence.